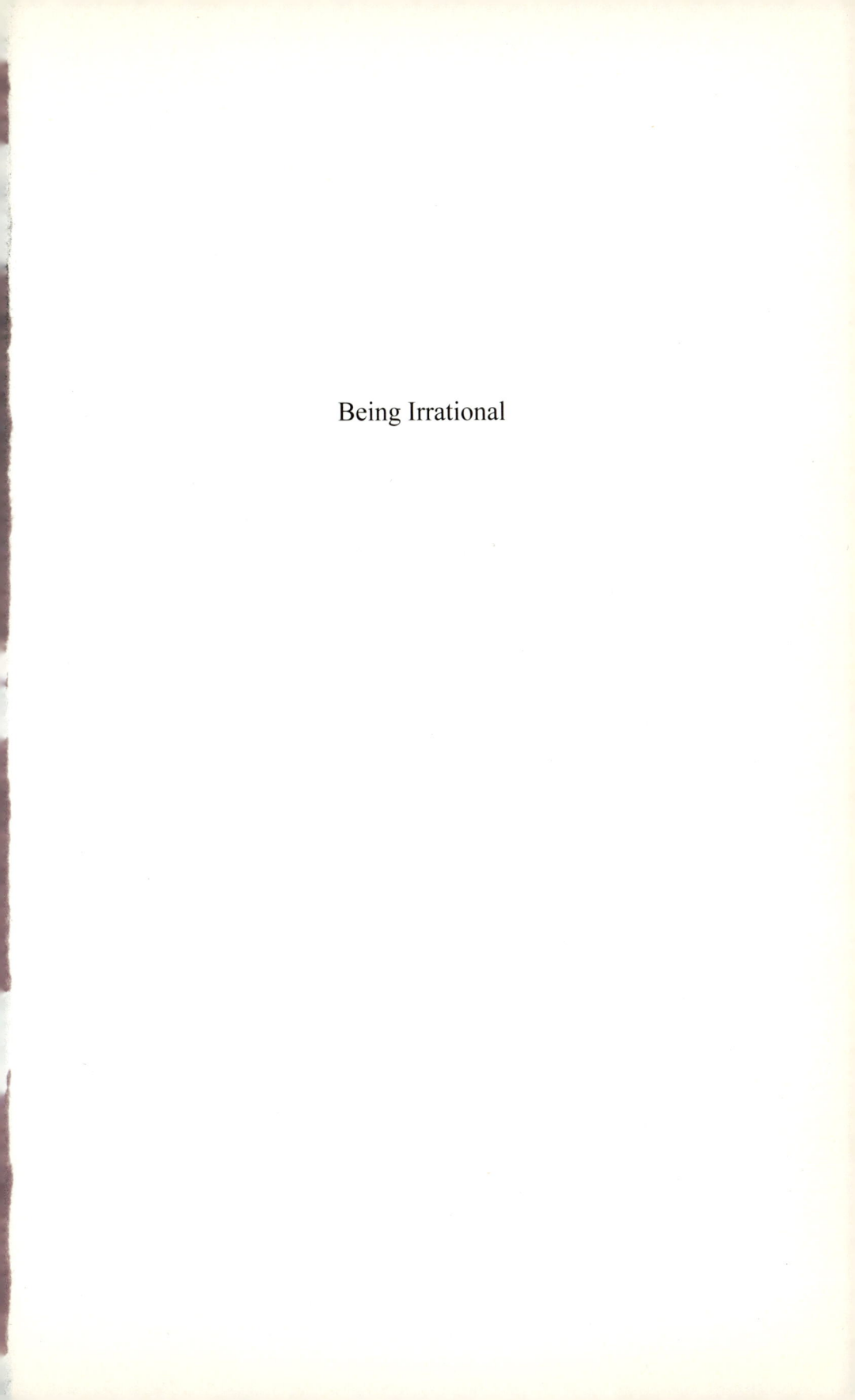

Being Irrational

Being Irrational

Lacan, the Objet a, and the Golden Mean

Shingu Kazushige

Translated and Edited by Michael Radich

Gakuju Shoin

Being Irrational: *Lacan, the Objet a, and the Golden Mean*
SHINGU Kazushige, M.D.
Translated and Edited by Michael RADICH

Originally published as *Rakan no seishin-bunseki* by Kodansha Ltd in 1995.

Gakuju Shoin, Publishers Ltd.
4-60-1 Minamidai Nakano-ku Tokyo 164-0014 Japan
http://www.gakuju.com

ISBN4-906502-28-8

© 2004 Shingu Kazushige
© 2004 Michael Radich   (English translation)

All rights reserved. No part of this book may be reproduced in any form without written permission from the copyright holders.

This publication has been made possible with the support of Suntory Foundation.
Printed and bound in Japan

CONTENTS

Author's Acknowledgements
Translator's Foreword

CHAPTER ONE
THE PSYCHOANALYTIC ROMANESQUE
    One: Starting at the Very Beginning   1
    Two: Nadja and Breton   5
    Three: Aimée and Lacan   9

CHAPTER TWO
THE STAGE IS SET
    One: After Freud   15
    Two: Melanie Klein   17
    Three: The Controversy Between Klein and Anna Freud   22
    Four: Enter Lacan   24
    Five: Schism – 1953   29

CHAPTER THREE
ROME: THE CORNERSTONE
    One: The Politics of the Short Session   37
    Two: The Logic of the Short Session   41
    Three: Interpretation as Sonic Boom   44
    Four: The Efficacy of the Short Session   47
    Five: The *Objet a* is the Golden Mean   52

CHAPTER FOUR
LANGUAGE AS THE OTHER
    One: The Fundamental Epistemological Position of Psychoanalysis   61
    Two: The Discourse of the Other   67
    Three: The Desire of the Other   73
    Four: The Desire of Nature   79

CHAPTER FIVE
BECOMING OTHER
- One: The *Objet a* Within the Discourse of the Other — 83
- Two: The Murder of the Thing — 86
- Three: Repetition (I) — 93
- Four: The Theory of the Mirror Stage — 98
- Five: Repetition (II) — 110
- Six: Symbolic, Imaginary, Real — 112
- Seven: Schema L and the Mirror — 121

CHAPTER SIX
ALL ALONE IN PARIS
- One: The Unary Trait — 127
- Two: The Ecole Freudienne de Paris — 133

CHAPTER SEVEN
WAITING FOR THE *AGALMA*
- One: The Object of Psychoanalysis — 139
- Two: Socrates — 140
- Three: Irma — 144
- Four: In the Mouth — 150

CHAPTER EIGHT
THE DISCOURSE OF PSYCHOANALYSIS
- One: The "Pass" — 155
- Two: The Four Discourses — 160
- Three: The "Discourse of the Master" and Oedipus — 168
- Four: Towards the Place of the Impossible — 176
- Five: The Final Failure — 180
- Six: Encore, Lacan! — 188

Bibliography
Index

ABBREVIATIONS

Écrits	*Écrits* (Paris: Seuil, 1966). [French original]
Roudinesco	Elizabeth Roudinesco, *Jacques Lacan and Co.: A History of Psychoanalysis in France, 1925-1985,* trans. Jeffrey Mehlman (London: Free Association Books, 1990).
S I	*The Seminar of Jacques Lacan, Edited by Jacques-Alain Miller: Book I, Freud's Papers on Technique 1953-1954,* translated with notes by John Forrester (Cambridge: Cambridge University Press, 1988).
S II	*The Seminar, Book II, The Ego in Freud's Theory and the Technique of Psychoanalysis, 1954-55,* trans. Sylvia Tomaselli, notes by John Forrester (Cambridge: Cambridge University Press, 1988).
S VII	*The Seminar of Jacques Lacan, Edited by Jacques-Alain Miller: Book VII, The Ethics of Psychoanalysis 1959-1960,* translated with notes by Dennis Porter (New York: Norton, 1992).
S VIII	*Le Séminaire de Jacques Lacan,* livre VIII, "Le Transfert", ed. J.-A. Miller (Paris: Seuil, 1991).
S XI	*The Four Fundamental Concepts of Psycho-Analysis,* ed. Jacques-Alain Miller, trans. Alan Sheridan (London: Penguin, 1979).
S XVII	*Le Séminaire, livre XVII: L'envers de la psychanalyse,* texte établi par Jacques-Alain Miller (Paris: Seuil, 1991). Translation by Russell Grigg, *The Seminar, Book XVII: The Other Side of Psychoanalysis* (Norton, forthcoming).
S XX	*The Seminar of Jacques Lacan: On Feminine Sexuality, the Limits of Love and Knowledge, 1972-1973 (Encore),* ed. Jacques-Alain Miller, trans. Bruce Fink (New York: Norton, 1999).
SE	*The Standard Edition of the Complete Psychological Works of Sigmund Freud,* ed. J. Strachey with Anna Freud, 24 vols (London: The Hogarth Press, 1953-1964).
Selection	*Écrits: A Selection,* trans. Alan Sheridan (New York: Norton, 1977). [English translation]

Author's Acknowledgements

Freud held that the future toward which our dreams lead us is "moulded . . . into a perfect likeness of the past", in that it *re*-presents a time in which our wishes were already fulfilled, and our desires already realized. If this is so, then surely an author will meet his own past through his future reader. In the mind of the reader, the author's wishes for the import of his text are realized, and the author's past encounters, as they determine his writing, are represented for the author himself to rediscover. Until such a moment, whether the author merely dreams of writing this foreword, or whether he writes it in his reader's dream, he is confined to the realm of the dream; and it is precisely the promise of such realization that makes writing – to be so *read* – such a meaningful endeavor.

And who represents that reader to the author if not the editor who urges him to write his book? Clearly, the author can only meet the reader to come by her mediation. I thank Kawasaki Atsuko of Kodansha Publishing, therefore, for effecting this mediation in the first instance; for this English version, I am likewise indebted to Michael Radich, who, as if by chance, picked out the original Japanese version from among many books on the capacious and well-stocked shelf of a large bookseller in Osaka, and ultimately made the decision to translate it into English.

In fact, I recollect many such happy encounters along the way as I have pursued the study of Lacanian psychoanalysis. I have been lucky to have as teachers and stimulating interlocutors my many mentors and colleagues in the Japan-France group (le Groupe franco-japonais) of the Champ freudien. Many of them came to Kyoto to participate in the International Symposium held in 1990, including Jacques-Alain Miller and Judith Miller as special guests, Jean-Louis Gault from Nantes and Pierre Skriabine from Paris as secretaries of the group, as well as many members of the group from France and all over Japan. Later, with the kind assistance of the Foundation of the Champ freudien, I was able to visit Paris and Nantes, and also Angers, where Roger Wartel was the warmest possible host. This symposium and the intellectual exchanges that grew out of it were among the most important sources of inspiration for this book, and I offer my heartfelt thanks to all these people.

Except where otherwise noted, all clinical material is from my own practice. I would like to thank all the patients who gave me the analytic experience I have recorded in the following pages.

My thanks are also due to the Suntory Foundation for offering me financial help for the publication of the English version, and to Yoshida Kazuhiro of Gakuju Shoin, who always showed this project warm and genuine understanding.

Shingu Kazushige
Kyoto, March 2004

Translator's Foreword

This book was originally published in Japanese as *Lacan's Psychoanalysis (Rakan no seishin-bunseki)*, and under that title it is the best-selling and widest-read introduction to Lacan in Japan. It is my belief, however, that the specific insights it affords into the *objet a* will make it fruitful reading for a much broader audience than the one it is confined to in Japanese; for this reason, I gladly accepted when Professor Shingu kindly offered me the chance to translate it.

Professor Shingu and I have together chosen a new title for the English edition – *Being Irrational: Lacan, the Objet* a, *and the Golden Mean* - in keeping with the relevance we hope its unique exposition of the *objet a* in particular will hold for an English-reading audience. The *objet a* is a seminal notion in Lacan's thought, and Bruce Fink has justifiably remarked that an entire book would be required to explain it fully. While *Being Irrational* is not a systematic exposition of all the different formulations that have been given to the *objet a*, it is, in a sense, just such a book. It is ground-breaking in that it develops a hint from Seminar XX (along with a few pieces of algebra from Seminar XVII) to the effect that "the *objet a* is the golden mean", and makes of this notion a key to Lacan's entire theoretical edifice. This is the "being irrational" (or "irrational being") of the title. As we see in Chapters III and V, it is "irrational" both in the ordinary everyday sense of the word – emotional, and not amenable to "logical" understanding – and also numerically: the golden mean is an irrational number.

In addition to the change of title, various other changes were also made in the course of the translation. Quotations, theoretical concepts, and details from Lacan's biography have been sourced. References to Japanese culture that would be lost on an outside audience in their original condensed form have been expanded. The translator and author have also co-operated to modify the text slightly in places, to make it read smoothly in English. In achieving the latter aim, we decided to move paragraph divisions in places, and we have also introduced some introductory and conclusory sections at the beginning and end of structural units such as chapters and sections. All such changes were made with the author's careful approval. In the few cases where changes bear on content, or where substantial passages were added, the fact is noted.

A note is also required on the use of the pronoun "I". In many passages, I have decided after consultation with Professor Shingu to translate the Japanese first person pronoun *watashi* as "I", but to use the third person form of the verb with it (e.g. "I is an other."). In so doing, I hope to convey a peculiarity of the Japanese of the original text. Verbs in Japanese do not conjugate for person, and there are no articles, so that both "I am an other", for example, and "the 'I' is an other" would be expressed in exactly the same way: *Watashi wa hitori no tasha de aru*. Throughout the book, Professor Shingu talks about *watashi* ("I") in discussing the vicissitudes of the Lacanian subject, and in Japanese, these passages not only read as natural ways of phrasing an objective consideration of "the I", but also as bearing quite intimately on the person of the author and/or the reader: "I". Inspired by the Rimbaudian "I is an other" quoted at the outset of Chapter V, we decided to compromise between the personal "I" (as opposed to the distancing "the I") and the objectifying use of the third person. We hope that this phraseology, even if it reads strangely in English, will convey something of the double import of the argument, which implicates the person of reader, writer, and translator even as it is, at the same time, a universal consideration of human subjectivity as a category.

In the course of preparing this translation, I have been helped by a number of people, and I would like to thank Duncan Campbell, Bruce Fink, Russell Grigg, Jeffrey Hayden, Matsuzawa Tetsurō, Daya Nelson, Nikaido Kazuko, and Judy Wakabayashi. As always, my wife, Amanda Jack, has provided me with constant support in ways too various to count. My thanks, however, go above all to Professor Shingu himself, for so readily entrusting the translation of his work to an unknown quantity; for his meticulous explanations of troublesome details; and for the many kindnesses he has showed me personally. Any mistakes in the translation, of course, remain my responsibility and mine alone.

Michael Radich
Cambridge MA, 2004

Illustrations

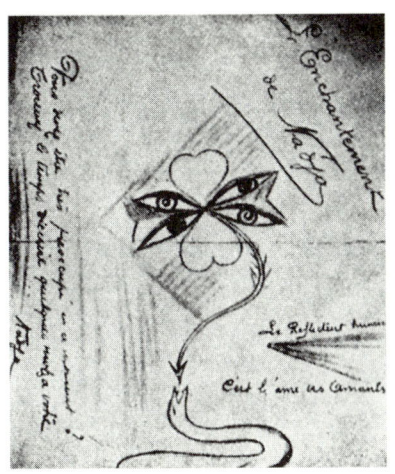

"The Lovers' Flower" by Nadja (see Chap 1)
Nadja, Gendaishichosha, Tokyo

René Magritte, "Reproduction Interdite", 1937
©ADAGP, Paris & JVACS, Tokyo 2004 (see p.124)

Ueno K., Torisu H., Hinohara A., and Hirai T. (University of Tsukuba School for the Blind), "The Town Where the Birds Come", Gallery TOM (see p.72)

Heironymous Bosch, "Music Hell", The Prado Museum (see p.75)

CHAPTER ONE

THE PSYCHOANALYTIC ROMANESQUE

One: Starting at the Very Beginning

A dream of tuna *sushi*
Whenever I come to discuss French psychoanalysis, and particularly that of Lacan, I cannot help thinking of one particular incident involving tuna *sushi*. Once, while working as a psychiatrist, I treated a woman who was a student majoring in French literature. One day we were out on the roof of the hospital, and I said, "Isn't the sun strong today! You need a hat!"

"Yeah," she replied, "but I want to wear a slipper," and she put her slipper on her head. Then, slowly, she brought the slipper down from her head to her mouth, and said, "I'd like to eat this."

"It's dirty," I warned her, as any sensible person might.

"Well then," she said simply, "I'd better put it on my foot." And she quietly did.

It was quite a moment. Before she could understand what I said to her so simply, she had gone through a great deal of confusion, and all the medicine we tried had not the slightest effect. At one point, she had risen from her bed to stare fixedly into the distance and shriek at the top of her lungs, "Don't die, Dr Shingu, don't die!" And yet I had been right there in front of her all the while. She had looked straight through me, the real me at least, to whatever she saw on her own horizon. Later, she told me that she had seemed trapped in a dream from which she would never wake. In that dream, her mother had already died four times, and reduced to a mere head, I was about to die too.

As can be seen from the fact that she wanted to eat it, the incident with the slipper was symptomatic of a period characterized by rampant overeating. More important, though, was her anxiety that she was suspected of eating everything from the shared fridges wherever she lived. Before she got sick and was brought to hospital, she got anxious about the fridge in her university dormitory, and now, in hospital, she got anxious about the fridge in her ward.

Eventually, however, she was able to announce that she had "eaten" something with a clear, untroubled expression on her face. It was after I had been away from the hospital for a while, attending a conference. At the conference, I had gone to an icebreaker party, and like many such events, it had been a standing buffet. Having eaten a little of the greasy, tasteless food at this party, I had felt like eating some tuna

Chapter 1: THE PSYCHOANALYTIC ROMANESQUE

sushi to cleanse my pallet, and had gone somewhere where I knew I could get some. But they no longer had what I was after, and I returned empty-handed. The next day I met the patient in her ward, however, and she told me, "Last night I dreamt I stuffed myself on tuna *sushi*." When she told me this, it raised a knot of mixed feelings in me. As one would expect, I was amazed by the apparent coincidence, but by the same token, I noticed that I felt as if it were almost a matter of course; in her dream, my patient had fulfilled for herself *my* unfulfilled desire of the night before.

Whenever I recall this experience with tuna *sushi,* the next thing that comes to mind is the dream about smoked salmon that Freud describes in *The Interpretation of Dreams.* A certain female patient of Freud's dreamt that she wanted to give a dinner party, but all she had in the house was some smoked salmon. She thought she would go out shopping, but then she remembered that it was Sunday, and all the shops would be shut.[1] In discussing this passage, Lacan says that the smoked salmon takes the place of the desire of the Other.[2] The difference between tuna and salmon aside, the two dreams share the point that they feature raw or half-raw, reddish eating fish, and in both dreams the fish is also given the role of bearer of the "desire of the Other" in the unconscious. This "desire of the Other" is an important point in Lacan's thought, and we will return later to examine it in in more detail.

Music

My patient's condition changed from day to day. She was in the state known as stupor, in which the patient looks as if they are completely asleep, and won't wake even if someone moves their arm around, for example. In fact, if you put the patient's arm into some unnatural position, he is most likely to keep it that way, and stay firmly stuck in his dream state. Even in this condition, however, the patient can still see very well everything that goes on in the world around him, with the difference that these real events undergo dream-like transformations; in my patient's case, for example, the hospital ward could become the site of a broadcasting station experiment, for example, or the voice of the nurse calling "Change sheets!" could be heard and registered in memory as "Change cheese!".

I used to play my patient Mozart's K 516 (String Quintet in G minor). Once, while still in her stupor, she went home for a night, and her mother took the tape of the Mozart with her and played it for her at home. She later recalled for me the way she had experienced the music.

> "When I left the hospital, the *moto perpetuo* was playing [in fact it was not], and it was like my little finger was playing part of it on the piano. The movement of my

---

[1] SE IV, 146-148.
[2] *Selection,* 262.

Chapter 1: THE PSYCHOANALYTIC ROMANESQUE

finger was somehow a promise between you [the author] and me.[3] When Mum played it for me at home, I felt chills all up and down my spine. I'd never felt like that before."

Even though she was still in her state of stupor when she heard the piece, she remembered it accurately, and could distinguish it from recordings by other artists. Perhaps the perception of music is different from other senses. In any case, the tune certainly was a link between her and me.

Her delusions eventually changed into dazzling strings of phonemes, which were like a kind of music to my ears. It was my turn to listen, and her turn to play.[4]

"I think that I'm Red Riding Hood and I've swallowed the poison apple [sic],[5] it's my Mum, you think, "Yeah [*un* - a play on *unchi*, 'poo']," right? Then my hemorrhoids [*kireji*] burst [*kireru*], but of course it's nothing like flirting, dahling; oh, Doctor, I need you more than anything! - if only I could make you see that, I think I wouldn't need any more caregiving [*kaijo*], I think I wouldn't need any more monsters [*kaiju*], you know, if you think, "Leave me alone, will you [*kureyo*]!?" then the next thing that pops up is a crayon [*kureyon*], right? And a crayon is a pastel [*kurepasu*], right? And you know, I think you could say, "Hi there, Natchan Lemon! Hi there, Natchan Lemon!" too."[6]

"I want to start right from the very beginning, well it is the very beginning, and it's not, I mean it's already begun, you taught me that, Doctor, the very beginning is inside Mummy's tummy. You might say, though, that even Mummy doesn't know what's inside her herself, but you could say that I know too, inside Mummy's tummy it was a sea of blood. I really feel [*tsukuzuku*] how good it is to be alive, a cicada [*tsukutsukuboshi*] is crying."

---

[3] In Japan children clinch a promise by clenching little fingers with each other – Trans.
[4] There are several untranslatable plays on words close in sound in the following quotes from the patient. I have included the original Japanese in brackets at relevant points so the reader can get some sense of these. – Trans.
[5] I would like to read the patient's blurring of the distinction between Snow White and Little Red Riding Hood less as a symptom of the breakdown of her mental faculties, and more as an instance of "wit" (*Witz*) in the sense analyzed by Freud in *Jokes and Their Relation to the Unconscious* (SE VIII). By means of this flash of wit, the patient gives succinct, humorous expression to the crisis of identity in which she finds herself. The reference to Snow White also hints at the connection between the crisis in her own identity and the confusion that had invaded her relationship with her (m)other. [Note added by the author for the English edition – Trans.]

Chapter 1: THE PSYCHOANALYTIC ROMANESQUE

The road to France

My patient was heavily caught up in French literature. She studied French with enthusiasm, and had French friends. I, on the other hand, was interested in the psychoanalysis of Melanie Klein, which we look at in the next chapter, and hoped to go to England, where Klein's ideas had taken root and flourished. But by the time her treatment had been completed and a few years had passed, the situation was completely different. It was I who went to France. Meanwhile, she changed majors to English literary theory when she advanced to graduate school. Was this all coincidental? No. We had done a swap. And what had we swapped? The *desire of the Other*. She yielded her desire to study in France to me, and took away with her my desire to learn more about English thought.

To use an old psychoanalytic term, what happened to us could also be called an exchange of "ego ideals". Ideas like "France" or "England", which have to some degree been symbolized, can include within them a mark that guides the subject along its path to socialization. This is the ego ideal, and it is what we had exchanged between us. There is a very close relation between the desire of the Other and the ego ideal, and it is because we carry the desire of the Other that we end up on the wild goose chase for an abstract ideal in the first place. The desiring heart, to some extent, already belongs to the other.

My relationship with my patient was a *mutual* psychoanalysis, and in psychoanalysis we experience the movement of the desire of the Other in forms like those I have described. If I had not been the recipient of her desire, then no doubt I would never have gone to France, and this book would never have been written. In a sense, the "cause" of this book lies in her "madness", insofar as it was brought into the relation between us. Similarly, although she was studying French with a passion, she still had no idea what she should focus on for her graduate research. It seems to me that the desire she took away from me decided for her the path she took.

When a person puts something into action, then, it is not her own desire that is at work. "Man's desire is the desire of the Other."[7] This dictum, extracted by Lacan from the Hegel he learnt under Kojève and of paramount importance to psychoanalysis, can be seen at work in the actions of myself and my patient. Both the appetite for tuna *sushi*, and the aspirations for the future indicated by the names "France" and "England", were *transferred* (in the technical sense of psychoanalytic transference) through the mesh of the desire of the Other. Seemingly telepathic phenomena like this occur relatively frequently in psychoanalysis, and in the thirtieth lecture of his *New Introductory Lectures to Psycho-Analysis*,[8] Freud himself writes with respect of people in analysis communicating their desire to one another

---

[6] "Natchan Lemon" is a brand of soft drink. – Trans.
[7] S XI, 235.
[8] Freud, *New Introductory Lectures to Psycho-Analysis,* SE XXII, 36-56.

pseudo-telepathically. In saying this, I do not mean to mysticize psychoanalysis – indeed, I would argue that it is far more mystical to think that humans are free to subjectively desire whatever they please. The modalities of human desire are, rather, predetermined in the realm of the symbol.

So I trod the paths of the desire of the Other all the way to France, and when I got there, I was excited to find that it was possible to have tuna *sushi* very cheaply, not in the Japanese restaurants of Paris, but at the fishmonger's. There you find huge tuna lying unadulterated, with their eyes goggling at you. The fishmonger asks how many grams you want and cuts it for you. If you cook some rice and make it yourself, you can eat as much tuna *sushi* as you want. Certainly, this is not to say that I *did* actually go to the trouble of making it – it meant more to me just knowing that it was *possible*. No doubt my desire for tuna *sushi*, which my patient took over from me at the time of the dream, was right from the start a desire with symbolic meaning, and that is why it was transferred into her dream.

My patient often spoke to me of André Breton's novel *Nadja*.[9] When she ran as if on thin air up and down the hospital corridors, drifting between madness and sanity, she often used to mutter, "I am Nadja" to herself. It was inevitable that I be Breton.

Two: Nadja and Breton

Record of a "successful" treatment

Psychoanalysis was introduced to France in the 1920s, following World War I. Henri Claude, professor of psychiatry at the Université Paris, showed himself receptive to psychoanalysis, and a research group made up primarily of doctors was formed there. Several other groups of doctors and psychologists interested in psychoanalysis were also established, and not long after, in 1926, the Société Psychanalytique de Paris (SPP) was officially founded. Many of the founding members were of the so-called orthodox school. Among them were the Greek princess Marie Bonaparte, an analyst herself and the eventual patron of the whole psychoanalytic movement in France, and Loewenstein, who later conducted Lacan's training analysis before emigrating to the USA and becoming a central figure in ego psychology.

There was another current that ran parallel to this, however, which also played a large part in bringing psychoanalysis to France – surrealism. It is a well-known fact that several exchanges took place between André Breton, leader of the surrealist movement, and Freud, and despite his disappointment at Freud's caution and his demands that Freud adapt a more radical posture, Breton never lost his respect for Freud as the master who had cast light on the positive meaning of the dream. In his

---

[9] André Breton, *Nadja*, translated by Richard Howard (New York: Grove Press, 1960).

surrealist venture, Breton aimed to thoroughly relativize reality, and so for him, the symbolic activity of the dream was especially valuable. He had originally hoped to go into medicine, and seems to have been haunted by an almost predestined sensitivity to madness.

Breton's novel *Nadja,* published in 1928, begins when its protagonist ("I") meets the sick Nadja on a street corner,[10] and is drawn into the long and involved tale of her life and her fortunes. *Nadja* is a kind of *roman à clef,* and can be read as the record of a treatment, although it would be inappropriate to maintain fixed ideas about who is treating who. The point is that the work clearly deals with psychoanalytic "transference".

When psychoanalysis was introduced to France by the medical groups mentioned above, there was a tendency to see the unconscious as a biological function. The incorporation of psychoanalysis into medical psychology amounted to no more than the addition of a new element, namely sexuality and its repression, to a system that explained everything, from pure biological fact to social phenomena, in the monistic terms of instinct, reaction, and heredity. But in Breton's case things were utterly different. Without having developed a sufficient understanding of the order of experience called "transference", he flew into it head first. It is only when transference arises between two people that the unconscious becomes plain, and when this happens we see that the unconscious is not merely a minor appendage at the bottom end of the nervous system, an organ of the individual *qua* biological organism. The novel shows this very clearly.

Once the psychotic Nadja has made her entrance, the novel describes the way the liaison with her completely drains the narrator "I" of all his spirit and vigor. In her guileless way, Nadja gradually draws the protagonist away from reality. For example, in the following scenes she seems to wield a kind of clairvoyant power.

> "Nadja's eyes now sweep over the surrounding houses. "Do you see that window up there? It's black, like all the rest. Look hard. In a minute it will light up. It will be red." The minute passes. The window lights up. There are, as a matter of fact, red curtains. (I am . . . unable to do anything about the fact that this may exceed the limits of credibility [. . .]) I confess that this place frightens me, as it is beginning to frighten Nadja too."[11]

Such is the power that Nadja has over the narrator ("I") by this point that he can no longer think of a reasonable explanation for this event, such as, for example, that Nadja always passes this way, and so would know roughly what time the light goes on in the window. In another passage, Nadja says that she and the narrator lived

---

[10] *Nadja,* 64.
[11] *Nadja,* 83-84.

Chapter 1: The Psychoanalytic Romanesque

together in the time of Marie Antoinette, and then asks who he was in those days:

> "She . . . wanted to walk back toward the Conciergerie.[12] She is very abandoned in her behavior, very sure of me. But she is looking for something . . . 'It's not here . . . . Listen, tell me why you have to go to prison? . . . I've been to prison too. Who was I? It was ages ago. And you, then, who were you?' . . . She wonders who she might have been, in Marie Antoinette's circle."[13]

Nadja's question rattles the narrator. Who am I? You might think that you know nothing better than the answer to this question, but in fact it is very hard to answer. The novel itself actually starts with this so-called problem of identity: *Qui suis-je?* ("Who am I?")[14] And in this scene, the narrator seems on the brink of a precious insight into the answer – "'I' am the man who lived with this woman called Nadja long ago, in the age of Marie Antoinette. That's it! It is precisely in being this man that 'I' am myself." The idea of "past lives", normally the brunt of so much scorn, suddenly takes on an air of reality with the discovery of this gentle companion from a former existence. Thus the relation between Breton and Nadja transcends time and space, to attain reality in "another scene" (*ein anderer Platz*).[15] Looking back on these events, Breton writes:

> "I . . . [had been] lying at Nadja's feet like a lapdog. By what latitude could we, abandoned thus to the fury of symbols, be occasionally prey to the demon of analogy, seeing ourselves as the object of extreme overtures . . .? How does it happen that, thrown together, once and for all, so far from the earth, in those brief intervals which our marvelous stupor grants us, we have been able to exchange a few incredibly concordant views . . .? I have taken Nadja, from the first day to the last, for a free genius, something like those spirits of the air . . . which we can never overcome. As for her . . . she takes me for a god, she thinks of me as the sun."[16]

This passage depicts superbly the weird magnetic field of the transference. But there is nothing in such a relation of the logic required to make a life together. For that, what is needed is what we might call the plane of a horizontal relation, within which to understand one another, whereas Nadja rises and falls on a sheer vertical

---

[12] The prison in Paris where prisoners awaited execution during the Revolution.
[13] *Nadja*, 84-85.
[14] *Nadja*, 11.
[15] Cf. Freud's famous formulation of the unconscious as "another scene". GW II/III, 51, 541; SE IV, 48, and V, 536.
[16] *Nadja*, 108-111.

axis.[17]

Having learnt that Nadja has debts, the narrator offers her both financial support and the warmth of his embrace, but even so, he says, "For some time, I had stopped understanding Nadja. Actually, perhaps we have never understood one another . . ."[18] In the end, Nadja, having "indulged herself in . . . eccentricities . . . in the hallways of her hotel,"[19] is taken off to the asylum, and the relationship is broken off. If Breton was the therapist, then the treatment ends in failure, but if the therapist was Nadja, then we must concede that it was a success, insofar as it inscribed in Breton's heart a "book" which would never be closed again.

Nadja and psychiatric medicine

Later in the book, Breton writes of mental hospitals, "Unless you have been inside a sanitarium you do not know that madmen are *made* there, just as criminals are made in our reformatories."[20] He further describes Professor Henri Claude, who we noted above was so receptive to psychoanalysis, with biting invective, speaking of "the cheek of people who question you when you want to be left alone, like Professor Claude . . . with his dunce's forehead and that stubborn expression on his face."[21] It was only natural, then, that *Nadja* should provoke criticism when introduced to the world of psychiatry. Everyone attacked Breton – including Clérambault, whom Lacan was later to laud as his "master" – and Breton picked up the gauntlet in response. This same Breton had originally aspired to a medical career and served as a kind of intern, and now he found himself at odds with medicine socially, on the strength of the transferential reality between himself and Nadja. He subsequently wrote *The Communicating Vessels*,[22] in which he attempted to dispute Freud's theories.

Perhaps, through the experience of *Nadja*, Breton had at some point become an analyst, without ever plying psychoanalysis as his trade. The "transference" had relativized his identity. If "I" for Breton was not the "lapdog" that had lain at Nadja's feet in the apartments of Marie Antoinette, then what good would it do "I" to be anything or anyone, in the context of the worldly world? If Breton *had* become an "analyst" in this sense, however, he was flying in the face of a countervailing trend in analytic theory. At the time, an orthodoxy was gradually taking shape within psychoanalysis that the aim of the treatment was for the analysand to identify with the analyst. Identification with the healthy ego of the analyst, it would eventually be

---

[17] "[In] the world which was Nadja's . . . everything so rapidly assumed the appearance of a rise and a fall." *Nadja*, 135.
[18] *Nadja*, 130.
[19] *Nadja*, 136.
[20] *Nadja*, 139.
[21] *Nadja*, 138-139.
[22] André Breton, *The Communicating Vessels*, trans. by Mary Ann Caws and Geoffrey T. Harris, with notes and introduction by Mary Ann Caws (Lincoln: University of Nebraska Press, 1990).

argued, would stabilize the patient's identity, and show them the way to a well-adjusted social existence. Now, Lacan declared out-and-out war on this view (taking his weapons from his well-stocked arsenal of irony);[23] more to the point, Breton's experience with Nadja was also the direct inverse of the situation envisaged in this model of analysis.

Lacan himself passed in and out of the surrealist coterie in the years when he was just starting out as a psychiatrist, and he probably met with Breton, five years his senior, on a number of occasions.[24] The two shared a common goal of opening humanity up to an alternate reality, and a passionate drive to discover within us something of an entirely different order to the ego identity based on social productivity.[25] However, Lacan was not the pariah Breton made himself, at least not initially. He rather received his psychoanalysis through the more institutionalized of the two channels through which it flowed into France – the medical and psychiatric groups touched on above – even as he maintained contact with Surrealist currents as well. We now turn to looking at Lacan's early encounters with psychoanalysis, and his own Nadja-like muse, the psychotic patient on whose case he based his doctoral dissertation.

Three: Aimée and Lacan

The master, Clérambault

Jacques-Marie Lacan was born into a Catholic bourgeoisie family in Paris on April 13, 1901. His father was a high-ranking executive in a trading company that dealt in foodstuffs, primarily vinegar, and his mother's side of the family was strongly

---

[23] "Any conception of analysis that is articulated – innocently or not, God only knows – to defining the end of analysis as identification with the analyst, by that very fact makes an admission of its limits. Any analysis that one teaches as having to be terminated by identification with the analyst reveals, by the same token, that its true motive is elided." S XI, 271.
[24] Of course, Lacan learnt a great deal more from Salavor Dali than from Breton himself. When his vigorous intellectual ambition first drew him to the surrealist group, it was Dali that he telephoned directly and asked for a meeting. See Roudinesco, 110.
[25] In a paper entitled "Écrits 'inspirés': Schizographie", written in collaboration with J. Lévy-Valensi and P. Migault in 1931, Lacan writes of Breton's *Manifeste du surréalisme* (1924) as follows: "The experiments undertaken by certain writers in a mode of writing that they call 'surrealist', the method of which they have described quite scientifically, show the remarkable degree of autonomy that can be attained by graphic automatism, quite apart from any hypnosis (Les expériences faites par certains écrivains sur un mode d'écriture qu'ils ont appelé surréaliste, et dont ils ont décrit très scientifiquement la méthode, montrent à quel degré d'autonomie remarquable peuvent atteindre les automatismes graphiques en dehors de toute hypnose)" *Annales Médico-Psychologiques*, XIIIe Série, 89e Année, T. II, No. 1, p. 520.

Chapter 1: THE PSYCHOANALYTIC ROMANESQUE

religious. After a brother who died in infancy, he was followed by his sister Madeleine, two years his junior, and Marc-François, five years younger again.[26] It seems likely that the mother's influence decided the complementary courses of the two sons: Lacan himself turned away from Catholicism, only to seek so restlessly after a system of knowledge that could match it, while his younger brother Marc-François chose the path of a Benedictine monk.[27]

The young Jacques is said to have read everything he could lay his hands on, to have collected various objects, and to have shown a keen interest in money.[28] Lacan thus clearly evinced an anal tendency. Now, psychoanalysis holds that anality is the basis of characterological interests in religion, money and order, and throughout his life, Lacan remained in a tense relation with this characteristic anal tendency in himself. He professed atheism in his role as psychoanalyst, and yet he habitually read religious works, and identified with certain mystics. He was dispassionately aware that if the mission of psychoanalysis is to minister to the mind, mundane matters of money nonetheless have an inalienable role to play; neither did he hesitate to accumulate wealth himself and to use it to political ends. He fired broadsides at the guild order of psychoanalysis at every opportunity; and yet, at the same time, he also maintained a cool distance from revolutionaries of various stripes.

In the next few years, Lacan began his medical studies, and Lacan's parents moved to Boulogne, on the outskirts of Paris.[29] In 1926 he began his basic studies in neuropsychiatry. Beginning in 1927, he continued these studies under Professor Henri Claude,[30] whom we encountered earlier, and from 1928, he studied under Gaëtan de Clérambault, who as chief physician with the Paris Police specialized in forensic psychiatry.[31]

Clérambault, who we saw earlier locked horns with Breton over *Nadja*, conducted extensive research into a psychopathological phenomenon he called "mental automatism", which lies hidden at the base of all delusion and hallucination.[32] Clérambault's "mental automatism" denotes the work in the mind of automatic ideation, that is, ideation that transcends the intentions of the individual. It is thereby linked, beyond what Clérambault himself might have intended, to the notion of the unconscious found, for instance, in surrealist "automatic writing". Clérambault considered mental automatism an expression of an organic dysfunction in the brain, and the surrealists, of course, saw things differently; this difference,

---

[26] Roudinesco, 103-4.
[27] Roudinesco, 102.
[28] Roudinesco, 103.
[29] Roudinesco, 104.
[30] Lacan, *De la psychose paranoïaque dans ses rapports avec la personnalité, suivi de Premiers écrits sur la paranoïa* (Paris: Seuil, 1975), 9.
[31] Ibid.
[32] Roudinesco, 105-8.

however, is not of interest to us here. What does matter is that Clérambault saw a radical disjunction in principle between the individual or social consciousness, and what was variously termed the unconscious, subconscious, or pre-conscious. This disjunction contrasts starkly with the continuity perceived by the French psychology of the time, as represented by Pierre Janet.

Clérambault himself was not interested in Freud. But Lacan found in his work, much more than that of Janet and Claude, a framework within which the Freudian unconscious could be correctly located. Freud's unconscious is not a part of the subject that, if integrated into the subject, will set the subject on the path to self-realization and make of it a more complete being. The unconscious is cut off from "I" by a radical discontinuity. Even if I could somehow make it conscious, it would already have moved on, be elsewhere; nevertheless, the relation with it cannot be avoided. This fundamentally and ineradicably alien aspect of the Freudian unconscious is shared by Clérambault's "mental automatism". Both are indifferent to the mind, but still affect its functioning persistently. Lacan elaborated on these characteristics of both constructs in his concept of the "signifying chain".[33]

Clérambault never married, and spent every day at the police station seeing criminal psychotics. He ended his life by shooting himself before a mirror.[34] He had observed the destructive tendencies in humanity from the viewpoint of objective medical science, always carefully to keep his distance from his patients, but at some point that destruction had sneaked up on him and wormed its way inside his heart. Perhaps he simply collapsed under the weight of accumulated transference. The course of his life stands in stark contrast to that of Lacan; but Lacan, too, as we will now see, laid the foundation of his theories through intimate acquaintance with a criminal psychotic.

Paranoia – the departure point
Lacan was given his theoretical starting point by a female paranoiac, who attacked an actress, "Z", at the theatre with a knife. The victim severely injured her hand when she sought to fend off the blows, and the attacker was taken to Sainte-Anne Hospital in Paris, where Lacan kept her under observation.[35] He called her Aimée, and made her case history public in his 1932 doctoral thesis, "On Paranoiac Psychosis in its Relation to the Personality".[36]

Aimée had written a great deal, in the hope of becoming a writer. She suffered delusions of persecution for a period after she turned thirty, and spent time in hospital. After being discharged, she sent a manuscript to a certain publisher, and

---

[33] *Selection*, 215.
[34] Roudinesco, 108.
[35] Roudinesco, 112-3.
[36] Lacan, *De la psychose paranoïaque dans ses rapports avec la personnalité, suivi de Premiers écrits sur la paranoïa* (Paris: Seuil, 1975). Details of the case study taken from this work, 153-205.

on being rejected for publication composed a bill of complaint with the intent of suing. After making an attempt on a member of the publishing company office staff, she was taken into the custody of the police. On this occasion, she got away with just a reprimand, but she soon developed delusions: the actress "Z" was writing a novel about her in collusion with the writer P. B.; "Z" was trying to kill her child. It was on the basis of these delusions that she attacked "Z".

The germ of her delusions could be traced back to the moment when she lost her first child immediately after it was born. At the time she already had the idea that her older sister had stolen her child.[37] This idea was transferred first onto the person of a friend and then to "Z", not fading even when she gave birth to and raised a subsequent child. It is relatively easy to see that these female images, in which her aggression found its objects, were expressions of her idealized self. Once she had engaged in the destructive behaviors described above, the tide of the delusions ebbed, and ultimately they vanished. Utilizing Freud's observations of the aggressive component contained in homosexual attachment, or cases where the feeling of guilt precedes the crime and is eased by the crime, Lacan gave her case the name of "self-punitive paranoia".[38] In putting herself in the position of the criminal, Aimée orchestrated matters so that she was punished, deserted, and abandoned by the women who represented her ideal. This was the only way she could gain some peace of mind. The fact that primal human aggression lies somewhere in the field of the identification of self and other became, for Lacan, an almost unshakeable theoretical starting point. The theory of the mirror stage, which we look at in Chapter V, was an inevitable outgrowth of these beginnings.

Aimée's son and heir
The relationship between Aimée and Lacan did not come to an end even when Aimée left the hospital and Lacan published his thesis. Because of his mother's condition, Aimée's son was raised by his aunt. After graduating from university he set out to become a psychoanalyst, and as his training analyst he chose Jacques Lacan. He was unaware that Lacan's "Aimée" was his own mother, and it also escaped Lacan's notice that this Didier Anzieu was Aimée's son, grown into a young man. Lacan accepted Anzieu into analysis. Since Aimée had gone by her maiden name when treated by Lacan, it was some time before either side noticed the connection.[39] Had each known who the other was, they would surely have avoided one another, or refused the analytic relationship.

But can we not see unconscious desire at work in the strange course these events took? Anzieu knew that his mother had suffered from psychosis, and must have

---

[37] Roudinesco, 113.
[38] Mehlman's translation. See Roudinesco, 113.
[39] Roudinesco, 120-1.

realized that there was at least a possibility that Lacan had treated her. On the other hand, it seems highly unlikely that Lacan had never heard that Aimée's married name was Anzieu, or that her son was called Didier. It is more natural to assume that each knew unconsciously who the other was, and that they chose one another precisely *because* they knew.

This was not the only subsequent connection between Aimée and Lacan. After she was discharged from hospital, Aimée was cared for by her sister, and hired by the owner of a country home in the area as a cook. As her employer's main house was in Boulogne, Aimée in time became the cook there too. But Boulogne was where Lacan's father and mother lived. When Lacan's mother died in 1948, his father took on a certain skilled cook as housekeeper, and when he visited his father one day, Lacan learnt that this housekeeper was none other than Aimée.[40] We can be sure that he ate her cooking together with his father.

Don't we get the sense that the chain of fate had come full circle? The transferential relation between Lacan and Aimée was apparently more intense than can be seen from the doctoral thesis alone. The internal structure of that transference had expanded and taken on concrete form, and was even now developing before Lacan's very eyes. Within the transference, Aimée was identified with Lacan's mother, and Lacan reenacted his relation to his mother in becoming Aimée's son. This transferential structure was made real by the *choice of Lacan's father*. At the time of his thesis, Lacan had in a sense been brought into the world as an analyst, and that analyst was already possessed of the desire to become Aimée's son. There is thus not the slightest shred of coincidence in the fact that his father searched Aimée out and installed her in Lacan's mother's place just at the moment Lacan's work as analyst was crowned with success. Similarly, when Lacan accepted Didier Anzieu for analysis, it is not stretching interpretation too far to see the workings of the unconscious desire to experience what it was like to be Aimée's son by putting himself in Didier's place.

How must it have been for Didier? Doubtless his mother's psychosis had brought him no small measure of suffering, and no doubt his biggest dilemma was how, or if, he could recognize his real mother, Aimée, *as* his mother. It was thus inevitable that he receive analysis from Lacan.[41] All he needed to do to accept Aimée as his mother was to swap unconscious desires with a person who wanted to be Aimée's son, and no-one could have fit the bill better than Lacan. Didier Anzieu eventually became an independent analyst, wrote a book on Freud's self-analysis,[42] and made a name for himself. But was he able to successfully take over from Lacan the desire to be

---

[40] Roudinesco, 121.
[41] We might say that it was *necessary*, in the full philosophical sense of the term. See Chapter VIII on Lacan's use of Aristotelian modal logic.
[42] Didier Anzieu, *L'auto-analyse de Freud et la découverte de la psychanalyse* (2 vols.) (Presses Universitaires de France, 1959).

Chapter 1: THE PSYCHOANALYTIC ROMANESQUE

Aimée's son? The record, understandably, is less eloquent on this point.

The desire of the Other provided the driving force of the analysis between Anzieu and Lacan, then, just as it did between myself and my psychotic devotee of French literature; as it ramified beyond the bounds of the analytic situation as such, it stitched together a patchwork of encounters across generations much like a Romanesque family novel. As Lacan rose to pre-eminence as a psychoanalyst, his deep-rooted desire for recognition as son and heir to the throne of the paranoiac woman he called "Aimée" must have exerted a subtle influence on his relations with the women who stood at the center of the psychoanalytic movement. In the next chapter, we will see how Lacan's relations with these psychoanalytic matriarchs played out, as we continue to follow Lacan's intellectual formation, and the human dramas that surrounded it.

CHAPTER TWO

THE STAGE IS SET

One: After Freud

Two essays: 1930 . . .
Psychoanalysis was a brainchild of a single man, Sigmund Freud, and during his lifetime, the entire psychoanalytic movement was grounded on and driven by his presence. Did it continue to exist at all, then, in his absence? And if so, did it persist unaltered in its essence by his death? This is the problematic of the "post-Freudian" era, and in thinking about this problem, we must first of all define our terms. If we are to posit such an "after Freud" in the history of psychoanalysis, where exactly should we begin? One important watershed that springs to mind is Melanie Klein's essay of 1930, entitled "The Importance of Symbol-Formation in the Development of the Ego".[1]

In 1917, Freud wrote an essay entitled "On the Transformations of Instinct, as Exemplified in Anal Erotism".[2] In it he describes how the feces are symbolically transformed into babies, money, and an obstinate personality. While these various objects are of different orders in everyday life, they form a common plane in the unconscious, and are exchanged with one another as the need arises. Like Freud's essay, Klein's theorizes the origins of symbolic activity; unlike Freud, however, Klein deals not with the anus, but with "inside" the mother's body.[3] This "inside of the mother's body" is something like a dark cavity, and in the mind of the troubled child it shifts chameleon-like through a rapid succession of different forms.

Klein had undertaken the treatment of a young boy called Dick. When Dick said the word "station" as he played with a train, Klein said, "The station is Mummy."[4] Dick then went into the shadow behind the door and said "Dark,"[5] almost as if in

---

[1] Melanie Klein, "The Importance of Symbol-Formation in the Development of the Ego", in *The Writings of Melanie Klein,* under the general editorship of Roger Money-Kyrle in collaboration with Betty Joseph, Edna O'Shaughnessy and Hanna Segal, 4 vols. (London: The Hogarth Press and the Institute of Psychoanalysis, 1975), vol. 1, 219-232.
[2] Freud, "On the Transformations of Instinct, as Exemplified in Anal Erotism", SE XVII, 127.
[3] Klein, 225.
[4] Klein, 225.
[5] Klein, 225.

reply to what Klein had said. Klein then said, "It is dark inside Mummy."[6] When Dick showed interest in a wash-basin, Klein again said that the concave part of the basin was "the mother's body".[7] As they played, Dick thus formed relationships with a whole series of different "insides", and the work of interpretation was able to confirm shared meanings which ran through them like a common thread. In a sense, we might say that in his play Dick connected all these various objects, using his own body as the equals sign needed to do so.

Freud's essay and Klein's essay alike deal with the origins of symbolic activity. But Freud's essay could also be read as an account of the dynamics of regressive libido, and some commentators would interpret this libidinal analysis in turn as a sort of biological myth, with no relation to the psychoanalytic situation per se. Klein's essay, on the other hand, does not admit of such a biologistic reading in the first place. There is no distinction between symbolic exchange in the unconscious and the act of understanding the world linguistically. Psychoanalysis deals with this activity directly, at the coalface and as it happens. The analyst reads the flow of symbols, and what characterizes Klein's particular analytic practice is that she orients the symbolic field around her own person in order to understand it. When Klein says "inside Mummy" to Dick, it means not only the inside of the child's actual mother, but also inside the body of Klein herself. By this means Klein creates transference, even in the case of child analysis. Positing the "interior of the mother" as the first object with which the child must enter into relations, Klein forged steadily ahead with her audacious linguistic interpretations, aiming to draw onto herself a transference from this most fundamental of all objects.

Lacan takes up this Klein article in detail in the seminar of 1954.[8] According to Lacan, Klein implants a viewpoint in Dick's world with her interpretations.[9] This fundamental signification, and the position of the subject who receives them, run through a plurality of actual things and bind them together, and together they constitute a function that saves the subject from his psychotic leanings. Klein proffered this function again and again to Dick with the words "inside Mummy", and in his relation with Klein the therapist, Dick obtained the point of view he required to answer the question, "What am I?"

... and 1932

Klein went on to publish a book, *The Psycho-Analysis of Children*, in 1932.[10] Through copious case studies, this work vividly describes the ceaseless flow of the symbolic

---

[6] Klein, 225.
[7] Klein, 226.
[8] See S I, Chapters VI and VII, 62-88.
[9] S I, 87.
[10] Melanie Klein, *The Psycho-Analysis of Children*, trans. Alix Strachey (New York: The Free Press, 1975).

Chapter 2: THE STAGE IS SET

function, as it arises between the child and the analyst and operates in relation to the inside of the mother. Even at a tender age, we see, the child is driven to the brink of distraction, occupied day and night by a structuring narrative woven about the mother's body. Klein's book hit the world of analysis like a bomb.

Even though Freud was still alive, I would argue that "after Freud" begins in 1932, even if solely for the publication of Klein's radical text. But Klein was not all. In the same year, there also occurred other incidents that are writ large in psychoanalytic history.

The first of these incidents was the Nazi seizure of political power in Germany. Thanks to this turn of events, a mounting tide of German-speaking analysts was ultimately to flee to America, among them Loewenstein, who had been Lacan's training analyst. The psychoanalysis that found its way to America subsequently developed in a direction different to that of Europe, acting as the basic theory underpinning psychiatry (psychopathology). So we could also say that this was the year that a second "after Freud" was let loose, to eventually burgeon on the far shores of the Atlantic.

1932 was also the year that Lacan published his doctorate thesis, based on the case study of Aimée.[11] As a whole, the thesis could hardly be described as a psychoanalytic text. But it did announce the radical, French-Lacanian reception of Freud. Moreover, Lacan sent a copy of the thesis to Freud, and received a thank-you card in return. This exchange was to be the sole direct contact the two ever had.[12]

1932 was thus the year of the Kleinian explosion; the year which provided the political conditions for the development of the American school of ego psychology (who were to become Lacan's sworn enemies); and the year in which Lacan himself first took up the study of Freud in earnest. Thus began the era of "after Freud", and Lacan threw himself into these new currents with full abandon. Before turning to Lacan, however, we will take a look at his theoretical antecedents in the work of Melanie Klein, whose flagship work was the watershed among watersheds that marked the turning point of 1932.

Two: Melanie Klein

The first symbolic equation

Melanie Klein was born in 1882 in Vienna, making her nineteen years older than

---

[11] Roudinesco, 112-116.
[12] Roudinesco, 133-4. On Lacan renouncing a chance to meet with Freud at the house of Marie Bonaparte when Freud passed through Paris on his way to his final exile in London, see Roudinesco, 134.

Lacan, and twenty-six years younger than Freud. She occupies an extremely important place in the formation of Lacan's thought, and we can be sure that the specifics of her theories, particularly as laid out in *The Psycho-Analysis of Children*, will help us greatly in understanding the theoretical developments of Lacan's formative period.

We touched earlier on Klein's notion that the basis for all symbol formation, including linguistic activity, is a process of ongoing substitution of various things for the "interior of the mother". She held that this substitution is set in motion by a particular kind of anxiety caused in the child by the relationship it enters into with the mother's "inside". The cause of this anxiety is the feared penis of the father, which the child imagines lurks in hiding within the mother. The child's intellectual curiosity regarding the inside of its mother's body is checked by its terror of the father's penis, and its intellectual development grinds to a halt. Klein considered this configuration an early form of the Oedipus complex. Since this movement of the symbol, in which the child flees the mother's interior and substitutes a chain of other objects for it, is connected to real intellectual development, the reference curiosity maintains to the original "inside of the mother" must inform every one of these symbolic substitutions. This reference sustains the equivalence between the result of the substitution and the original term it substitutes for. Here we see the germ of an advanced symbolic capacity, similar to the manipulation of equations by which we place two completely different things on either side and then join them with an equal sign, and Klein quite correctly calls the substitution games seen in children the "symbolic equation".[13]

The origin of anxiety

In her account of symbolic development, Klein depicts a dualism of difference and identity that structures the symbolic process. The "interior of the mother" stimulates the child's curiosity and promotes its intellectual development, and the reference to it constitutes a concealed core of unchanging self-identity at the heart of the symbolic process. On the other hand, this "inside of the mother" provokes anxiety, and compels the subject to replace it with other things. If anxiety is present in manageable quantities, we can expect it to stimulate both curiosity and the substitution process. But when it becomes too severe, the substitution process loses the reference that serves it for an equal sign, and degenerates into pure panicked flight. The world of the child gets stuck at the level of the disorganized collection of sensory images encountered at each moment.

Anxiety is thus the key. Where does it come from? From 1932 and *The Psycho-Analysis of Children* onwards, Klein pursued this question in her theoretical explorations. As we noted earlier, Klein found the cause of this anxiety in the fearful

---

[13] *The Psycho-Analysis of Children*, 57, 83 n. 2.

penis of the father, which the child imagines is contained in the body of the mother. Subsequently, however, she came to the view that the relationship of the child to its mother, itself, contains an element that inevitably produces the anxiety in question.

Klein found that the breastfed child must, in fact, grow anxious in direct proportion to the degree of bliss it finds in its relationship with its mother. The suckling baby feels that the breast holds everything it could ever want: specifically, infinite supplies of milk and love. Because the breast is infinite and possesses infinite treasures, it can share all with the infant and still remain undiminished. The child wants this inexhaustible infinity all for itself; but that is exactly what the breast will never give the child. In so monopolizing infinity, the breast is perceived as miserly and mean, and the infant is insatiably greedy in its craving for what it cannot have. No matter how generously it is provided with nourishing milk, the child is weighed down by the grim fact that it has no way of getting hold of that milk by its own efforts. The child knows that if it should ever be deprived of the breast, it would undoubtedly suffer more than ever. What the child needs, then, is not the milk or love *per se*, but the power to give them.

As its greed for the omnipotence of the breast mounts, a destructive impulse rears its head within the child. What it can't have, it may as well smash to smithereens. Klein called this impulse envy, as distinct from jealousy.[14] Spurred by this envy, the infant, in its fantasy, invades the inside of the breast, sucking it dry like a vampire and scooping out its contents. It also attacks the breast with corroding urine and explosive feces, ruthlessly pursuing its utter destruction. While invading and violating the breast like this, however, the infant takes its mother's milk – the ruins of the obliterated breast – in through its mouth, and this introjected breast now threatens the child from within. The breast, having been smashed, now starts plotting its revenge, and attacks the child from within in an effort to break it to pieces. Host as it now is to such a terrifying internal object, the child perceives this object deliberately inflicting harm in even the most innocuous sensations of biological displeasure – hunger, for instance, or the urge to urinate.

When it can stand this fearsome object inside it no longer, the child projects it back into the outside world in an attempt to avoid the pain it brings. In other words, the child projects the bad object back within its mother. For a fleeting instant, the child feels that the one suffering internal attack is its mother, not itself, and it gains a brief respite. Before it knows it, however, the child is no longer sure if it is the mother suffering, or itself; for the distinction between itself and its mother is wiped out by the bad object that shuttles back and forth between them. This state of affairs is known as "projective identification", and in it, the external world into which the bad object has been projected takes on the malevolence of the object, accumulates it, and multiplies it. Eventually, strive as the child might to sense the world simply as it

---

[14] Melanie Klein, *Envy and Gratitude*, (New York: Basic Books, 1957).

is, every single thing that presents itself to the senses as part of the world seems poised at the ready to wipe the child from the face of the universe. The infant ends up caught between the internal and external worlds, wracked from all quarters by the anxiety of being persecuted and finally hounded to complete annihilation.

Thus, if we trace this persecution anxiety to its root, it originates when the infant seeks omnipotence in the mother's breast. The greedy mind of the infant destroys the "good breast", with its hidden store of infinite power for the good, and transforms it into the "bad breast", which burns with the thirst for revenge.

Ethicizing instinct – the "paranoid-schizoid position" and the "depressive position"

This, then, is the sort of unconscious drama in which the anxiety that ferments around the notions of the breast and the interior of the mother's body has its source. Anxiety becomes overbearing and symbol formation is thwarted, a scenario that speaks eloquently of just how virulent the greed and envy of the infant are. But more than this, the infant's anxiety is also the prototype of the delusions of persecution seen in schizophrenia and paranoia, and the worlds of these mental maladies are structured by the anxiety that greed and envy bring in their wake. Klein explains greed and envy, in their turn, as having their origins in the "death instinct".

But just what sort of instinct are we talking about here? We are dealing with this process: the infant feels that the power of the breast is infinite, and wants to wield such power itself; in other words, the object is structured as an ideal of unblemished perfection, and identified with. Can we really speak of such a process as an "instinct" – a term that is, after all, borrowed from biology?

I would contend that this capacity to think of the object as absolutely good already amounts to ethical demand. The process of ongoing identification of the self with such an absolute good, of transcending the reality of the self in the direction of an impossible mirage, is an operation spiritual in the extreme. Klein's claim was that this sort of ethical demand is to be found already in the infant in its first year. While it is true that she does describe this as the activity of the "death instinct", she means by "instinct" not something biological and inborn, but rather an irreducibly fundamental mental unit.

This particular rendering of "instinct" is captured in Lacan's notion of the "drive". Among the fundamental theoretical Lacanian terms, we find need (*besoin*), demand (*demande*), and desire (*désir*), which with the drive (*pulsion*) form a conceptual set. While we would expect the need of any living creature to be biologically appropriate, humans are captured from a very early stage by the sort of demand Klein describes, and begin the quest for perfection. From the intractable gap that yawns between need and demand springs the drive – and desire. As Klein says (in the name of "instinct"), the drive is a movement that, in the form of greed and envy, never lets up from destroying the object, and is haunted by the object's ruined remains. The subject of volition is here perceived as somehow falling on the side of the object, and it is difficult for the human subject to become the subject of her own drive. Desire comes about with the subject's realization that the object of the drive is a lost object, one that can never be possessed.

According to Klein, this realization gives rise to consciousness of wrongdoing (guilt), because it was the subject herself that destroyed the breast beyond all hope of regeneration. The awareness of sin against the object of desire comes to the human subject simultaneously with the awareness of desire itself. Because of the wrong it has done the object, the subject longs to get hold of the object again, this time to pour on it the balm of love. This longing is desire. But because the original breast has been destroyed – in fact, obliterated completely – all the subject can ever lay hands on is something other than the true object of desire. All we ever obtain through desire is something that stands in for the breast – in other words, a symbol of it.

Here, the process of symbol formation as Klein conceived of it reaches completion. Only when the guilty subject desires does the original symbol appear. Klein called this set-up, where the subject frames itself as guilty, the "depressive position", because guilt is the single largest structural element in depression. She holds that the subject assumes this position anytime from three to six months after birth. The period prior to this, dominated by greed and envy, she called the "paranoid-schizoid position". What Klein refers to here as "paranoid" is the persecutory terror the infant has of the bad breast, while "schizoid" refers to the split between the ideal breast and the persecuting breast, and the split in the ego as it identifies with each respectively.

Klein saw the origin of delusions of persecution in the imperative to identify with the power of the ideal breast. Though there is a certain discrepancy in developmental periods, this notion of Klein's is in line with Lacan's attribution of the origin of paranoia to the identification with the ideal image made at the mirror stage. Both emphasized that the human subject enters very early into a relation with an object which has deviated from the natural, biological balance, and that the subject is caused suffering by the absolute demand awakened by that object. It was left to Lacan, however, to try to theorize more clearly than Klein the way this *angst*-ridden condition is brought on by the fact that humans use language to think, and we will pursue the development of this idea in Lacan's thought throughout the bulk of this book.

Three: The Controversy Between Klein and Anna Freud

Freud's "daughters" and the "matriarchal" period of psychoanalytic history

Soon after conducting a lecture series in England in 1925, at the invitation of Freud's direct disciple, Ernest Jones, Melanie Klein moved there from the continent, and together with Jones began forming what could well be called the "English school" of psychoanalysis. At the same time, in Vienna, birthplace of psychoanalysis, the position of Freud's youngest daughter, Anna, as his successor and heir grew more and more secure. Like Klein, Anna Freud also turned her hand to child analysis, and the opposition between the two only grew sharper as time went on.

Klein recognized true transference in children as well as adults. Transference is constituted when the death instinct, originally active between the infant and the mother's breast, moves into the relation between the analyst and the child patient. This transference jump-starts the stalled process of symbolization and sets it back in motion. In order to reduce the anxiety stemming from the death instinct and promote symbolization, the analyst must give a strict linguistic interpretation to the transference through the medium of the child's play.

Against this, Anna Freud held that the analyst has an educational responsibility to the child, and that the first requirement is to win the child's trust. She therefore held that the antagonistic feelings that arise with ordinary psychoanalytic transference are disadvantageous to the establishment of the therapeutic relation, and furthermore that no efficacy can be expected from the interpretation of such transference in any case. This is because the child still lives within a strong realistic relationship to its parents, and this relation has an immense power, far in excess of that of the transference. Whereas Klein's ideal was that all children would normally undergo analysis, Anna Freud held that psychoanalysis ought to base itself on the concept of normal development that had emerged from received pedagogics and psychology: psychoanalysis, in this case, would be a supplement applied only where there was a particular need.

Klein saw the internal bad object as the most rudimentary incarnation of the superego, the seat of the internal moral faculty. The inception of the superego is thus relegated to a developmental phase far earlier than that ascribed to it in ordinary Freudian theory. For Anna Freud, naturally, this sort of revision to orthodoxy was difficult to countenance. From her point of view, the child was still deficient in the experience necessary to form a superego, and there was a requirement for the analyst to enter into the position where the future ideal ego would eventually form, and meet the child with a correct and authoritative attitude.

The opposition between Freud and Klein did not stop at matters of theory, however, developing into what was clearly a plain power struggle. Continental

Chapter 2: THE STAGE IS SET

analysts issued a string of criticisms of Klein, including the charge that Klein's theories were not borne out empirically by the observation of children. At last, when Anna Freud sought exile in London with her father in 1938, there could no longer be any skirting around the opposition between the two women. At the time, Jones was in a position of responsibility in regard to the psychoanalytic movement not only in England but in all of Europe, and he managed to protect Klein's original work, masterfully parrying even complaints from Freud senior himself to the effect that the English school was waging a campaign against his daughter. At the same time, he also protected Anna's position out of respect for his long-standing relationship with Freud. Through his diplomacy and tact, Jones managed to avert the very real threat of a split in the Psychoanalytic Association.

Flexing political muscle on Anna Freud's side of the fight was another psychoanalytic matriarch: Marie Bonaparte, who brought her noble identity as the grand-daughter of Napoleon's younger brother and a Greek princess to her activities as a psychoanalyst. Bonaparte was a born politician, as evidenced by the role she played in helping Freud flee to London via Paris when the Nazis took over Vienna. She lent financial support to the psychoanalytic cause, and gave Anna Freud her patronage. At the same time, however, she read *The Psycho-Analysis of Children,* and sure enough, she felt the shock-waves from Klein's bomb. Bonaparte realized that Klein could not simply be written off as a heretic, however, and she was ultimately to work with Jones in navigating the troubled political waters between Anna Freud and Klein and steering them towards mutual co-existence.

Bonaparte centered her activities in Paris, and she thus cast a long shadow over Lacan's early movements in the psychoanalytic world. She did not consider it appropriate that Klein establish her own, separate school, as we have seen, and perhaps this was because she was aware that without tolerance of a certain degree of theoretical difference, psychoanalysis as a movement could easily be eviscerated. In Lacan's case, however, the possible benefits to the psychoanalytic movement as a whole of tolerance failed to outweigh the repugnance she felt for the idea of working together with him. Her repugnance was perhaps intensified by the fact that with Lacan she would have to co-operate at close quarters – unlike Klein, who was at least at the safe remove of London. Little by little, it became clear to Bonaparte that Lacan had to be removed.

Not without reason, then, is this period sometimes called in jest the "matriarchal" era of psychoanalysis. The air rang with the clashing swords of Klein, Anna Freud, and Marie Bonaparte, and if we want to add them, Helene Deutsch and Karen Horney too, both of whom raised objections to Freud's theorizations of femininity. This matriarchal age was the age in which Lacan became an analyst. If Lacan was put on the path to becoming an analyst when he plunged himself deep in the paranoid world of a woman called Aimée, then, perhaps for him the collegial world of analysis at the time was just an extension of Aimée's world. Whether he liked it or not, he was bound to end up embroiled in a tangled web of proliferating transferential and counter-transferential relations when he first plunged into that world. We now turn to examining the splash he made.

Four: Enter Lacan

The tightrope-walk from Anna Freud to Klein

Lacan made his analytic debut when he delivered his paper "The Mirror Stage" at the International Psychoanalytical Association's conference in Marienbad in 1936. Lacan wrote later that his delivery was interrupted after ten minutes by Ernest Jones, who was in the chair.[15] A much revised and extended version of this paper was finally delivered in 1949 in Zurich, and then published under the title "The Mirror Stage as Formative of the Function of the I as Revealed in Psychoanalytic Experience".[16] Its companion piece is the essay "Aggressivity in Psychoanalysis", published in 1948.[17] In "The Mirror Stage", Lacan mentions Anna Freud, and in "Aggressivity", he refers to Melanie Klein.

In "The Mirror Stage", Lacan argues as follows. For a period after birth, the animal called "man" is characterized by the fact that the nervous system does not function in a harmonious or integrated fashion. Thanks to their developed sense of posture, adults can feel the unity of their own body form even with their eyes shut, but infants have no such experience of coherence. When an infant between six and eighteen months of age in these circumstances comes in contact with its own reflection in a mirror, it *visually anticipates* the unity of its nervous system. The child assumes the mirror image with much jubilation, as an ideal "I" through which it attains unity much earlier than through its internal experience of itself. Useful comparisons can be made in this respect to the animal world. In birds, the sight of another individual functions to greatly accelerate sexual maturation, and experiments have shown that a similar power is inherent in the sight of the individual's own reflection in a mirror. The mirror image impels both bird and baby towards a kind of maturity.

On the basis of such reflections, we can assume that the jubilation of the human individual when it comes face to face with its own mirror image springs from an admixture of ego unification and sexual activity. At that same time that it assumes the mirror image as its ideal self in this stage of its development, the human subject also takes this self as the object of its sexual interest. This is the structure of

---

[15] Roudinesco, 133.
[16] *Selection*, 1-7. On the Zurich congress, see Roudinesco, 145.
[17] *Selection*, 8-29.

narcissism. In the virtual dimension of the mirror, the sexual objective and the ideal self are welded firmly together.

It is not long before this "mirror I" lurches off in the direction of the "social I". In place of the mirror there appear the images of the subject's brethren, *qua* the vehicles of social value. This swing in direction is oriented to secure the subject as a meaningful constituent of human society, but at the same time, it renders the subject captive to society, and prepares the structural ground for paranoiac madness. This process will be examined in greater detail when we take up the theory of the mirror stage once more in Chapter V.

In a work similarly dating from 1936, Anna Freud, too, describes children mimicking the facial expression of a teacher who is scolding them, or thinking that ghosts are not scary if they themselves turn into ghosts too, gathering such phenomena under the rubric of "identification with the aggressor".[18] When the child enters into human social relations or a belief system, it generally identifies itself in this way with an aggressive adversary. We can see a commonality between the swing from "mirror I" to "social I" described by Lacan, and the identification here identified by Anna Freud. Both concepts share the denial of the real distinction between self and other, and the latentization into the self of an aggressive component that lies between the two. For this reason, it was only natural that Lacan would refer to Anna Freud in "The Mirror Stage". The reverent tones in which he does so, however, smack of political considerations, and in fact work to obscure the conceptual continuity of his work with hers.[19]

The mention of Melanie Klein found in "Aggressivity", by contrast, is much more explicit and systematic, and clearly evidences the overlap, not to say the competition, between Lacan's and Klein's theories. Lacan recognizes fully that the "bad internal object" spoken of by Klein is found in actual psychoanalytic experience. The analysis is therefore a locale in which the subject re-experiences a world of persecutory anxiety like that attested to in Klein's writings. One of the greatest tasks incumbent upon the analysis is to accept the projection of the "bad internal object" and manipulate it. This projection resembles the swing towards paranoia described earlier, but through the analysis, it is possible to filter it and check its flow.[20]

Lacan touches next on Klein's "depressive position". First, he interprets the shift Klein describes from the gruesome fantasy world of the paranoid-schizoid position to

---

[18] Anna Freud, *The Ego and the Mechanisms of Defence*, trans. Cecil Baines (New York: International Universities Press, 1946).

[19] Lacan says, "[O]ur experience . . . teaches us not to regard the ego as centred on the *perception-consciousness system,* or as organised by the 'reality principle' . . . . Our experience shows that we should start instead from the *function of méconnaissance* that characterizes the ego in all its structure, so markedly articulated by Miss Anna Freud." *Selection*, 6.

[20] *Selection*, 15.

the depressive position as signifying "the subjectification of a *kakon* (evil)".[21]   Lacan then claims that we must recognize in this moment the origins of the structures of the ego, comprised of narcissism and the denial of the other.   It seems entirely plausible that Lacan, at that time engaged with the problem of the advent of the ego, was here comparing his theory of the mirror stage with Klein's concept of the depressive position.

Lacan concludes his discussion of Klein with the comment, "[There is a] passionate desire peculiar to man to impress his image in reality,"[22] a very apt description of the world of Klein's "projective identification".   In fact, if we read Klein's accounts of projective identification with reference to identification as it is found in Lacan's mirror stage, we can sympathize with the struggle of the human subject to register itself in a world that transcends its own limitations.   This is linked to the problem of relating the internal world to the *Umwelt*; that is, the problem of positioning the self in the social context; or, to use concepts later developed by Lacan, the problem of supporting the reality of one's own existence in the relations of the Symbolic realm.

We see, then, how Lacan locates his own thought between two of his predecessors in psychoanalytic theory, Anna Freud and Melanie Klein.   At the same time, we are also surely justified in saying that he is like a character in a French court drama, jockeying for a tenable position between two female antagonists locked in a naked power struggle.   But politics aside, what does Lacan add to psychoanalysis here, theoretically speaking?   While Anna Freud emphasized the power of society to influence the child, and Melanie Klein grappled with destructive fantasies that arise directly within the child's mind, Lacan synthesized these assertions, and attempted to verify them theoretically with findings from ethology.   The formalization of the mirror stage theory, accomplished on the basis of Henri Wallon's accomplishments in psychology, was firmly in the tradition of the French humanism, which tied physiological fact, mental experience, and social structure neatly together.   It could be argued that with the theory of the mirror stage, Lacan was attempting to incorporate this tradition, epitomized in the exquisite writing of Maurice Merleau-Ponty, into the body of psychoanalytic thought.

Lacan's reference to Klein thus goes beyond mere matters of politics – we can also read into it a theoretical pedigree.   Right up until he attained complete independence with the establishment of the École Freudienne de Paris in 1964 (the so-called "second schism": see Chapter VI), Lacan frequently made reference to the comparisons between his own concepts and those of Klein.   We now turn to examining another of these points of contact between Klein's and Lacan's ideas, in Lacan's reading of the Freudian notion of *das Ding*.

---

[21] *Selection*, 21.
[22] *Selection*, 22.

Chapter 2: THE STAGE IS SET

The place of *das Ding*
As we have seen, Lacan deals with Klein's essay on "Symbol-Formation" in depth in the seminar of 1954. Here, he holds that Klein was grafting the language of the symbolic world onto the world of the child, albeit by her own peculiarly "brutal" method.[23] He recognizes that Klein's account vividly presents the nascent subject in the throes of its struggles within the structure of the "Symbolic", and that it indicated precisely the correct position for the analyst to take. His approach here represents an attempt to clarify matters further through the application of his own theoretical apparatus.

To anticipate still further, in the seminar of 1959-1960 ("The Ethics of Psychoanalysis"), Lacan takes up Klein's work once more, this time in connection with the pivotal concept of *das Ding*.[24] Lacan makes reference to Klein's theory that when the child realizes it was he who destroyed the primal object inside his mother, he assumes the depressive position, and gives himself up to the impulse to compensate for the destruction. The fountainhead of art is to be found in this restorative activity, which in the child is accomplished in fantasy and in play.[25] What does this have to do with *das Ding*? If, as Freud thought, mind can be understood as a mental apparatus, then there must be some thing which flows into the apparatus from outside it, and which the apparatus processes. This important constituent was simply called *das Ding* (the Thing) in Freud's writings. Like any normal German noun, it is written with a capital letter as a matter of course, but when Lacan singled it out as a concept and brought it into French, he retained the initial capital. Lacan argues in this seminar that Klein's "primal object" inside the mother is constituted by the insertion of the mysterious body of the mother in the place where this *Ding* ought to be.

In the seminar of the following year, Lacan dealt with the transference, and in that context, he elaborated still further his readings of both *das Ding*, and of Kleinian thinking.[26] Just as Klein focuses on transference as the transference from the interior of the mother to the interior of the analyst, for Lacan, also, the supposition that *das Ding* is inside the analyst is an important element in the formation of the transference. Because *das Ding* exists inside the analyst, the patient gets the impression that it is something extremely valuable, something that must be had no matter what. Lacan calls this object the *objet a*, and it is an indispensable element in his theoretical system. We will return to the importance of this concept in the next chapter, and again a number of times in the course of this book.

---

[23] See S I, 68.
[24] S VII. For Klein and *das Ding*, see particularly 115-117.
[25] Melanie Klein, *The Writings of Melanie Klein, Vol.I, 1921-1945: Love, Guilt and Reparation*, 176, 335-338.
[26] S VIII.

Chapter 2: THE STAGE IS SET

Lacan meets Klein

At the conference in Zurich in 1949 where he delivered his "Mirror Stage" paper, Lacan encountered Klein in person, and expressed a wish to translate her *The Psycho-Analysis of Children* into French.[27] Klein gave her consent immediately. Soon afterwards, a young French woman analyst[28] expressed the same desire, and Klein turned her down on the grounds of the prior arrangement. Obviously, she had taken Lacan at his word.

But time passed, and no translation was published. Rumors that Lacan had abandoned the project reached Klein's ears, and it was taken over by René Diatkine, who at the time was still one of Lacan's disciples.[29] As Diatkine was more at home in German than English, Klein provided him with the German original (*The Psycho-Analysis of Children* was published in the original and in English translation virtually simultaneously). Diatkine translated half of the book, and Lacan then instructed a woman analyst, also one of his pupils, to translate the remainder. This analyst was Françoise Boulanger (née Girard), the same young woman who had asked Klein permission to translate the book after Lacan.[30]

Boulanger approached Lacan to say that she would like to have access to the manuscript of the translation prepared by Diatkine. Lacan ought to have had the manuscript in his care, but it turned out that he had, apparently, *lost* it. Boulanger and her husband at the time, Jean-Baptiste Boulanger, contacted Klein directly, and *La Psychanalyse des enfants* was finally issued in their translation in 1959, the first of Klein's works to appear in French.[31] Klein sent the following letter to the translators.

> "I very much wish that I could have put the work in your hands . . . when Madame Boulanger first offered . . . . [H]ow much worry and trouble I should have saved myself! But . . . I could not take it away from Lacan. However . . . I am very happy that the work is at last progressing."[32]

Why would Lacan have lost interest in the translation, and why would he have lost Diatkine's manuscript (assuming that Boulanger's story is accurate)? As it turns out, there is a facet to Lacan that enables us to describe him as a past master of the political blunder. Ultimately, Lacan was to strike out on a theoretical path very different from that trodden by Klein, and perhaps in so doing he was led by his own

---

[27] Phyllis Grosskurth, *Melanie Klein: Her Life and Her Work* (New York: Knopf, 1986), 377, 389.
[28] Françoise Girard – Trans. Grosskurth, 377.
[29] Grosskurth, 389-390.
[30] For this and following paragraph, see Grosskurth, 391-392.
[31] Melanie Klein, *La psychanalyse des enfants*, trans. J.B. Boulanger (Paris: Presses universitaires de France, 1958, 1998).
[32] Grosskurth, 391-392.

parapraxes.

Estrangement
Despite their theoretical overlap, or perhaps, indeed, because of the competition between them, the relation between Klein and Lacan quickly went sour, and the same was also true of the Kleinian and Lacanian schools. After founding his École freudienne de Paris in 1964, Lacan made very little reference to Klein, and Kleinians, too, preferred to shy away from the topic of affinities with Lacanian theory. Even the conservative group of French analysts, who were originally much closer to Anna Freud, are now working to take Klein's ideas on board, but they still continue to foreclose the arena to Lacan. In South America, also, Lacanians and Kleinians are rivals for the lion's share of the psychoanalytic "market".

Within the International Psychoanalytical Association (IPA), Klein's ideas have already secured a place as an important pillar of theory. In recent years, the leadership of the IPA (which has close ties to the Klein school) has sought to open dialog with the Lacanian school, but negotiations ended in breakdown, and the central bodies of the Lacanian movement have chosen to travel their own, independent road. A new international organization, L'Association Mondiale de Psychanalyse (AMP), was formed in February 1992 to vie with the IPA. At present, each pursues its own particular structural and theoretical course. The IPA operates out of England, bringing schools of varying tendencies throughout the world together under one umbrella, and the AMP, based in France, unites the Lacanians who have spread throughout the Latin world to Spain and South America. We will now close our chapter with a brief look at the first stage in the drama that produced this impasse.

Five: Schism – 1953

The princess's power-play
Lacan was married in 1934, and fathered three children,[33] but from 1939 (while his wife was still pregnant with their third child) he became intimate with the actress Sylvia Bataille, wife of the writer Georges Bataille.[34] Sylvia had been estranged from Georges since 1933, and he and Lacan were friends, having been classmates in the lectures of the Hegelian scholar Kojève. In 1941, a daughter, Judith (now Judith Miller) was born to Sylvia and Lacan, but at the time Sylvia was yet to be divorced from Bataille.[35] She and Lacan were only officially married in 1953, a year in which

---

[33] Roudinesco, 129.
[34] Roudinesco, 147.
[35] Roudinesco, 147.

was significant for Lacan in that, apart from being the year of their union, was also the year that Lacan split with the IPA. Why did this split take place, and how did it come about?

The oldest psychoanalytic body in France, the Société Psychanalytique de Paris (SPP), had commenced activity in 1926, and after the Second World War the baton was passed to the so-called "second generation". While Marie Bonaparte always retained a great degree of influence, the central figures in this generation were Lacan, Daniel Lagache, and Sacha Nacht. These leading figures differed on the fundamental issue of how psychoanalysts ought to be chosen and trained. Nacht held that psychoanalysis ought to place itself at the service of the overall rubric of neurobiology (an idea satirized ferociously by Lacan in his later "Rome Discourse"[36]), and he sought to lay down forceful controls for the systematic organization of psychoanalysts, centered on the medical field. The problem of whether or not it was essential for psychoanalysts to have a medical grounding was one that had remained unresolved ever since the time of Freud. Marie Bonaparte, who did not herself have a medical background, cautioned against Nacht's medical controls. Lagache, for his part, was a trained doctor, but was by temperament more a creature of academe, and envisaged a liberal psychoanalytic organization grounded in psychology. The bulk of the SPP's members were behind Lagache.

Lacan, meanwhile, had developed a practice known as the "short session". While the date of the short session's origin and the details of its development are hazy, by the time Aimée's son Anzieu entered analysis in 1949, Lacan's "analytic hour" had already fallen in duration to around half of the customary fifty-five minutes,[37] and two years later was said to have shrunk even further, to twenty minutes. Many people speculated that these short sessions had been introduced as a way of coping with the drastic increase in those seeking analysis with Lacan, and that it had brought him no meager increase in fees.

Marie Bonaparte repeatedly took Lacan to task for his short sessions, and Nacht, too, demanded explanation. Lacan proved a slippery adversary. Each time that he was admonished to follow usual practice, he equivocated, expressing a public resolution to conform to the system while in fact carrying on business as usual.[38] Whatever the motives that occasioned it in the first place, Lacan apparently felt that, with the short session, he had come up against something important, something that drove straight to the root of psychoanalysis – something not to be relinquished lightly. And yet, he showed little inclination to set that something forth in a clear theoretical form. Perhaps, at the time, he still hoped to avoid a showdown of principles, and

---

[36] Lacan, "The Function and Field of Speech and Language in Psychoanalysis", *Selection*, 30-113.
[37] Roudinesco, 229 ff.
[38] Roudinesco, 236, 239, etc.

find a political settlement to the issue.

In terms of the standoff between the Nacht and Lagache factions within the Society, Lacan's position was in reality closer to that of Nacht. Nacht was given the helm of a consultative committee looking into the training and accreditation of analysts, and he submitted the draft of a code that would have established a psychoanalytic research institute, headed by himself, to govern such matters.[39] The draft met fierce opposition from Bonaparte and the liberal faction.[40] Nacht withdrew for the time being to regroup his forces, and Lacan, who had mediated the conflict, decided to draw up a revised draft, in which he incorporated the notion that psychoanalytic principles could be reduced to neither medicine nor psychology.[41]

In this draft, however, Lacan neglected to give Marie Bonaparte an honorary title,[42] and there is speculation that this blunder exerted a subtle influence on the Princess's subsequent political moves. The elections for the presidency of the SPP were just around the corner, and when they were held the following year, in 1953, Bonaparte ran against Lacan. Lacan was elected in a third round of voting,[43] and a further revised draft of the research institute code, this time authored by Nacht himself, was approved. In Nacht's final draft, however, nobody forgot to attach all due honorary titles to the Princess's name.[44]

The discrepancy between Lacan's and Nacht's views must have already been growing apparent, but at least at this juncture, it appeared that their alliance had outmaneuvered the Bonaparte-backed Lagache liberals. It seems, however, that the Princess had already had a certain change of heart in the course of the wrangle. She seems to have come to the conclusion that her fight was in fact not with Nacht's ideology of medical supremacy, but with what she saw as Lacan's technical arbitrariness – with the short session. The events that followed made it clear that at some point, she and Nacht had reached a sort of cease-fire agreement behind the scenes.[45] Nacht brought the prerogative of his new training institute to bear, and officially required Lacan to respect the standard analytic hour.[46] Before Lacan had made any clear reply, the liberal faction, with the backing of Marie Bonaparte, issued a motion of no confidence in Lacan's presidency on June 16, 1953. A ballot was taken, and Lacan was forced to resign.[47]

Almost nobody anticipated what happened next. On Lacan's resignation, Lagache,

---

[39] Roudinesco, 223, 237.
[40] Roudinesco, 237.
[41] Roudinesco, 238.
[42] See Lacan, *Television: A Challenge to the Psychoanalytic Establishment,* trans. Jeffrey Mehlman (New York, London: Norton, 1990), 60; Roudinesco, 239.
[43] Roudinesco, 239.
[44] Ibid.
[45] Roudinesco, 239.
[46] Ibid, 239-240.
[47] Roudinesco, 249.

who had been vice-president, became acting president in his place, and Lagache himself, Françoise Dolto, and J. Favez-Boutonnier immediately announced their resolution to withdraw from the SPP.[48] The split in the Society was plain for all to see. Lagache was of the opinion that, rather than continuing his struggle with Nacht, who now had control over the training and approval processes, he would do better to create a new association, within which he could move freely. He had been preparing his move for some time.

Fresh from his forced resignation, Lacan himself joined the dissident move,[49] with a most peculiar result – Lacan, the target of a liberal vote of no confidence, was now shoulder to shoulder with Lagache. Lagache, however, had informed Lacan the night before of his plans,[50] and we can be quite sure that Lacan at least had time to consider his options. Probably Lacan realized that there was no longer any chance of Nacht's support, and that the Princess, aware that she would have to tolerate either Nacht's medicalism or Lacan's short session, had chosen to go with Nacht. Even if he were to comply with Nacht and come to a compromise with Marie Bonaparte, he would be fighting a lost battle.

The new group that Lagache, Dolto *et al* created with Lacan was named the Société Française de Psychanalyse (SFP), and was officially announced under Lagache's name on June 18, two days after the dramatic schism.[51] At this point, it became clear that Lagache and his followers had made a rather peculiar miscalculation. They had been under the impression that, even if they did pull out of the original official association (the SPP), they would not forego their status as full members of the International Psychoanalytical Association (IPA). It turned out they were wrong. Resignation from the SPP also implied resignation from the IPA. This fact made itself clear when members of the Lagache faction were unable to take part in the international congress in London, which was close to hand.[52]

Before the congress, the IPA executive deliberated about whether or not to recognize this new French group (the SFP). If we read the minutes of this discussion,[53] we see that Loewenstein and others advocated compromise for the sake of damage control. Against this, however, Marie Bonaparte, without actually raising Lacan's name, spoke with subtlety and finesse, narrowing the focus solely to the problem of non-standard session length. Recall that Bonaparte had indirectly supported the liberals in their opposition to the medical control of analysis. Even so,

---

[48] Ibid.
[49] Roudinesco, 250.
[50] Roudinesco, 249.
[51] Roudinesco, 251.
[52] Roudinesco, 250.
[53] International Psycho-Analytical Association, "Report on the Eighteenth International Psycho-Analytical Congress, President's Report", Dr. Heinz Hartmann, *International Journal of Psycho-Analysis* XXXV (1954), 271-279; 272-278 reproduced in *Television*, 71-74.

once they strayed from the fold of the official body, she made no effort whatsoever to intervene on their behalf in the IPA. It is clear that she took this attitude because Lacan was now among them. The meeting concluded by entrusting the problem to an investigatory committee headed by Winnicott, a disciple of Klein considered capable of exercising independent judgement in the matter.[54] A year of investigations culminated in a decision to keep the SFP beyond the pale.[55] Negotiations with the renegades, however, were to continue for some time to come.[56]

The "cornerstone" of the short session

In his famous "Rome Discourse", Lacan describes in very clear terms the weight his presence carried within the SFP. "Rome Discourse" is the common name for a lecture entitled "The function and field of speech and language in psychoanalysis",[57] delivered at the conference for Romance language psychoanalysts in Rome in September 1953. This paper was as good as a de facto manifesto of the new Société, and as it declares the position of a new school of analysis, it simultaneously lambastes all existing schools.

Biologism and resistance analysis come in for particularly harsh criticism. Biologism is accused of committing fundamental errors: it relegates the unconscious to the realm of lower-level brain function, and also circumvents the division of the human mind from itself by expounding the congruence of body and consciousness. Resistance analysis is attacked as nothing more than a reheated version of Hegelian notions: it holds that the new ego, which is conscious of the resistances, transcends the old resisting ego in the direction of a synthesis of the whole personality. Both seek to cancel out Freud's discovery that consciousness is in fact the puppet of that of which the subject is not conscious. By contrast to these heterodoxies, the "Rome Discourse" conceives of the unconscious not as some low-level brain function, nor as an irrational tendency which needs trouncing by a powerful ego, but as a linguistic activity rather like polyphonic music. The human subject is born into a network of social relations that is already structuratred linguistically, and in the process, a linguistic activity prior to all subjective consciousness is implanted in the heart of the subject.

Also significant for us here is that in this paper, Lacan publicly recognizes the short session as the technical bedrock of his ideas. One reason for this was doubtless that, having parted ways with Nacht and Bonaparte, Lacan no longer needed to beat around the bush. At the same time, however, we can speculate that in Lacan's mind, the recognition of the unconscious as a linguistic structure was linked to the

---

[54] Roudinesco, 252.
[55] Roudinesco, 319.
[56] See Roudinesco, 319-350.
[57] *Selection*, 30.

elaboration of theoretical justification for the short session. Let us consider how this might be so.

The subject conveys itself to others by speaking, and the act of speaking is realized in a linear linguistic structure. This linear structure is elaborated within time, and time, in turn, is the defining condition of all mortal life. It follows, then, that the speech act is a unique means for the subject to enter a relation with time, and so stages an encounter with the temporal limitation of the subject's life. This relation between the fact that the subject speaks and its realization that it itself is a temporal being is essential to psychoanalysis. Psychoanalysis, as technique, can only be applied through the act of speaking, and arguably, this implies that what the analysis handles *is* nothing other than the relation with time.

When we look at things like this, we must realize that the process of beginning and ending speech in psychoanalysis is an essential element of analytic technique. This temporal articulation, therefore, surely needs to be managed with awareness and sound methodology, and not just left up to the mechanical workings of the clock. There is good reason to believe that the division of time, whether intentional or not, already carries all the weight of interpretation.

Lacan thus set out to proactively reclaim the short session as his own unique discovery. Both the SPP and the IPA insisted that total hours in analysis be calculated when approving qualification of analysts, and thus divorced analytic technique from a reality that was one of its greatest assets. The most important reality for the subject comes to light not in the accumulation of standardized analytic hours, but precisely in the moment of cut-off. Lacan retrieved this discarded reality from where standardized technique had cast it aside, and sought to make it the "cornerstone" of the house he was to build. In the theoretical moment represented by the "Rome Discourse", then, Lacan not only declared a new psychoanalytic group; he also revealed to the world the uniqueness of his own theory. We can be sure that as he did so, he braced himself for what it would bring.

Oedipus starts his journey
The loss of the Klein manuscript; the shortening of the session; the pregnancy of his lover Sylvia; the omission of the Princess's title; the mistaken impression that one could resign from the SPP and remain in the IPA – from this string of accumulating parapraxes and blunders, Lacan *qua* Lacan was born. And in the retrospect of this moment, it becomes possible by "deferred action" (*Nachträglichkeit*) to ascribe meaning to these various parapraxes – to see in hindsight that they all pointed in the same direction. A model of the way the subject realizes its subjectivity in psychoanalysis is thus embodied in the political trajectory traced by Lacan himself. In other words: just as what gradually becomes clear in psychoanalysis is unconscious desire, the trajectory that Lacan stitched together from his various blunders looks like it was sustained by a desire that not even he knew about. What sort of desire was it?

Chapter 2: THE STAGE IS SET

How did it feel to Lacan himself as he experienced the bitter drama of schism, which looked so much like a ritual scapegoating?

Later, in the seminar of 1961, Lacan was to speak of ancient Greek tragedy.[58] He said that without anyone being to blame, the moral debts of humanity accumulate, until they bear down on a sacrificial lamb, who is punished without having done anything to deserve her fate. The sacrificial victim "does not know" (does not know what, if anything, she has done wrong, for instance; she acted unknowingly), but her own unconscious desire brings the weight of the moral debt down on her. Ultimately, all the scapegoat can do is accept her fate. The classic prototype of this scapegoat is Oedipus, and Lacan says that the reason Freud chose the Oedipal myth as the archetype of his discoveries lies precisely in the appeal exerted on Freud by this notion of "not knowing".[59]

Lacan himself seems to have been unable to avoid overlaying his own political fate onto that of the protagonist of the Greek tragedy. A psychoanalyst to the core, he seems to have recognized that his own unconscious desire was pulling him in the direction of an Oedipal fate. But in 1953 this French protagonist was still wrapped in the protective tolerance of his associate Lagache, two years his junior. With the two of them at its center, the SFP set up shop and started business, confident in the hope that, someday, it would win consent from the IPA. We will return to their story, and see how they fared, in Chapter VI.

---

[58] S VII, *The Ethics of Psychoanalysis*.
[59] S VIII, 157-9.

CHAPTER THREE
ROME: THE CORNERSTONE

One: The Politics of the Short Session

The Rome Discourse

In September 1953, a conference was held in Rome for psychoanalysts speaking the Romance languages. Due to the schism described in the previous chapter, Lacan, Lagache and the others of the SFP found themselves in a very delicate position. The organizers on the Italian side, however, decided to go ahead as originally planned, and Lacan was given the chance to speak. Still fresh from the heat of forging a new school of analysis, the SFP, he was to deliver a talk entitled "The Function and Field of Speech and Language in Psychoanalysis",[1] generally known simply as the Rome Discourse.

The text of this imposing essay, as it is found in *Écrits,* comes to 86 pages. In the preface he added to it for publication, Lacan conveys amply the sense of the extraordinary that he felt under the circumstances. He saw the fact that the conference was held in no less a place than Rome as something more than mere coincidence; indeed, he felt that his address was no less than the infantile stammerings of a certain history, beginning there to speak of itself. He even hoped to secure an audience with the Pope during the time he was in Rome for the conference, and to this end put out feelers (ultimately unsuccessful) to the Vatican through his younger brother, Marc-François, a Catholic monk, and also through the French embassy.[2] Given the import of the occasion, we might imagine that, to paraphrase Verlaine, he felt he "knew the ecstasy and terror of being chosen" (used as the epigraph to Dazai's *Bannen*);[3] that he suffered the *trema* that presages the onset of psychosis; or even that manic megalomania stirred within him.[4] But the address he

---

[1] *Selection,* 30.
[2] See Roudinesco, 261.
[3] "J'ai l'extase et j'ai la terreur d'être choisi." Verlaine, "Sagesse", in *Oeuvres Poétiques Complètes,* ed. Y.-G. Le Dantec (Paris: Éditions de la Nouvelle revue française, 1938), 176. Used as epigraph in Dazai Osamu (1909-1948), *Bannen* [My Late Years], in *Dazai Osamu zenshū* [Complete Works of Dazai Osamu] (Chikuma Shobō, 1976), vol 1., p. 5. Translation modeled after *Poems by Paul Verlaine. Selected and Translated, with an Introduction, by Ashmore Wingate* (London: The Walter Scott Publishing Co), 173.
[4] For *trema* as the first stage of psychosis, see Klaus Conrad (1905-1961), *Die Beginnende Schizophrenie* (Stuttgart: G. Thieme, 1958).

delivered – the Rome Discourse – is an intellectual work prodigiously encyclopedic in scope, and yet meticulous to the last detail.⁵ From among the various threads of its polyphonic structure, let us first take up the problem of the "short session", which as we have seen was the focus of controversy in the drama of the schism. We will first look at the implications of the short session for Lacan's status as master.

He who comes in place of Freud
The short session is more than just a technical innovation; it symbolizes the uniqueness of Lacan's entire position. In *Écrits,* Lacan uses the biblical passage, "The stone which the builders rejected, the same is become the head of the corner," (Matthew 21:42) to mark that fact that, by refusing to abandon this technique, he had marked a whole new departure for psychoanalysis.⁶ This turning point occurred in 1953.

Freud most certainly did not think of psychoanalysis as something like a school lesson, to be measured by the clock. However, he did think it appropriate to regulate a fixed minimum of hours or years to qualify aspiring analysts, in order that psychoanalysis might be transmitted as science and technique.⁷ In order that psychoanalysis might be passed from one generation to another, that is, so it did not come to an end with Freud and his peers, the idea of regulating the length of the session, or total years in analysis, became central to psychoanalytic debate.

In insisting on the short session, Lacan was announcing willy-nilly that he was beyond such constraints – that he was not bound by the rules crafted for self-protection by those who proclaimed themselves Freud's heirs. In other words, Lacan was declaring himself to be not a disciple of Freud, but one who came in Freud's place. People were presented with a forced choice: to acknowledge, or not, that Lacan had somehow acceded to the place apparently left vacant by Freud's death. Lacan was no longer simply someone who transmitted Freud's teachings.

The act of manipulating the timing of the session at one's own discretion thus assumed extraordinary significance, providing symbolic support for the place of the transcendent Lacan as he who came in place of Freud. If, for the sake of comparison, we say that Freud was Buddha, then Lacan corresponded to Bodhidharma, Shinran, or

---

⁵ Lacan was unable to deliver the address as it is written due to considerations of time. See Roudinesco, 265. For a record of what Lacan did in fact say when he took the podium, see "Actes du Congrès de Rome", *Psychanalyse* I (1956), 202-211. This same record has also recently been republished in Jacques Lacan, *Autres Écrits,* ed. Jacques-Alain Miller (Paris: Seuil, 2001), "Discours de Rome" 133-146, "Réponses aux Interventions", 146-164.
⁶ Footnote 106 to "The function and field of speech and language in psychoanalysis" (the Rome Discourse), *Selection,* 112.
⁷ See, for example, SE XX, 233 "The Question of Lay Analysis": "I lay stress on the demand that no one should practice analysis who has not acquired the right to do so by a particular training."

Chapter 3: ROME: THE CORNERSTONE

Nichiren:[8] just as people believe in the Buddha and take refuge[9] in him, they also believe and take refuge in these figures, and similarly, the place that Freud occupied in people's hearts was now occupied by Lacan. This sort of conceptual status is what Lacan demanded with his insistence on the short session.

We can fully expect that, if the significance of the short session is indeed to be found in this sort of symbolic value, difficulties will arise in handling this technique as a mere technique. Most particularly, such difficulties arise in the transmission of that technique; if the short session is a special symbolic privilege granted only to the *master* who takes the place of Freud, then we cannot expect that any *disciple* would possibly be able to put it into tangible practice. And indeed, not a single one of Lacan's followers did ever succeed in doing so. But does a technique that cannot be taught warrant the name of technique at all? On the one hand, if Lacan himself failed to pass on this technique to any of his disciples, however, Lacan was, in fact, not functioning as master at all; on the other hand, if the short session is indeed essentially a technique, then it is precisely here that his disciples could have expected to find the unique Lacanian teaching.

Of course, the failure of Lacan's disciples to practice the short session was underpinned by a kind of political circumspection – considerations of the criteria for membership in the IPA. No doubt it was indeed counter-productive to have the IPA think that Lacan was, through his followers, proliferating the practice of the short session, when the IPA found that practice so unpalatable. As the possibility of admission to the IPA became more and more concrete, it must have seemed safer to not be practicing the short session. But this attitude was a contradictory one, the product of setting too much store in admission to the IPA. When the IPA later conducted its hearings, the bulk of Lacan's followers reported that they were not practicing the short session, even as they defended analysis as practiced by Lacan. They would surely have been hard pressed for an answer were they asked why, if they believed that Lacan's methods were the best, they were not practicing those methods even on their own patients. There is no way to account for such a contradiction. Of course, the unspoken answer to the question this contradiction poses was already fixed. It was, no less, that Lacan was a patriarch, a founder in the true sense, with all the special mandate that implies.

In this way Lacan, whether he meant to or not, had placed his followers in a

---

[8] Bodhidharma (d. 536?) was a (possibly legendary) Indian monk who established Ch'an Buddhism (antecedent of Japanese Zen) in China. Shinran (1173-1262) and Nichiren (1222-1282) founded respectively the True Pure Land (Jōdo Shinshū sect) and the Nichiren sects of Japanese Buddhism. The relevance of the comparison here is that all three are held by followers to have instantiated the essence of the Buddha in one way or another – Trans.

[9] "Taking refuge" (Jpn. *kie*), a Buddhist term for declaring one's faith in and reliance on the Buddha, the teachings (*dharma*), and the community of renunciate monks and nuns (*saṃgha*) for salvation – Trans.

contradictory political position, and by so doing, was at last making clear his own status as something above and beyond the law. This status could not be established merely by Lacan's own disciples recognizing him as the founding father in place of Freud, but if Lacan's new organization, the SFP, were granted entry to the IPA *en masse*, then the IPA itself would also by this act have given him *de facto* recognition. The IPA could never be expected to consent to such a thing. Fundamentally, the IPA, and with it all other professional psychoanalytic bodies, was comprised of people who proclaimed themselves *followers* of Freud. It would not do to have one single himself out from their number, and go around declaring himself a *substitute* for Freud. As we shall see in Chapter VI, the IPA would ultimately demand that the SFP strike Lacan from its register of training analysts. This was logically inevitable, and at the same time, we could even go so far as to say that it was the direct result of Lacan's own desire to elevate the symbolic value of the short session. Once more, we can ask here whether Lacan really "did not know" that this is how things would work out.

There is something we must bear in mind at this point. It is by no means rare, in psychoanalytic *practice*, for the person of the analyst to be overlaid onto that of Freud or Klein in the mind of the patient. All insightful analysts take note of this phenomenon, and consider how they ought to go about conceptualizing it, whether it contains a grain of reality, or is just sheer fantasy. Analysts, therefore, do indeed occupy the place of Freud in the reality of analysis, even as, in all interactions with their professional guilds, they vociferously declare that they are *not* a replacement for Freud. To some extent, then, the analyst must equivocate.

But is this double mental life really acceptable in someone devoted to the truth of being, as an analyst is? If a certain kind of analyst, while acknowledging himself capable of playing Freud's part in relation to the patient, believes it wisest to refrain from proclaiming himself Freud's substitute to his colleagues and peers, he is guilty not just of theoretical inadequacy, but also a failure of moral courage. Lacan, on the other hand, was faithful only to the reality of psychoanalysis, and demanded that he be acknowledged as he who had come in place of Freud. The majority of Lacan's followers acquiesced to this demand, and put themselves forward, voluntarily or unknowingly, in the role of the defenders of this notion to the IPA. By 1964, and the decisive parting of ways between Lacan and the IPA, Lacan was devoting his seminar to delving deep into the question of the nature of Freud's desire, and the idea that each individual analyst must assume that desire as his or her own.

If this theorization of the analyst's desire is correct, then each individual analyst is one who takes Freud's place, at least so far as desire is concerned, and we will return to take up this central theme once more, in Chapter VI. In the meantime, it suffices to observe that on one level, the short session was highly politicized, and symbolized Lacan's position in his conflict with the IPA. But this is by no means to say that there was no substance to it as an element of technique. In the Rome Discourse, we see Lacan's efforts to provide theoretical support for the short session as technique, although as a theoretical argument, it could hardly be called systematic or ordered. It is to an examination of that theoretical argument that we now turn.

Two: The Logic of the Short Session

Scansion – punctuating the analysis

As we saw in passing in the previous chapter, the defining characteristic of the technique of the short session is to be found in the introduction of temporal structure into the thinking and speaking subject. Now, in psychoanalysis, the timing of the end of the session is decided by the analyst; even where the length of the session has been fixed beforehand, it is difficult to bring the session to a close without the analyst sending the analysand a message of some kind. It follows that the termination of the session is a part of the analyst's task.

It is further possible for this act of termination to bear great significance as an *interpretation* on the part of the analyst. This is because the act of interrupting the discourses originating in various levels of the mind and structuring the analytic situation is, more than a simple interruption, no less than the insertion of a punctuation mark into the text within the patient – an act of scansion.[10] We can illustrate this point with an analogy. In the classics of both Japan and the West, the text is unpunctuated. By putting periods to the text, it is possible to bring out new meaning, or indeed, to be led into erroneous readings.[11] The ending, or "scanding", of the session likewise has an important function as just such a "period" – as a moment of punctuation.

While the analytic endeavor does fall into the same broad category as the exploits of the adventurers who interpret canonical texts, it must also give rise to a meaning peculiar to analysis and analysis alone. What sort of meaning are we referring to here? And what mode of punctuation, what sort of interpretative methodology, is capable of precipitating meaning of that kind? Let us examine this notion of "scansion", and its theoretical background, in a little more detail.

---

[10] To use Bruce Fink's word, the analyst "scands" the patient's discourse. Fink says, "I prefer to use the neologistic 'scanding' as the verb form of scansion, since 'scanning', the accepted verb form, has rather different connotations which could lead to considerable confusion here: looking over rapidly, quickly running through a list, taking ultrathin pictures of the body with a scanner, or 'feeding' text and images in digital form into a computer. All of the latter should be clearly distinguished from Lacan's idea of cutting, punctuating, or interrupting something (usually the analysand's discourse or the analytic session)." Bruce Fink, *The Lacanian Subject: Between Language and Jouissance* (Princeton: Princeton University Press, 1995), 187 n. 22 – Trans.

[11] *Selection*, 98-99.

Chapter 3: ROME: THE CORNERSTONE

The race against time (*sekitate*) to determine self[12]

One of the keynote theses of the Rome Discourse is this: In psychoanalysis, we re-enact the moment when the desire of the animal called man is made human through the "discourse of the Other". Eight years earlier, Lacan had written an essay called "Logical Time and the Assertion of Anticipated Certainty: A New Sophism",[13] in which he had outlined the process whereby the human subject determines for itself that it is human, and internalizes that determination of itself. "Logical Time" theorizes this process as a function of time, and in the Rome Discourse, this essay is taken up once more, and used as theoretical support for the short session.[14]

At the core of Lacan's argument is this notion. The "short session" should be analytically punctuated (scanded) so that a particular meaning emerges retroactively from its text – the mechanism whereby the subject determines for itself that it is human, and also the frailty of that mechanism. Let us first look at this mechanism, which Lacan articulates into the following three steps:[15]

(1) A man knows what is not a man;
(2) Men recognize themselves amongst themselves to be men;
(3) I declare myself to be a man for fear of being convinced by men that I am not a man.

How must psychoanalytic experience be temporally structured to produce meaning of this order? To elucidate this point, Lacan uses the "Parable of the Three Prisoners".

There were once three prisoners. The superintendent of the prison came to them and said, "I have here five cards, three white, and two black. I will stick them to your backs. You may look at the backs of the others, but you may not speak, and anyone who can discover what color his own card is, and give me a correct logical explanation

---

[12] In this and following sections, a pivotal Japanese term, *sekitate* (here "race against time"), draws out links between a number of situations where a feeling of haste, pressure for time, or of an impending cut-off point rushes a subject into a particular action. Lacan calls this factor in his sophism "urgency" (*Selection*, 34). It has proved difficult to translate *sekitate* with a single English term. The Japanese is given in parentheses wherever it occurs, in the hope this will help to pull together the disparate threads of the argument.

Some sense of the movement involved here is conveyed by the various senses of the English "precipitate": as a verb, "to cause to happen too soon or sooner than expected; bring on"; as an adjective, "rushing ahead", "done rashly or with undue haste", "sudden and brief"; and also, as a noun, the solid left behind by a process of chemical precipitation, which separates a dissolved substance from a solution as a solid. This latter calls to mind the subjective truth that is "precipitated out" of the analytic discourse by the "precipitate" ending of the session – Trans.

[13] Lacan, Jacques, "Le Temps logique et l'assertion de certitude anticipée: un nouveau sophisme", *Cahiers d'Art* (1945), 32-42. *Écrits* 197-214. Translated as "Logical Time and the Assertion of Anticipated Certainty: A New Sophism", by Bruce Fink and M. Silver, in Ellie Ragland-Sullivan, ed., *Newsletter of the Freudian Field*, vol 2 (1988), 4-22.

[14] Lacan takes the sophism up at several points in the Discourse: *Selection* 34, 48, 75, 77, 95ff.

Chapter 3: ROME: THE CORNERSTONE

of how he knows it, can go free." The superintendent then put a white card on the back of each of the three prisoners. The result: all three prisoners went to the superintendent at the same time, and, having laid out the same logic before him, all three were set free. How did this happen? The logic the three used was as follows.

Let the three prisoners be represented by A, B, and C respectively. A sees that the cards on B and C's backs are white. A thinks, "If my card was black, then B would be able to see one white card and one black. If that was to happen, then no doubt B would think, 'If my card is black, then C would be seeing two black cards. If that were the case, then C would surely run off to the superintendent, since there are only two black cards, and he would know he is white. But C has made no move. In which case, my card must be white. I'd better go to the superintendent!' But *B hasn't run out, any more than C has*. In that case, my initial hypothesis must be wrong. Which means I must be white." In this way, A determines his own identity, and runs off to the superintendent; and the same logical structure arises in B and C, so that all three go to the superintendent at the same time.

It is clear that the time factor here is decisive. The vital thing is that there is an instant when all three prisoners each "see that the other two have not made any move". "I" can make a dash for freedom, by virtue of the logical process described above, only because the other two make no move, and only for so long as this is so. In fact, it is perhaps even more accurate to say that this logical process itself allows one of the three prisoners to come to being *as* the subject "I": the I that looks at the backs of the other two and thinks the problem through is, itself, anticipated as a potential on the premise that it does not lag behind the other two in making its break for freedom. There must, therefore, be a certain sense of urgency (*sekitate*), which lies behind this logical process and supports it – which *precipitates* it; anyone who is even a split-second slower off the mark will no longer have the option of pursuing the logic of the sophism. For the prisoners, self (identity) cannot be determined without this accompanying temporal function, namely the sense of urgency (*sekitate*), and it is by a process exactly like that whereby each prisoner determines he is "white" that we, too, as subjects, affirm ourselves as human.

To return to our original question: these considerations bear on the analytic situation because it is precisely this logic of humanization that the analysis must re-enact. This means that the psychoanalyst must listen with an ear to the *tempo* of the patient's speech. The analyst's role is to pick up and carry the hustled feeling (*sekitate*) that comes into being within the discourse of the patient, to tune her ears in to the rhythm of the discourse's movements, and pace her footsteps to the shifts in tempo within it. At this point the short session comes into its own, picking up the pace and hustling the session towards its cut-off point – the point of scansion.

---

[15] *Écrits* 213; Fink and Silver, 18.

Three: Interpretation as Sonic Boom

Beyond the speed of logic

If we continue with the analogy of the prisoners, what constitutes the walls of the prison? They are, of course, walls of words (*logos*); they are walls of logic (*logos*), because it is impossible, merely from the static fact that of five cards, three have been used, and that two of those used are white, to deduce logically the color of the remaining card, that is, the card that is stuck to one's own back. It is necessary to step outside these walls of logic.

It is useful to consider what sort of speed we must attain to make this step. If we allow that logic is constructed from language, then the speed of logic must be the speed of sound. (The notion that logic is omnipresent, and therefore that the speed of logic is infinite, is no more than a misconception caused by considering only logic as already-made, and not logic in the making.) After all, language is also sound. Therefore, in order to "break the logic barrier," all we need to do is to exceed the speed of sound. Now, when something breaks the sound barrier, a sonic boom occurs: an airplane, for example, carries around it the sound waves it produces, and when the plane itself breaks through this envelope of sound waves, a violent explosion is heard – the sonic boom. In similar fashion, a subject that moves faster than its own thought, logic, and language also produces a sonic boom.

In discussions at the time of the Rome Discourse, Lacan used this analogy to explain psychoanalytic interpretation.[16] The interpretation, he suggests, is thus not some procrustean bed of meaning, to which the discourse of the analysand is fit by force; it is rather something which is heard as pure sound, prior to all meaning, when a subject breaks through this "language barrier". There is no particular reason why this sound should not bring the session to a full stop: the analyst can intervene at this point, and cut the session off by means of some act or other.[17] From within the discourse that is thus punctuated by this interpretative ending of the session, the meaning of the subject wells up and is marked and recorded, like an historical narrative.[18]

---

[16] "Actes du Congrès de Rome", *La Psychanalyse*, I (1956), 252.

[17] Just as the sonic boom was once celebrated as a kind of military salute, but is now classified as a species of noise pollution, so the patient can take the sonic boom either way. Whether the analytic boom salutes or pollutes depends entirely on the content of the session.

[18] It is here that we also find the pertinence of Lacan's comparison of the short session to Zen: in Zen, interviews between master and disciple are cut off by voice as not meaning but sound. The *katsu!* of the Zen master is nothing other than the sonic boom. [Lacan refers to Zen at *Selection* 100-101. The interviews referred to here are *mondō*, face-to-face encounters between master and adept, which especially in Rinzai Zen are often part of the training centered around *kōan* or Zen riddles. *Katsu!* is a sudden shout, pure exclamation, something like "Yah!" or "Ha!", often used by Zen masters – Trans.]

Chapter 3: ROME: THE CORNERSTONE

This, then, is part of the theoretical underpinning of the notorious "short session"; it aims to produce a sense of urgency, the pressure of which, like the race against time in the sophism of the three prisoners, *precipitates* the analysand's coming to being as subject in the intersubjective space; the precipitate speed of this process hurls the subject through the "language/sound barrier", and produces the interpretative "sonic boom", a forceful irruption of language as pure physical sound that outruns meaning. How, then, does this theoretical structure look in practice? We now turn to an instance of the incidence of this interpretative moment in the clinical setting, taken from my own clinical experience.

The precipitate of full speech (*parole pleine*)

One day, during analysis, a male patient said that he wanted to go to the toilet. He was in the middle of speaking about his memories of the past: at a time in his life when his younger brother had been born, and his place in the family threatened, he had stood on a bridge watching the muddy water of the river as it flowed beneath his feet, when suddenly a plastic bag with a fetus in it had come floating past. As soon as he had said this, he went to the toilet. When he came back, I gave him the following interpretation.

> "You thought that the fetus in the plastic bag was your brother. The reason you wanted to go to the toilet just now is that you were equating the flow of your urine with the river. Your wish to wash your brother away down the river appeared to you as the urge to urinate, and when you went to the bathroom just now, your act was mentally equivalent to flushing your brother away down the toilet."

At this point it was apparent that an essential cut-off point had arisen in the session. Even more than that, it was clear that, in the act of leaving to go to the toilet, the analysand himself had in fact put a period to the session.

The problem for us here is not to determine whether what he caught sight of, as he stood on the bridge and watched the river go by, was in fact a real fetus, or whether he just saw a fetus in some indeterminate piece of rubbish. More important than whether it was reality or fantasy, is the fact that this fantasy-reality gave rise to a new reality in his mind – the reality of his brother carried on the stream of his urine. In psychoanalysis, fantasy is treated as real. Fantasy is not a so-called conceptual product, but rather, is supported within the body by reality of this order.

As the psychoanalytic discourse is woven into being, the scene of analysis is thus overlain onto the scenes of the past – the scene of a murky river flowing through a downtown neighborhood gets mixed with the flow of words through the analysis – and then takes concrete form as the flow of urine the analysand senses in his experience right here and now. His own body, and the analyst's room, all meld completely into the scene from the past of which he speaks. In this past world, our

Chapter 3: ROME: THE CORNERSTONE

analysand interrogates himself as to whether or not he has really been accepted into the social body, considering the question through the lens of his brother's birth. He knows that his brother is soon to be born, and thinks to himself that he also is in the process of trying, in similar fashion, to be born into the community. Both he and his brother are sitting on the cusp of being feasibly included in the group.

Here we find a situation identical to that which obtains in the case of the three prisoners: the patient's brother is on his way into the world, and before the brother's birth process is complete, the patient himself must make the dash that will establish him as a member of the social body. He entrusts the image of what might become of him, should he lag from the starting blocks by even a hair, to the fantasy of his brother stillborn, or the fetus floating in the cloudy river. He hurriedly stands and dashes from the room. This hurriedness, or urgency (*sekitate*), overlaps with the pressure of his physical urge to urinate, and produces a *stretta*, as it were – a modulation in the discourse, and an increase of tempo, directed towards the session's final cadence.

In this case, then, the physiological function of urination proved capable of moving faster than the exchange of speech that constitutes the analysis. Even before he was offered any interpretation, the patient had anticipated the content of that interpretation (that he wanted his brother dead), and declared his murderous intent towards his brother in the toilet, through his act of urination. As we have already seen, in the Rome Discourse Lacan describes the unconscious as a polyphonic discourse. The polyphony is comprised of voices like memory, perception, and the body, and the body in particular takes the role of the "silent part"[19] in this polyphony. This internal discourse between the sense of the body and the conscious subject, the conduct of which is an extremely commonplace element of ordinary life, was precipitated from within our patient as speech of such speed and density as to condense both *past* and *present*. The present (urge to urinate) became a vehicle for the past (his fratricide), and the act of urinating, which as linguistic activity normally falls into the category of the meaningless, was suddenly brimful of language. In the Rome Discourse, Lacan calls this sort of precipitate *parole pleine*, "full speech".

As we have seen, then, the efficacy of the short session, which Lacan presented through the model given in "Logical Time", is that it works to establish a self-determining, subjective I. However, as we can see from the case study given above, this I stands out more for its flimsiness than its solidity. If I is set up on nothing more substantial than the empty feeling of letdown after urinating, what sort of an I can it be? We now turn to looking at some perhaps unexpected consequences of the short session, and the advent in "full speech" of the I thus established.

---

[19] *Partie muette.* See *Écrits*, 251; *Selection*, 43.

Chapter 3: ROME: THE CORNERSTONE

Four: The Efficacy of the Short Session

Paranoia games

It may be slightly improper to compare the discourse of the analyst to a hard-sell sales patter, but the "morning-after feeling", the sense of post-toilet emptiness we just traced to the root of our patient's identity, might remind us of the sense of futility one feels when hustled into (*sekitate*) buying some meaningless article by the placards saying "Today only!" and the salesman's cries of "Going cheap!" The sense of being rushed into a purchase, too, is close to the urgency of the prisoners' situation, or the pressure of the patient's toilet urges (*sekitate*). In order to protect itself from this sense of futility, "I" might even proclaim that the junk I have bought is a rare find, a treasure, and go round bragging about it to people!

As we saw earlier in Lacan's three-stage formula, I first learns what it is that "is not human" (and this is already a denial of our incapacity to know ourselves). I then looks around it, and ascertains that it is among humans (at this stage I is a team player, loyal to the group cause). Finally, fearing that these others will tell it, "You are not human," I beats them to the punch and declares itself human first (make your break while you've got the chance – look after number one!). Does this whole scenario not remind us of the power plays of intersubjective politics: of discrimination, social distinctions, and the game of insider/outsider, for example?[20]

In the brief scenario of Lacan's sophism, in fact, we find the full set of structural requisites to paranoia – the deep-hidden sense of frustration and impotence; the group awareness that exists solely that we might not be left on the outer; the sense of righteousness that logically justifies the self by rationalizing one's actions. Does the

---

[20] In Japanese culture we find cultural terms that illustrate the stages of this Lacanian model. The concept translated here as "team player" (Step 2 of Lacan's dialectic) is *rentai*, "solidarity", a term used in analyzing the famous group imperative of Japanese culture, especially in the context of the modern labor movement. Betraying the group cause to save your own skin, or to advance your own interests (Step 3), is called *nukegake*, "to run out on" (your fellows), "to get the jump on, steal a march on" (someone), recalling the moment where the prisoners must make a break for the superintendent and freedom. Needless to say, bucking the group like this is generally frowned upon.

In Japanese society we also find instances of the "power games" that pivot around these poles of participation in, or copping-out/exclusion from, the social contract. An instance for that is the range of behaviors called collectively *kirisute*. The term originally referred to the prerogative of ruling samurai during the Edo era (1600-1867) to cut down all social inferiors on the spot [cut down here is literal, i.e. with a sword – Trans.]. *Kirisute* survives as a concept to label, for example, any social policy that demands some sector (usually the weak or disadvantaged) to be neglected (i.e., in Lacan's terms, relegated to the "inhuman") for the sake of the "greater common good". [This note expands greatly on brief hints in the original text aimed at a Japanese readership. It was added for the English translation with the author's co-operation – Trans.]

analysis create paranoia, then? Isn't it supposed to build personal character instead? Lacan's answer to this question is quick and simple: paranoia and character are in fact the same thing.[21] His doctoral thesis, which was mentioned in Chapter I, was entitled "On Paranoiac Psychosis in its Relation to the Personality";[22] he was later to criticize this title himself, however, for if personality is paranoia itself, it is little better than a tautology.

Is Lacan's thesis correct? Is what we call "character" (in both the neutral sense and in the value-loaded sense of "a man of character") nothing more or less than paranoia? By and large, it seems that Lacan is right. From a number of excellent biographies, we have now been made fully aware of the perplexing degree to which people who are praised for great "character" are ruled by self-righteousness and a strong sense of victimization, bringing home the ease with which human values, and the social sphere, can be controlled by such paranoid structures.

The question of paranoia and its place in subjective and social structures was to occupy Lacan throughout his career, and we will return to it in Chapter V. In the meantime, let us rather turn to a deeper look at the first term of Lacan's three-step model, i.e. "that which is not human".

I as *objet a*

There is a certain instant in which I, as it stands in logical time, sees that the other two prisoners are yet to make a move. This "seeing" is the basis for the logical structure of I; its status is something like that of evidential fact supporting an argument. But this "seeing" cannot become fact if I fails to anticipate the other two in flying into action. The fact that I "saw" is constructed only because I leaps into action, and only then is the logical construct that follows is made possible. There is no leeway for even the slightest tardiness. The fact of having "seen", which seems so much like an objective given, is in fact something I *constructs* for itself. I creates for itself the ground for its being human and being one of the "whites". In throwing up

---

[21] In this passage, the words "character" and "personality" are used to translate the same Japanese word, *jinkaku*, which means both "character" in the value-loaded sense of "a man of character", and also "personality" in the sense it is a technical term in psychology. In order to cover the whole range of the term it was necessary to juggle with two English translations, but the reader should bear in mind that Lacan's term is "personality", and that this book is not attempting to set up "character" as a further concept somehow distinct from Lacan's usage – Trans. For personality and paranoia as identical, see *Séminaire* of December 16, 1975, texte établi par Jacques-Alain Miller, *Ornicar?* 7 (juin-juillet 1976), 7 : "The only reason I have so long resisted the republication of this book is simply that paranoiac psychosis and personality have no relationship – because they are the same thing (Si j'ai si longtemps résisté à la republication de ce livre, c'est simplement que la psychose paranoïaque et la personnalité n'ont pas de rapport. Parce que c'est la même chose.)."
[22] Lacan, *De la psychose paranoïaque dans ses rapports avec la personnalité* (Paris: François, 1932) (Thèse pour le doctorat en médecine, Diplôme d'état). Republished as *De la psychose paranoïaque dans ses rapports avec la personnalité* (Paris: Seuil, 1975).

Chapter 3: ROME: THE CORNERSTONE

this construct, of having seen that the others have yet to make a move, as its past, I breaks through the wall of language and is thrust into the present.

But let us recall what met the gaze of these two who "did not make any move" – the black card that I posited it had on its back. As I guessed at what the other two were thinking, the hypothesis that the card on I's back was black was absolutely essential. Another I – an I bearing the black card – existed within the other two prisoners, as a down-payment that underwrote the hypothetical thought processes I supposed in its two fellows. But when I constructed the past given of "having seen that the others had yet to make a move", and at the same moment broke into flight, this other I was banished into the past – interred in the gaze, thought and movements of the other two prisoners that I left behind. This other I, immured in the retroactively posited past, is where we find "the thing that is not human", the first step of Lacan's sophism – in something we cannot see even if we use a mirror: the view of ourselves from the back.

This thing, buried inside the other – this thing that we ought to see in the mirror and yet somehow cannot, which is inhuman and remote and alien to I, and yet which is most certainly a part of I – this thing, to which each I clings as to a ground when it determines itself as human, is what is called, in the Lacanian terminology, "the *objet a*". The classic instances of the *objet a* are the fourfold set of the breast, the feces, the voice, and the gaze; and these various objects, which insinuate their way most cunningly into all the images of analysis, had long before Lacan already been called "part objects" by Abraham and Klein.[23] In Book 8 of the seminar (1960-61), Lacan gives these "part objects" pride of place as one of the most important discoveries of psychoanalysis.[24] In this period, he gave new names to the concept of the part object – names like "agalma", discussed in Chapter VII, or "*objet a*" – and set about developing it greatly, as the pivot of his whole theoretical system.[25]

---

[23] K. Abraham, "A Short Study of the Development of the Libido, Viewed in the Light of Mental Disorders" (1924), in *Selected Papers on Psycho-Analysis* (London: Maresfield Reprints, H. Karnac, 1979), 497: "In the stage of 'partial love with incorporation' . . . the love-object is represented by one part of itself. The small child has an ambivalent attitude towards that part (penis, breast, excrement, etc.); that is, he desires it and rejects it at the same time." Melanie Klein, *The Psycho-Analysis of Children,* 136: "As we know from Abraham, in an early stage of development both real and introjected objects are mainly represented by [the] organs [of the real and introjected objects, i.e. mother or parents]." Klein, "On the Theory of Anxiety and Guilt" (1948), in *Envy and Gratitude and Other Works, 1946-1963: The Complete Works of Melanie Klein, Volume 4* (London: Hogarth Press), 32: "The good internalized breast and the bad devouring breast form the core of the super-ego in its good and bad aspects . . . . The second important part-object to be introjected is the penis of the father to which also both good and bad qualities are attributed. These two dangerous objects – the bad breast and the bad penis – are the prototypes of internal and external persecutors."

[24] S VIII, 172.

[25] Incidentally, for readers who have an interest in psychoanalytic theory as a whole, it is worth adding that important developments of the Abraham-Kleinian part-object include

Chapter 3: ROME: THE CORNERSTONE

In Volume 20 of the seminar (1972-73), Lacan returns to the essay on logical time to locate the *objet a* in the I being looked at by the other two prisoners;[26] here, the *objet a* is "that which is not human," the first step of the sophism in "Logical Time". When I sees that the other two prisoners have not yet moved, and therefore concludes that it ought itself to make a break for it, the time lag between the *seeing* and the *concluding* approaches infinitely close to zero. This is because the slightest gap would allow the other two to leave the subject in the dust, and frustrate the consummation of the subject's logical process; I is thus urgently pressed (*sekitate*) to bring the conclusion of its logical process closer and closer to the moment of seeing.

Within the act of "seeing", then, is concealed I as that which is not human. At the same time, however, the act of concluding the train of logic signifies "I say I *am* human". For this reason, as the time lag approaches zero, a *contact,* in the sense of a kind of short circuit, is established between "being not human" and "being human", and at the logical extreme of the urgency that presses the subject (*sekitate*), that which is *not* human insinuates itself into the heart of the self-determination of the subject as that which *is* human. Moreover, the way in which this inhuman element muscles in on the action is utterly unique, because it is precisely by means of this long-awaited self-determination as that which is human that the inhuman something will inevitably be lost – and primordially so. It will always-already have been lost; it will never have existed in the first place. And this fact itself, bare and unadorned, marks the exit from the short session.

Even in psychoanalyses that do not utilize the short session, where the encounter is of fixed duration, the analyst still brings things to a conclusion by some act or other. This means, of course, that this same effect *does* also arise in these other situations, and in fact, analysts frequently whisper among themselves about patients who suddenly get down to the nitty-gritty five minutes before the end of the analytic hour. The short session simply takes this observation beyond mere whisperings, brings it out into the light of day, and gives it a place in the methodological structure.

The end of the short session is never fixed, and precisely because it is not fixed, the subject comes to interrogate itself, as temporal being. This is the efficacy of the short session, and even its defining characteristic; the short session is a practice which brings out, from within the very self-awareness whereby the human subject grasps itself as human, an inhuman object (like the fetal corpse of the patient's brother fantasized in the urine). This object inheres in the subject's self-awareness as both prior condition and necessary consequence, and even then only insofar as it will always-already have been lost.

What can be said of the "end of the analysis", in the sense of the end of a single

---

Lacan's *objet a,* Winnicott's transitional object, and Kohut's "self-object", though Kohut himself makes little mention of the connection.
[26] S XX, 48-49.

session, can also be said of the end of the psychoanalysis as a whole; it is not possible to fix the end of analysis, to pre-define a quota of years in analysis upon which all analyses will be complete. Let us take a look at this further implication, less often recognized, of Lacan's doctrine of analytic time – the problem touched on by Freud in "Analysis Terminable and Interminable" – and the political context in which Lacan issued his challenge to the orthodoxy.

That which marks the end of "analysis interminable"
In the Rome Discourse, Lacan takes up Freud's late paper, "Analysis Terminable and Interminable" (1937),[27] and says that the word "interminable", as Freud uses it, in principle means "limitless" or "boundless" in a sense that we could say is almost Wittgensteinian. In *Tractatus Logico-Philosophicus*, Wittgenstein says, "Our life has no end in just the way in which our visual field has no limits";[28] for as long as we are alive, or within life's horizon, then, we have no way of saying where the edge of life might lie. As Russell says in his "Introduction" to the same work, by way of expanding on Wittgenstein's point, "Our world may be bounded for some superior being who can survey it from above, but for us, however finite it may be, it cannot have a boundary, since it has nothing outside it."[29] "Interminability" in the psychoanalytic sense thus falls into the same category as this sort of limitlessness or boundlessness; once we are within the analysis, there is no way for us to say when it will end,[30] and this is as true of each individual session as it is of the analysis as a whole.

How, then, does this "interminability" of our life-world map onto the "interminability" of analysis? In Wittegensteinian terms, life's end, its boundedness, remains unknowable for so long as we are within life. Despite this, however, we do know that we will die sometime. In what way do we know it? Is it merely a matter of ordinary knowledge? It seems more likely that it goes beyond normal knowledge, into a different dimension. As we saw from the case history above, what is undertaken in the analytic session is a discourse aimed at defining oneself as human. For the duration of the session, this discourse (including silence) is overlain onto the continuum of our very life. If a session of "interminable" analysis is cut off (punctuated, scanded) by something internal, which arises at the behest of this self-definition as human (*sekitate*), then surely that same something will give an end

---

[27] SE XXIII, 216-253.
[28] *Tractatus Logico-Philosophicus: the German Text of Ludwig Wittgenstein's* Logisch-philosophische Abhandlung, trans. D. F. Pears and B. F. McGuiness (London: Routledge and Kegan Paul, 1961, 1988), 147.
[29] Ibid, xviii.
[30] Touching on the question of terminating the analysis, Lacan says, "Time plays its role in analytic technique in several ways. It presents itself first of all in the total duration of the analysis . . . . [I]t is now clear that this duration can only be anticipated for the subject as

not just to the session, but also to our (seemingly) "limitless" life. Our life, precisely in virtue of being *human* life, bears within itself the germ of its own limit, and this limit approaches us in the form of the "non-human". As the non-human – that is, the *objet a* – surfaces, we demonstrate that in fact we were party to a knowledge of our own death much more profound than ordinary knowledge.[31]

Is there not a danger that this essentially psychoanalytic process will be altogether lost sight of in methods where qualifying standards for analysts are fixed on the basis of length of each single session, number of sessions per week, and total years in analysis? As it happened, at the time of the Rome Discourse, the movement towards this sort of coercive standardization of the curriculum was growing very strong within the IPA and the SPP. In unveiling the technique of the "short session", Lacan was urging that this initiative be reconsidered, and demanding that people think about the relation between time and the subject within psychoanalysis.

It is now clear just how important a role the *objet a* plays in the practice of the short session; as we have seen, what the short session's treatment of time precipitates out is no less than the *objet a*. But in fact, this role of the *objet a* was only elaborated subsequently; several years were to elapse between the Rome Discourse, in which Lacan discussed in public his method of the short session, and the introduction of the *objet a* into his theoretical framework. I will now anticipate even more, to see how Lacan, after a gap of nearly thirty years, reworks his sophism and brings it into connection with the *objet a*, which he presents as the golden mean.

Five: The *Objet a* is the Golden Mean

In search of the golden section

At one point in Volume 20 of his seminar,[32] Lacan ties the *objet a* to the function of haste, or pressure for time (*sekitate*), which we discussed earlier, thereby hinting at a relation between the short session and the *objet a*. Lacan says that the *objet a* can be understood as the "golden mean".[33] Now, on the one hand, when the *objet a* shows itself inescapably in the analysis, it is often in such base forms as the breast, feces, the voice, the gaze, and so on; on the other, the golden mean could almost be called the patron saint of Beauty itself – what possible connection could there be between two such seemingly opposed quantities?

In order to bridge this apparent gap between Lacan's two terms, let us return to

---

indefinite" (*Selection*, 95).
[31] The latter half of this paragraph was rewritten in Japanese by the author for the English translation – Trans.
[32] S XX, 48-49.
[33] S XX, 49.

Chapter 3: ROME: THE CORNERSTONE

the example of the parable of the three prisoners. I, that is, one of the three prisoners, is looking at the cards on the backs of its two fellows. I attempts to extract, from the way the backs of I's two fellows look to it, knowledge of what sort of thing I itself is. Let us express this notion of "how things look" by means of a *ratio*, that is to say, a set of proportions; but also by means of *ratio* as in "ratiocination" and "rationality", that is, "reason" and "calculation". For instance, in relation to 2, 5 is $\frac{5}{2}$, that is, 2.5. In similar fashion, we will say that, in relation to I (x), the other (y) is $\frac{y}{x}$.

If the other as it is to I is $\frac{y}{x}$, then, how should we think about the question of what I itself is? We can be sure that the same I assumes a different significance for the people of the nation as a whole, for example, and for I's blood relatives. We can see, then, that the question of what I is (that is, what I am) must be asked in the following form: What is I, from the perspective of a particular type of whole? Returning to the perspective of the prisoner "I", the problem for I is: What is I, as I is within the whole formed by itself and the other prisoners (assuming that such a thing exists)? If we notate the line of sight common to I (x) and the other (y) as $x+y$, we can therefore express I as

$$\frac{x}{x+y}$$

i.e., "what I is to the whole comprised of I and the other". This is the I that we should properly seek – I as it appears in the perspective of the whole. This image of I, however, is originally and forever beyond our grasp; in fact, this view of I is precisely the essence of that which is known as the *objet a*.[34] In other words

$$\frac{x}{x+y} = a$$

It may be true that this image of I as it is for the whole is originally and permanently unobtainable for I. But what if this image of I were to appear to I from the midst of the way *the other appears to I*? That is to say, would it not be a stroke of luck if, just when I wanted to know what I was to the whole, this mode of I's being were inscribed in the others I was seeing? In a sense, this would make it possible for I to access the

---

[34] In the parable of the prisoners, for instance, "I as it appears to the whole" is precisely the impossible "view of oneself from the back" constituted by I as part of the overall intersubjective structure – the totality of (black and white) cards in the game – Trans.

Chapter 3: ROME: THE CORNERSTONE

view of itself from the back, even as I remained just as I was all the while.

As it so happens, this is precisely what did in fact occur for the prisoner "I". From the midst of the way I saw the others there emerged what I was for the whole, inclusive of I itself. (Of course, this could only have happened on the condition that I had already taken flight from the place where it happened, having made a hasty exit to see the superintendent). We can notate the state of affairs at this point in time as follows:

$$\frac{y}{x} = \frac{x}{x+y} \quad ①$$

i.e. I is to the whole comprised of I and the other as the other is to I. Since the right hand side of this equation is identical to a, we arrive at

$$\frac{y}{x} = \frac{x}{x+y} = a$$

From this we can discover that $y = ax$, and by substituting this into ①, we obtain

$$a = \frac{1}{1+a} \quad ②[35]$$

If we solve this, taking the positive solution, we derive the following value:

$$a = \frac{\sqrt{5}-1}{2}$$

This value is the golden mean (the golden section). We can see, then, that when "the way I sees the other" is equal to "what I is within the whole" like this, the other is the golden mean for I. What exactly does this mean?

We can see more of what this algebra implies by paraphrasing it in ordinary language. The golden section is "the proportion of the two divisions of a line segment such that the longer is to the whole as the shorter is to the longer." Taking a rectangle as an example, how long ought the short side be, in terms of the long side, for us to feel that this rectangle is as beautiful as possible? The standard answer is that the proportion of the short side to the long must be the same as the proportion of

---

[35] Formula ② appears in S XVII, 180-183. The other formulae do not appear in Lacan. I worked them up to help explicate and develop the implications of Lacan's formula, and the resulting algebra was the impetus for writing this book. For further developments of the mathematics presented here, see Chapter V, note 62.

Chapter 3: ROME: THE CORNERSTONE

the long side to the sum of the two lengths – and this proportion, again, is the golden mean. In the calculations we just performed, then, I corresponded to the long side of the rectangle, and the "other" to the short.   Incidentally, if we calculate the value of our answer, $\frac{\sqrt{5}-1}{2}$ is approximately 0.618, and in the case of the Parthenon in Greece, for instance, the ratio of the height of the building to the breadth of the main face is extremely close to this value.

Returning to equation ① above, the other is to I as I is to the whole comprised of both I and the other. Let us remove this formulation from the context of the parable of the three prisoners and consider it in a more general manner. The formula tells us that the other is to I as I appears from the perspective of a universal, God-like viewpoint made up of both the I and the other. It is a case of, "Love thy neighbor, because God sees thee from behind thy back even as thou seest thy neighbor." That is, when I regards its neighbor with the same regard that God has for I, I will be able to see itself as I appears to God, *in* its neighbor. At that point, I's neighbor will be the golden mean to I, i.e. the *objet a*. The importance of this is perhaps clearest only if we consider the state of affairs in reverse – i.e. at the moment when I perceives the *objet a* in its neighbor, I itself is seeing its I with the eyes of God.

I thinks that I is human. This universal judgement is odd, if you consider it – after all, the human species has two genders, male and female, and there is no way for I to change its gender; on top of this, there are many different races, and I is locked within its blood and heredity. Despite all this, however, I determines itself to be "human", just as if it were possible for I to experience all conceivable human standpoints. Ultimately, this means that, unawares, I has all along been in possession of a God-like viewpoint, comprised of the amalgam of other people and I. It also means that as the support for this viewpoint, we have all, likewise all along and unawares, been seeing in one another the *objet a*, which is nothing other than our self. In all likelihood, somewhere among these considerations lies the reason that the golden mean is considered so beautiful.

Let us try another example – love. Some time ago, there was a pop song called

"x + y = Love"   ③[36]

In Greek terms, the "love" here, comprised of both subjects, is Eros, god of love, a transcendent viewpoint that knows the hearts of both lovers. One can see that this viewpoint corresponds to what we already referred to above as the whole comprised of I and the other. Let us consider the classic angst of the earnest lover – "How do I see her? Do I feel *love*, or *lust*? Oh, I don't know!" If "I" gets to worrying like this,

---

[36] English in original.   Chiaki Naomi, *X+Y=LOVE* (Columbia, August 1970) – Trans.

all it need do is think as follows: "When I can see her just as God sees I, then I love her." Then, if I is *x*, and she is *y*, we can make the "god of love" given in formula ③ bearer of the transcendent perspective, and use the following equation to solve I's emotional problem. We arrive at

$$\frac{y}{x} = \frac{x}{x+y}$$

Of course, this is identical to equation ① above. To I, she is *a*, the golden mean. And, to God, I also is *a*, the golden mean. A happy identity between Agape and Eros, Christian and erotic love! It is a little worrying that $\frac{\sqrt{5}-1}{2}$ is an "irrational number", but it is also a "real number" all the same. We can at least use Pythagoras' theorem to diagram it on a number line. Unreasonable though it may be, it exists. Love is loving her as God loves I. "I" can accept that.

I think the meaning of the notion that the *objet a* is the golden mean should be fairly clear by this point. The *objet a* is the support that is necessitated when I comes to see itself from a transcendental perspective. This support appears in the people and objects around I, and helps I as it steals away, unbeknownst even to itself, to the transcendent viewpoint. Were it not for this support, I would never be able to see itself from outside itself at all.

In this way, the *objet a* appears whenever I enters into a relation with an other, and that relation is equal to the relation that this "we", as the set of both the other and I, enters into with I. Here the *objet a* shows itself as the ratio of the other to the I; an aspect of the other that is more a matter of relation (*ratio*) than positive entity. What, then, is the relation between the transcendent God's-eye perspective this "ratio"-nalization gives us access to, and the particular being of the subject that we find there? This is the question we consider next.

The "irrational" relation between universal and particular

When I feels itself to be something with identity (identity with itself, that is), I is, in a manner of speaking, "one" (= 1). At that point the *objet a*, best notated as $\frac{\sqrt{5}-1}{2}$, will surely appear within the other, and the transcendent whole comprised of both I and the other will without fail appear as the sum of I and the *objet a*: in other words, as $1 + \frac{\sqrt{5}-1}{2} = \frac{\sqrt{5}+1}{2}$. Now, if we look closely, we will see at this point that the *objet a*

Chapter 3: ROME: THE CORNERSTONE

and the value of the transcendent are inverses of one another: $\frac{\sqrt{5}-1}{2} \times \frac{\sqrt{5}+1}{2} = 1$.

Thus, I finds itself jammed between two mutually inverse irrational numbers, just barely able to maintain its identity, that is, the fact that I is one. When I is one like this, from the perspective of the transcendent whole that is $\frac{\sqrt{5}+1}{2}$, I becomes $\frac{1}{(\frac{\sqrt{5}+1}{2})}$, that is, $\frac{\sqrt{5}-1}{2}$. In other words, the I that maintains its self-*identity* - its oneness with itself - is the golden mean for the transcendent whole.

    The support of I's self-identity is the *objet a*, as the ratio of the other to the I. Naturally, the *objet a*, if it is a ratio, cannot be seen. As with all things, however, problems with this ratio become obvious only when things do not go right. When the ratio is even slightly disturbed, the *objet a* appears not as a ratio, but as the gaze, the feces, or in other concrete forms. The relation between I and other, as when I sees the other in terms of the golden mean, is from the first an unstable one. Here we should note that although we at first notated the other as it is for I in the form of the fraction (ratio) $\frac{y}{x}$, the answer that ultimately presented itself was an irrational number - and irrational numbers cannot really be written as fractions. For this reason, the relation between I and other is something beyond the fraction (ratio), that is to say, beyond reason (ratio). Just as the golden mean is an irrational number, love, so to speak, is a *numerically* "irrational relation" - its constant is this irrational number, and just as irrational numbers contain "irreducible radicals", love is also "radically irreducible". It oscillates forever about a radical core of ultimately indeterminable value, and like its value, our hearts too are never quite stable.

    In using equations to consider our problem, we have approached the equivalence of the viewpoint of the I seeing the other, and of the "we" as it looks at I. In this sense it is possible to say that we have been treating the identity of universal and particular, and it is precisely from this perspective of the essential difficulty of the identity between universal and particular that Lacan attempts to look at the human relation to language in the Rome Discourse. Our anticipatory detour through Lacan's later work and the *objet a* has thus brought us full circle, back to Rome and 1953. Lacan's incisive question in the Rome Discourse was: What might make it possible for I (the individual, the particular) to see itself as it truly is, from the universal viewpoint of language? He was to gradually prepare an answer to this question in the form of the subject's relation to the *objet a*, which thus takes the place of the Hegelian

Chapter 3: Rome: The Cornerstone

Absolute Spirit emergent from the synthesis of subjective and objective.[37]

Perhaps the equation we have been using might make a Japanese reader think of the Confucian dictum, "Be able to follow what your heart desires, without transgressing what is right."[38] But in Lacan's case, it is rather precisely when the relation of the subject to the other *is* congruent with the relation of the whole to the subject itself, that the appearance of the *objet a* within that congruency exposes the subject to an intense temptation from the Other side *to* transgress.[39] For the subject then runs the risk of reducing itself to a mere utensil of the desire of the Other, and forgetting its own desire in its stupefaction. In this sense, the relation of the subject to the *objet a* is, for the subject at least, conflictual enough,[40] and in this light, Natsume Soseki's notion of "*renouncing* self to conform to Nature" seems closer to our equation than the Confucian formula. What was important for Natsume was the enduring paradox that, the more he sought to subject himself to the requirements of natural law, the more insistent the voice of temptation became. In this connection, we might recall how the protagonist of *Light and Darkness*[41] was caught between his

---

[37] Lacan states his position on Hegel in the Rome Discourse. Insofar as Hegel conceives of the movement of Spirit as tending towards the synthesis of particular and universal, he is a precursor of psychoanalysis; however, only with psychoanalysis is the conclusion of this movement correctly recognized. "But if there still remains something prophetic in Hegel's insistence on the fundamental identity of the particular and the universal, an insistence that reveals the measure of his genius, it is certainly psychoanalysis that provides it with its paradigm by revealing the structure in which that identity is realized as disjunctive of the subject, and without appeal to any tomorrow" (*Selection*, 80). A little further on, Lacan points out that within language itself, there exists a duality of universal and particular that it is extremely difficult to resolve. Human being becomes human by awakening to its most *particular* desire, but it cannot but use *universal* language to do so. Lacan puts it this way: "In the symbolism brought to light in analysis, it is certainly a question of a language. This language, corresponding to the playful wish to be found in one of Lichtenberg's aphorisms, has the universal character of a language (*langue*) that would be understood in all other languages (*langues*), but, at the same time, since it is the language that seizes desire at the very moment in which it is humanized by making itself recognized, it is absolutely particular to the subject" (81) [Note added by author for English edition – Trans.].

[38] See *Analects*, "Weizheng". "The Master said, 'At fifteen, I had my mind bent on learning. At thirty, I stood firm. At forty, I had no doubts. At fifty, I knew the decrees of Heaven. At sixty, my ear was an obedient organ for the reception of truth. *At seventy, I could follow what my heart desired, without transgressing what was right*'" [emphasis mine – Trans.]. James Legge, trans., *The Chinese Classics with a Translation, Critical and Exegetical Notes, Prolegomena, and Copious Indexes* (Hong Kong: Hong Kong University Press, 1960), Vol. 1, 146-47.

[39] "Other side" here means the place of the Other, but also something like the Buddhist *higan*, the "other shore" of enlightenment or *nirvāṇa*. For *higan* see Chapter IV, note 25 below – Trans.

[40] These two sentences were added by the author for the English version – Trans.

[41] See Natsume Soseki, *Light and Darkness*, trans. V. H. Viglielmo (London: Owen, 1971). The notion of "renouncing self to conform to Nature" (*sokuten kyoshi*) mentioned above does not appear in the novel itself, but was used by Natsume in discussing the work, and is a staple of criticism.

aspiration to lead a life in harmony with nature's dictates on the one hand, and an ill-advised love on the other.[42]

In fact, the sense of the "numerically irrational relation" is missing from notions like the Hegelian "Absolute Spirit" and the Confucian formulation. We find rather more of an affinity to it in Descartes' *cogito* ("I think, therefore I am"), and in the seminar of 1969-1970 (*Seminar* Vol. 17), Lacan experimented with expressing the *cogito* by means of a formula which utilized the golden mean[43] – the formula given as ② above. For the meantime, however, let us leave the mathematics there, and rather continue our examination of the relation between the "desire of the Other" and the *objet a*.

The desire of the big Other

As we saw previously, the way "I really am" (the way I really is) can only be made clear from the universal viewpoint of the "we" that includes I. That which I supposes looks at I from that viewpoint is the *other*, in the strict sense of the term – in other words, the "big Other".[44] We speak of this sort of other as the "big Other" because Lacan always wrote the term with a big 'A': *Autre*.[45]

It is imperative that I finds out what it is to this big Other. This question is interchangeable with the question of whether, seen from the perspective of the big Other, I is good, or bad; loveable, or something to be discarded. The question that presses on I is this: Can I construct its being as something whose existence is an

---

[42] This sentence was modified by the author for the English version – Trans.
[43] S XVII, session 11, "Les Sillons de L'Alèthosphère", 175 ff.
[44] In this book, I will generally use the term "big Other" in terms of this most general and abstract definition. This is the basis that makes the mathematical reasoning presented in this and subsequent chapters possible. However, the big Other can also be considered in various quite concrete guises, and Jacques-Alain Miller gives four principle concrete instances:
  (1) The linguistic structure itself, divided again into three principle aspects: (a) the phonemic battery; (b) *langue,* as the lexicon of the language; and (c) *langue* as syntax. This is what Lacan refers to as the "treasury of signifiers".
  (2) The sum of all concrete discourse. This is a "limit concept", which taken to an extreme refers to all that has ever concretely been said by anyone in all of human history – a vast body of discourse which the individual subject traverses in her own specific way.
  (3) Culture or civilization: for instance, what Lévi-Strauss described as the "fundamental structures of kinship", the various ideals of a specific civilization.
  (4) The family, as cause of the various complexes: for instance, Freud's "Oedipus complex" can be situated in the place of the big Other.
Of these four specific guises of the big Other, it is especially (2) that is closest to the sense in which the term is used in Chapters IV and V of this book.
[For Miller, see Kazushige Shingu, ed., *Beyond Meaning: Lacan in the Clinical Setting* (*Imi no kanata e: Rakan no chiryōgaku*), (Kongō Press, 1996), 243-244 (in Japanese). This note added for the English edition – Trans.]
[45] In English works about Lacanian theory, this other is called the "big Other", or just "Other"

inevitable necessity, utilizing for the task the viewpoint of language common to us all – the logic of the big Other? This question can also be read as the central problem that troubles the human heart: Does the big Other desire my existence? In everyday terms: Am I wanted? Lacan repeatedly stated that the fundamental form of human desire is the desire for recognition from the big Other. This thing called language insinuates itself into I's entire being, and through the paths and byways of that language, I must ascertain for itself whether its being is right or not – whether or not I is to have freedom to exist. In the next chapter, we will consider these problems, looking further at the links between the desire of the big Other as language, and the *objet a*. Our point of departure, once again, is the Rome Discourse.

---

with a capital 'O'. This convention has been followed throughout this book. – Trans.

CHAPTER FOUR

LANGUAGE AS THE OTHER

One: The Fundamental Epistemological Position of Psychoanalysis

Vanished childhood
Before it is anything else, Lacan's "big Other" is essentially a matter of language. How, then, is it possible for this Other to desire, exactly as humans desire? In order to answer this question, we must first return to look once more at psychoanalysis' fundamental epistemological take on human being.

In Freud's *The Interpretation of Dreams*, we find the following passage: "The earliest experiences of childhood are not obtainable any longer as such." Freud goes on to add that these memories are " replaced in analysis by 'transferences' and dreams."[1] In this casual remark, Freud marked a significant conceptual turning point. When we delve back into our memories, we somewhere encounter a point where they give out on us; nobody remembers their own birth. Nonetheless, we believe that our identity reaches back to birth in an integral, unbroken continuum, and we live life as if our amnesia *a propos* our earliest years is due to nothing more than a casual lapse of memory. In fact, however, it is no longer possible for us to experience for ourselves the factual link between our current body and whatever must have existed as a baby in the arms of our mother and father.

Psychoanalysis sets out from the acceptance that this impossibility is real; this is why Freud proclaims that "childhood is no longer obtainable". But lost as it may be, the vanished childhood continues to work on us: through symbols, it structures our unconscious, and dreams and the transference are systems of precisely this sort of symbol. Moreover, as long as we persist in seeking the ground for our existence within, we inevitably remain confined within the limits of these symbolic systems, even as we forge ahead with the search. As we work our tentative way towards this vanished ground of the thinking I, we ourselves construct the ground we thereupon tread. While this ground may well be gone forever, we would surely have been warranted, had it not vanished, in equating it with life itself. What we thus construct is the integral fabric of our very life – the sheer fact of our being alive.

This process of loss-and-construction of the primal ground of being sometimes can be seen in quite concrete terms in dreams. Once, for instance, when Freud informed

---
[1] Freud, *The Interpretation of Dreams*, SE IV, 184. Punctuation slightly altered.

a female patient of his theory that the first experiences of childhood were permanently lost, the patient had a dream in which she went to a butcher for something and was told, "That's not obtainable any longer."[2] She then went to a grocer instead, and the grocer tried to talk her into buying "a peculiar vegetable that was tied up in bundles but was of a black color", whereupon she said, "I don't recognize that; I won't take it." In this dream, the butcher represents Freud. The patient is in search of a childhood that, like meat, is brimful of unmediated life itself, but wherever she goes it is *all gone*. In its place she finds the outlandish vegetable – and as in this dream, we frequently encounter the use of vegetables as a symbol for lost vitality and life. The instant that this vitality, the original lost life of our beginnings, is recognized as lost, it is symbolically reconstructed within the mind, in a process that psychoanalysis refers to as "deferred action" (*Nachträglichkeit*) – here, when the dreaming mind of the patient replaced the "meat" with the "vegetable".[3] We cannot experience directly what the "life" that is thus reconstituted was originally like, and so the experience only survives within us in an already symbolized form, and this symbolic construct constitutes our standing-place as we carry on our lives, fall ill, and so on.

Freud's famous notion of "psychical trauma" is another instance of this "deferred action", whereby the lost ground of the subject is symbolically reconstituted, and we will now look at this concept in a little more detail.

Primal scene as trauma[4]
In *Project for a Scientific Psychology*, Freud describes the case of a female agoraphobic, who became incapable of going out because she was obsessed with the notion that she would be laughed at by shop assistants on account of her dress.[5] On analysis, it emerged that, when young, she had experienced the sexual trauma of having a shop-keeper grab at her genitals through her clothing, and she told the analyst that the shop-keeper had a grin on his face as he did this. Being young, the patient had not understood what the experience meant, and comprehension of the experience was *deferred* until she reached puberty, upon which it was repressed, and the symptoms were formed in its place. Within the symbolic complex of "having her clothes laughed at", *clothes* stands for the notion of "being touched *through her clothes*", while *being laughed at* stands for the gloating grin of the shopkeeper.

In this way, events and objects are made sense of through the process of "deferred action", but the inevitable price is the annihilation of the events and objects

---

[2] *The Interpretation of Dreams*, SE IV, 183 ff.
[3] See *Project for a Scientific Psychology*, SE I, 356.
[4] In Japanese the term "trauma" (*gaishō*) still retains its literal sense of "an external wound", while in English this original meaning has been obscured in common use by the analogous psychological usage – Trans.
[5] See *Project*, 353-356, for this episode and Freud's interpretation.

Chapter 4: LANGUAGE AS THE OTHER

themselves. In this example, the traumatic sexual experience was still within the range of possible recollection, and it was a real experience. But we can anticipate cases where the sexual trauma itself is largely fantastic in quality, and the symbolization of an even deeper trauma. In such cases, the fantastic quality of the sexual trauma ultimately functions as a *deferred* (*nachträglich*) symbolic understanding of some other matter, and in fact, psychoanalysis finds itself dealing with a great number of such cases. Patients are frequently troubled by a notion such as "If only, at such-and-such a time, such-and-such a thing had not happened, then surely my life would now have been natural and fulfilling." We can say that the lost vital ground of the self is here symbolically recuperated through the concept of "my natural life = vital force", which the subject supposes "would have been realized had such-and-such never happened".

Psychoanalysis can thus be viewed as a process of reconstructing a symbolic system in order to interrogate the vital ground of the self. A central concept in psychoanalysis is the "primal scene" (a scene of sexual intercourse between the parents, as actually witnessed or imagined by the child), which can also be understood in this context. The primal scene is traumatic not only because the parents, who ought to be moral paragons, were engaged in sexual behavior. Rather, as "I" searches for the inception of its own existence, it runs up against a dead end, an insurmountable darkness, and has no alternative but to set such a token image in its place. *This* fact is traumatic; the true primal trauma is the fact that each and every one of us is no longer capable of directly experiencing the inception of our own existence.

By putting this scene of the biological inception of existence in the place of the inaccessible origin of self, "I" confirms that its self did in fact have an origin. Yet the confirmation so obtained amounts to no more than a flimsy pastiche, if for no other reason than that, while there is any number of sexual unions, there was only ever one that produced I – and precisely this unique union is *a priori* impossible for I to witness directly. It has been decisively lost.

Thus, we see that as human beings, we find access to the origins of self absolutely impossible. It is for this very reason that we lap up such a plethora of myths and other fantastic constructs. Since we can never be sure where we really came from, we are set free to think that we were raised by wolves, say, or even that we came from outer space. Let us look at one example of such a myth – the comic *Dragon Ball*, by Toriyama Akira – and how the drive to reconstitute the origin is at work within it.[6]

---

[6] *Dragon Ball,* by Toriyama Akira, is one of the most popular cartoons (*manga*) of all time in Japan. It was originally serialized in the magazine *Jump* [*Janpu*], starting in 1985, and subsequently spawned a host of spin-offs – TV series, movies, video games etc. The comic has yet to be translated into English, though some episodes of the animated TV series have been dubbed or subtitled. See Ian Kelly (1997), *The Dragon World* [online], available from http://www.sas.upenn.edu/~ikelley/DragonBall/ [accessed October 24 1999]. – Trans.

Chapter 4: LANGUAGE AS THE OTHER

The Dragon Ball myth

In *Dragon Ball,* the protagonist Son Gokū really does come from outer space – he is sent to Earth soon after birth from a planet called Saiya. "Saiya" is an anagram on *yasai*, "vegetable", and Son Gokū's true name is Kakarotto, which plays on *kyarotto* ("carrot") – wordplay which recalls the symbolic operation in the dream mentioned earlier, whereby vegetables stood in for lost life and vital force. An old martial artist finds Son, takes him in and raises him. But on the night of every full moon he metamorphoses into a giant ape, and on one such occasion he tramples his foster father to death. Son's personality is split between his usual identity and the giant ape, with no communication between the two, and he is left with no recollection of the event. He then falls into a ravine and hits his head, whereupon he also forgets why he was sent from Saiya to Earth, and instead of fulfilling his mission grows up as a good plain Earthling. Here we see a complete Oedipal set: the problem of infantile amnesia, the myth of patricide, and a traumatic episode (the experience of an external wound). Freud never concealed his astonishment at the extreme facility with which poetic works embodied discoveries that cost psychoanalysis such hard work, and in this sense Toriyama Akira, the artist who created *Dragon Ball,* is surely a poet of the modern age.

Even in examples from poetry and comic books, then, it is plain to see that psychoanalysis has no monopoly on its characteristic mode of self-knowledge. The cognitive attitude psychoanalysis shares with these mythic and poetic forms is more than a matter of mere chance, and it is possible to see a tradition at work in the ways the psychoanalytic epistemological method and a variety of modes of knowledge are linked at a basic and essential level. I will now explore the similarities in cognitive structure between psychoanalysis and several other theories of knowledge.

The incompleteness of self-referentiality

First, we must look at the relationship between psychoanalysis and the Cartesian *cogito*. The formula of the *cogito* was born of Descartes' thoroughgoing consideration of the following problem: On what grounds could he be sure his own thought was correct? Perception cannot constitute the ground of correct thinking, since we cannot possibly be sure that even the testament of our own body is not illusory. Doubt as we may all that is reflected in the mind, however, it still seems beyond doubt there must be something in the eye of doubt's storm; an "I" that is doing the doubting. From such considerations arose the formula of the *cogito*, "I think, therefore I am", and with it, the stipulation that, to think, it is necessary to exist. Thought is thus supported by the thinking subject.

In fact, however, the Cartesian formula can be expanded to infinity: "I think, 'I think, "I think, therefore I am," therefore I am,' therefore . . ." and so on. In other words, there is absolutely nothing to say we can stop the whole process at the first "I am". Even if the thinking subject does exist, the certainty of its existence retreats

Chapter 4: LANGUAGE AS THE OTHER

forever beyond this feedback loop of thought. As Lacan points out, the thinking I and the being I of the *cogito* are thereby not, in fact, concentric at all.[7] Now, just as this I of being is both eccentric to the thinking I and also supports it, so also the past infancy of the I, while beyond and inaccessible to I, supports the current I, as we saw earlier in looking at the psychoanalytic project. The Cartesian being I and the psychoanalytic I of infancy obviously signify the same thing. Both, though posited as the ground of thought, cannot be grasped from within thought itself.

These considerations lead us once more the Wittgensteinian ideas we examined in the last chapter in connection with the "interminability" of psychoanalysis. In his *Tractatus Logico-Philosophicus*, Wittgenstein points out that, in principle, solipsism is correct. Solipsism holds that it is impossible to say that anything in the world is a reality independent of our experience, because it is only possible to judge the reality of things perceived and cognized from a standpoint within ourselves. We therefore cannot say whether the other actually exists, or not. For example, suppose I write a book called *The World as I Found It*.[8] Wittgenstein argues that in such a tract, the only thing of which we could say absolutely nothing would be the writing subject itself. In other words, if the world is nothing other than our own experience, nothing exists within that experience to assure us that we are indeed experiencing it. Deprived of all logical inevitability to its existence, the subject of experience is erased, and all that remains is a world of pure experience. Consequently, "solipsism, when its implications are followed out strictly, coincides with pure realism."[9]

Wittgenstein's conclusion is thus the exact opposite to that of Descartes. That is to say, he holds that "There is no such thing as the subject that thinks or entertains ideas."[10] But he also states that "The subject . . . is a limit of the world."[11] In other words, if we posit an ineffable subject that lines the spoken world (that adheres to its flipside, like the lining of a coat) and so lies just beyond it, then such a subject is admissible. Just as infancy in psychoanalysis can never be recovered in and of itself, the being of the subject that supports the world of thought can never be recuperated by the subject's thought. In this respect, both Descartes and Wittgenstein are describing something close to the epistemological position of psychoanalysis.

These similarities find still more formal expression in language theory. Here, the problem becomes the distinction between the "subject of speech" or spoken subject (the subject of the speech *content*) and the "speaking subject" (the subject of the

---

[7] "Is the place that I occupy as the subject of a signifier concentric or excentric, in relation to the place I occupy as subject of the signified? – that is the question." *Selection*, 165.
[8] *Tractatus Logico-Philosophicus: the German Text of Ludwig Wittgenstein's* Logisch-philosophische Abhandlung *with a new edition of the Translation by D. F. Pears and B. F. McGuiness* (London: Routledge and Kegan Paul, 1961, 1988), 117.
[9] *Tractatus*, 117.
[10] *Tractatus*, 117.
[11] *Tractatus*, 117.

speech *act*).[12] Let us look at what occurs when we fail to separate these two constructs. A classic example produces the "Liar's Paradox", which springs from the impossibility of determining if the declaration "I am lying" is true or false. If we assume I is telling the truth, then the content of I's declaration dictates that I must be lying. A contradiction arises. If we suppose I is lying, on the other hand, then the content of I's lie dictates that it must not be lying, that is, I must be telling the truth. Again, we contradict ourselves. Ultimately, even I who makes the statement doesn't know itself if it is lying or telling the truth.

This "semantic paradox" links directly to the following "ethical paradox". Let us assume that some circumstance forces I to lie. I then deeply regrets its lie, and realizes that lying is in fact I's true nature. I repents, and goes to church to confess and turn over a new leaf. At this point a paradox arises. If I is truly an inveterate liar, then that truth, itself, becomes untrue the moment I enunciates it. I's repentant mood, and the urge to confession, turns holus-bolus into lies too. If it is a lie that I is a liar, then in saying so, I must backhandedly declare its own truthfulness. In that case, there was nothing for I to repent in the first place. Either way, I is bound to be turned away at the church door – quite literally, damned if I do and damned if I don't. The fact remains that I did tell a lie, and must repent for it and reform; but again the same paradox awaits. The important thing here is that there is nothing I can do to convey its repentance to the church. Even if I did manage somehow to put what was on its mind into words, no-one would ever understand what I meant. This bind is devastating, and because of it I is rendered desolate.

There is more, however. The problem does not stop with lying. Say I takes it into its heads to do some good deed: if I is motivated by a desire to prove its virtue to itself, can we truly say that I has good in its heart? Isn't it moved more by hypocritical vanity than true good? The same is also true of love. Isn't what we think of as love no more than the selfish wish to use the other to our own advantage? We thus see that if the "I" that is making an utterance does not stand in truth, the content of any utterance collapses in ruins. This is true no matter how I expresses what goes on within it, and no matter how well its statements may be substantiated at the level of content. I hopes somehow to verify its own ideas about what goes on within it. But what if this "subject that thinks or entertains ideas" does not in fact exist? As the anguish of the logical paradox presented above suggests, "I", as that which guarantees that our sense of things is correct, in fact *cannot* exist. While it seems that there *is* a speaking subject that supports the subject of the utterance, any such subject has in fact been lost somewhere along the line – and that is the reason that people sometimes need psychoanalysis.

A number of epistemological traditions thus emerge which are linked by structural

---

[12] Lacan calls these "le *je* de l'énonciation" and "le *je* de l'énoncé", translated by Sheridan as "the *I* of the enunciation" and "the *I* of the statement". S XI, 139.

homology (albeit rather schematically) to the basic epistemological take of psychoanalysis on the human. Let us set out the correspondences between terms in these different epistemological theories (see figure):

Psychoanalysis	Childhood	System of symbols
Descartes	Existing "I"	Thinking "I"
Wittgenstein	Subject as boundary of world	Thinking and signifying subject
Language theory	Speaking subject	Spoken subject

In the row for each of these respective epistemologies, the item on the left can be read as something that has disappeared in some sense. These disappearances share a common cause – the structure of logical incompleteness found in the paradox arising from self-referentiality. For simplicity's sake, I will refer to this as "the incompleteness of self-referentiality". If we take Wittgenstein's "What we cannot speak about we must pass over in silence"[13] as the incompleteness thesis in the context of modern philosophy, then we can equally say that the psychoanalytic "Childhood is not obtainable any longer" is the incompleteness thesis in the context of modern anthropology.

Thus far, we have seen that the ground of the human subject is primordially lost; that we compensate for this loss by (re)constructing the ground for ourselves in symbol, myth, and analytic theory; that psychoanalysis shares its recognition of this basic loss with several other epistemological traditions; and, finally, that the ground is whipped out from under the speaking subject's feet by a common cause, the logical incompleteness that arises out of self-referential utterances. As it turns out, this self-referentiality is inescapable wherever the subject seeks to represent its own being through language – the instance that Lacan called the "big Other" – and it is to this relation between subject and signifying system that we now turn.

Two: The Discourse of the Other

"Even the same that I said unto you from the beginning (arkhē [14])"
We have seen that our own century seems to have first logically and mathematically formalized the perception that the existential ground of the signifying, thinking subject has disappeared. It is vital to realize, however, that the problem itself was

---

[13] *Tractatus*, 151.
[14] *Arkhē* is Greek for 'beginning', as in English "archaeology", "archaic". Greek in original. – Trans.

Chapter 4: LANGUAGE AS THE OTHER

sensed and located a great deal earlier.

If we turn to the Bible, for instance, we find a passage where Jesus says, "I am the light of the world" (John 8:12).[15] To this, the Pharisees say, "Thou bearest witness of thyself; thy witness is not true." (8:13) In other words, the Pharisees attempt to pull the ground out from under Christ's feet through recourse to the logical incompleteness of self-referentiality. In response, Jesus says, "Even if I bear witness of myself, my witness is true: for I know whence I came, and whither I go." (8:14) This response might read as a declaration that the incompleteness of self-referentiality does not apply to Him. This is because while He is one, He is simultaneously one with the Father who sent Him, and thus also two. He says, "I am he that beareth witness of myself, and the Father that sent me beareth witness of me." (8:18)

Soon after, one who is with them poses a question even simpler than that of the Pharisees: "They said therefore unto him, Who art thou?" (8:25) To this, Christ answers, "Even that which I have also spoke unto you from the beginning (*arkhē*)." (8:25) Indeed, Jesus has already touched on the answer to their question ("I am the light of the world"). But we must not fail to note that Christ's words resonate with a further meaning: "That of which God has spoken ever since the beginning of all things (*arkhē*)". Lacan takes these words of Christ as the epigraph to the second section of his "Rome Discourse".[16]

This "What am I?" ("Who art Thou?"; "What is I?") is the only question that we cannot answer for ourselves. At this point, the capacity to exercise language in the making of meaning is wrest from us. But does this imply an imperative to get our neighbor to verify for us what we are? Does it mean we should have our neighbor bear us witness that we are indeed good? Surely that would come to no more than the fabrication of an alibi, and such fabrications are powerless to confirm what we are in truth. Ultimately we must return on our *own* behalf to the beginning of all things, the *arkhē*, and hear and answer our *own* prayers for knowledge of our true nature.

And so the psychoanalytic project of retracing our memories to their source is thrust upon us. At the point of *arkhē*, someone spoke of what and who we are; we suppose that we must have preserved that someone's words, somewhere inside us. In all likelihood we will blurt those words out unawares during the psychoanalytic discourse – falteringly, perhaps, or in some miscarriage of speech – and the analyst ought to be one who has the power to hear "full speech" (*parole pleine*) in those scrunched-up scraps of language forgotten in the closet. This is the reason that Lacan takes this biblical passage for his epigraph.

---

[15] All quotes from the Gospel are taken from the *Gideons International New Testament*, parallel colloquial Japanese and American Standard Version (Tokyo: Nihon seisho kyoukai, 1967).
[16] See *Écrits*, 266; *Selection*, 56. Lacan too quotes the Greek.

Chapter 4: LANGUAGE AS THE OTHER

The ordeal of language [17]

We, too, are often pressed by someone to articulate what we are, just as the Pharisees pressed Christ. If we look within, we can often catch a glimpse of ourselves, nose to the grindstone, slaving to have some answer ready for this question. When this scramble to furnish ourselves with alibis threatens to go awry, we become anxious; we then seek relief in applying a technical psychological label like "identity diffusion"[18] to this anxiety. If it is an abnormality that is known to psychology, we think, then some positive empirical cause for it will probably be found in our life or in society. Thus we attempt to dispel our anxieties through scientific posturing.

In fact, however, it is not some fantastic crowd of Pharisees around us that presses us to say what we are, but just the plain fact that we speak in language. Given that we use language, we find ourselves in a position where it is simply imperative that we can say *in* language what *we* are. Otherwise, the content of our language is drained of all truth-value. Our linguistic activity itself becomes meaningless. The absolute absurdity of the situation, however, is that regardless of this necessity, the incompleteness of self-referentiality has rendered us incapable of saying any such thing in language at all. We are being given the third degree: "You! Talk! Say what you are!" But in spite of this, the words we should use to do this talking were not made for the job. Here we see the cruelty of human existence *qua* speaking being. Indeed, more than that, it is here that we also find the wellspring of many an illness. Lacan expresses this painful condition of speaking being in a nutshell, in his concept of "the relation between the subject and the signifier".[19]

In Chapter I, I described how the patient of the tuna *sushi* dream said, in her delirium, "I want to start right from the very beginning". These words expressed her will to return to the *arkhē*, and answer for herself her query as to who or what she had been there. But even as she said, "The very beginning is inside Mummy's tummy," she also told us that "You might say, though, that even Mum herself doesn't know what's inside her." This signifies that the incompleteness of self-referentiality already afflicts the Other, from whom the subject nonetheless hopes to learn the truth of what the subject is. Here, our patient's demented speech is an absolutely rigorous logical language.

Incapable of giving, ourselves, the evidence of what we are, and yet required to establish the verity of our linguistic activity, our only option is to fling the question back at the language that demands this evidence itself. In other words, we must obtain the meaning of our existence *from* language, *qua* that which was there from the beginning of all things (the *arkhē*). The capacity to create meaning is no longer

---

[17] The word "ordeal" here translates Japanese *junan*, which is also translated "suffering" in the key phrase "helpless suffering [being]" in this and following sections. Note that it also has the meaning in Japanese of "passion" as in the Passion of Christ. – Trans.

[18] I refer here to the ideas of Erikson.

[19] *Selection*, "On the possible treatment of psychosis", 183.

Chapter 4: LANGUAGE AS THE OTHER

within us; it is therefore posited as existing within language itself. Language appears as that which has been there right from the start (*arkhē*) and gives meaning to what we are, and in fact, this Other called language, from which we must obtain meaning, quite clearly *did* exist long before us. We were born, ignorant of our own nature, into the midst of others who behaved just as if they *did* know what we are. People were already speaking to one another about us, and we could not be party to that discourse – the "discourse of the Other".

In this sense, our initial encounter with language was an ordeal, an experience of helpless suffering.[20] One reason for this is that at the time of this ordeal, when just to be at all was to be utterly and helplessly passive, we were literally "in-fant" – we could not talk. We cannot just chalk the ordeal up to the natural consequences of biological prematuration, however – adequate explanation demands more of us. As can be seen by comparing the various lines of the table above, this incapacity of speech is actually a logically inexorable condition. Just like our patient's (m)Other, the linguistic Other already has the hole of inadequate self-reference gnawing at its heart.

When the human subject *qua* speaking being comes to speak of itself, then, it finds itself incapable of maintaining logical consistency, and this incapacity is a structural inevitability of language. Consequently, it seems, something *external* to language must uphold the fact that the speaking being itself does exist – the support must be sought *outside* speaking being. The real being that supports the truth of our speech is, however, ultimately revealed as exactly the being that helplessly suffers the discourse of the Other, and which has vanished without trace beneath the accumulated discourse of the Other past. This Real, then, enjoys existence *in* the discourse of the Other, as its object, and must be discovered *through* the discourse of the Other. If indeed it is possible to become this Real, then surely, when the time comes, we need only open our ears to the dinning discourse of the Other, keep our peace, and ask no more whether we are alive or dead.[21]

All the while when we speak, we are actually this speechless being in the unconscious, and it is the Other which speaks of us. For this reason, Lacan defined the unconscious thus: "The unconscious is the discourse of the Other."[22] He also

---

[20] "Suffering" translates *junan*. See note 17 above.

[21] This paragraph concerns the Lacanian Real as "the impossible", a term whose relation to the Other is conceived as a spatial paradox. Simply because the subject cannot attain its support *in* language does not imply we can facilely conclude it must seek that support *outside* language. For, when the subject does find that support, it turns out that it is not entirely outside language either. Lacan theorized this paradoxical both/neither in-nor-out relation of the Real to the Other with his neologism *extimité*. *Extimité* plays on *intimité* ("intimacy") by replacing "in" with "ex", outside. It thus means something external in the very heart of that to which it is external, a within/without relation. See Chapter V, Section Six, and S VII, 139.

[22] "If I have said that the unconscious is the discourse of the Other (with a capital O), it is in order to indicate the beyond in which the recognition of desire is bound up with the desire for

often put it like this: "It (*Es*) speaks." In either of these formulations, "I" is the *spoken object*, and enjoys an existence as the *object* of speech/discourse. Some time after the Rome Discourse, Lacan stated that phrase "I heard" (*J'ouïs*) resonates with a corresponding imperative from the Other: "Enjoy!" (*Jouis!*)[23] In Japanese, this perhaps matches the correspondence between *kiku* ("to hear") and *kiku* ("to work, to have effect", "I can feel it!"). Any being that does not *hear* (*kiku*) the Other, loses all *efficacy* (*kiku*), that is to say, it loses all reality. Thus, that which spoke of what we were at the point of *arkhē* or absolute beginning, still speaks as the unconscious within us, even now.

The family romance
As we have seen, then, the incompleteness of self-referentiality prevents us from articulating anything about our origins for ourselves, and through this impossibility we see what it means that language is a thing of the Other. We concomitantly recognize ourselves as something helpless and suffering, the object of the discourse of the Other. Lacan's "discourse of the Other" is a structural successor to Freud's concept of the Es, and what I have called "helpless suffering" is connected to what Freud termed "helplessness" (*Hilflosigkeit*). Concrete instances of the "discourse of the Other" are many and varied – the telepathy touched on in Chapter I in the dream of tuna *sushi*, for example. Another such instance is Freud's "family romance".

"Family romance" is the phenomenon whereby patients imaginatively revise their relation with their family, and we find classic examples in the fantasies of the abandoned child and the foundling. While these fantasies are quite common, they also have some relation to clearly pathological phenomena, like the fantasies of noble lineage found in psychosis. In such fantasies we see the efforts of the subject to ascertain its own status in the context of the "discourse of the Other", here in the form of kinship and genealogy. If we delve deep into the fantasies of individual patients, then, we recognize structures like myths, which have been passed down through the family since before the patients themselves were even born. For example, in some cases the patient is seen as the reincarnation of a miscarried child, or a grandfather or grandmother who has recently died. The subject is assigned its position within such structures groundlessly, by pure chance, and it is within this big Other that the ground of the subject comes to being and precipitates the subject's "ordeal".

This "Town Where The Birds Come"
It is in dreams that we find the reflection of the age when the subject was a

---

recognition." *Selection*, 172. See also p. 312.
[23] See *Selection*, "The subversion of the subject and the dialectic of desire in the Freudian unconscious", 319.

unilaterally passive recipient of the discourse of the Other that was exchanged all around it. The majority of dreams are set in the past – a person who has moved is likely to often dream of their old house, for instance – and this past refers generically back to the prehistoric past of suffering abjection before the discourse of the Other. If we allow that the discourse of the Other regarding the subject was, for that subject, a riddle, then that riddle is preserved as riddle in the dream. For so long as we are dreaming, we cannot move, and under these natural conditions, we return to the past, when we merely listened to the discourse of the Other. In the effort to interpret this enigmatic discourse, we cobble some images together and jerry-rig a makeshift meaning, and this interpretation is the production that we stage in the dream. The subject itself is most often transparently visible in this context, working frantically to keep the theatre of the dream in motion. At times, however, this effort reaches its limit and the discourse of the Other intrudes directly into our mind. At such times the dreamer will hear a sort of "speaking in tongues", a gobbledygook auditory illusion, and awake with a start.

We have seen that, even in dreams, we can experience only rarely this pure state wherein we receive the discourse of the Other as it is, shorn of all mediating visual or dramaturgical interpretation, and enjoy a speechless existence. Is such a state then even possible at all? Even if it is, can it be expressed? I believe that there are indeed expressions of this state, and one extremely beautiful example of such an expression is a piece called "The Town Where The Birds Come", created by pupils at a school for the blind and introduced by Ichikawa Hiroshi in "In Search of Omens" (see illustration, page xiii).[24]

What are the "birds" in this piece? Discoursing voices, no more and no less. The birds' cries figure the extreme beauty of the discourse of the Other as sheer quality; naked voice stripped of all raiment of meaning. The spiral shaped "town" we see here, on the other hand, is none other than that very blind being the discourse envelops all round. The form of the spiral no doubt also corresponds to the helix of the cochlea inside our ear.

At some point in the growing process, we leave this sort of being behind, and pass over to the side of the discourse of the Other. The words that we speak now when awake are in fact mere fragments of a past discourse of the Other. In analysis, one task of the analysis is done when we notice this fact. At that point, the desire revives to resume the position of passively suffering the discourse of the Other, rather than be the subject who speaks that discourse. We find such a position in the dream, and Lacan says of this, "Here, in the field of the dream, you are at home."[25]

---

[24] Ichikawa Hiroshi, "Yochō wo motomete" *Critical Space* (*Hihyō kūkan*) 1991, No 1.
[25] S XI, 44.

Chapter 4: LANGUAGE AS THE OTHER

Three: The Desire of the Other

Am I wanted?
But really, can we successfully catch the meaning of our existence from the Other by just *being* quietly before Its discourse, as in "The Town Where the Birds Come"? Perhaps. But even so, the question remains of how we would express the meaning so obtained. Regardless of how we represented it, our utterance would doubtless be robbed of all force once more by the self-same incompleteness of self-referentiality.

We are spoken of in the discourse of the Other. However, this discourse cannot be recuperated *qua* meaning back to within ourselves. We cannot say how we are placed within the discourse of the Other, nor as what it is that we occupy that place. Why is it that the Other goes on speaking of us in such a cryptic manner? Perhaps we should rather say that, for so long as we attempt to understand this discourse of the Other, the Other can speak of us in no other manner. And all the while, the Other discourses on. It is precisely the discoursing Other's desire to speak of us continually, and nothing else, that emerges as the meaning we obtain for our existence at the point of origin, or *arkhē*. We may well be unable to say exactly how the Other speaks of us, or as what, but we take the sheer fact that the discourse never lets up to mean that we do indeed exist.

At this juncture, let us briefly retrace our tracks. In order to hear what the Other has to say about our being, we have returned to the *arkhē* or point of origin. What we found there, however, was not meaningful speech, but rather the desire of the Other, which remains an enigma. The discourse of the Other conveys not meaning, but desire, to the subject. It follows that the answer to the question of what we are is given in this form: "I am the object of desire of the continually discoursing Other." In 1961, Lacan set out very clearly the relationship between the "desire of the Other", introduced in the Rome Discourse, and its object, the later formulated *objet a*:

> "The subject is called on to be born again – as the *objet a* of desire; as that which it was for the Other when it came to life; as the *wanted* or *unwanted*[26] as which it came into the world – in order to find out if it really wants what it desires. This is the sort of truth Freud brought to light with the invention of analysis."[27]

If, as this passage suggests, it is through the desire of the Other that the born-again subject comes to grasp that which it wants itself, then the subject will also in the process internalize the desire of the Other and make it its own.[28] The subject has no

---

[26] *Wanted* and *unwanted* appear in English in Lacan's original. — Trans.
[27] "Remarque sur le rapport de Daniel Lagache", 1961. *Écrits*, 682.
[28] This means that the subject's desire is not her own, but something she gets from the other

−73−

Chapter 4: LANGUAGE AS THE OTHER

way of knowing whether this desire of the Other is a good thing or a bad. Of itself, the desire means literally "nothing" (*kū*).[29] However, we become conscious of ourselves by virtue of being wanted or unwanted by this desire, and are born again as speaking subject. For better or worse, the coming to being and growth of any subject that speaks of itself hinges entirely on the desire of the big Other.

Those who speak of the desire of the Other

There is one group of people who employ markedly desperate measures in seeking to prove the desire of the big Other, and who thus relate most eloquently just how vital that desire is to the subject's growth. We call these people *psychotic*. They know full well that we are only truly born in the moment when we feel the desire of the big Other directly upon us. And at the moment when a person knows this, something which has heretofore been hazy clears, and in a flash he becomes transparent to himself.

This, however, is also the moment when schizophrenia crystallizes into being. The absolute conviction of one's own delusions, which is vital above all else in characterizing paranoid schizophrenia, is at the same time both certainty of the desire of the Other, and also certainty of one's own existence. Let this conviction once be verbalized, though, and its quality shifts. It must secure the assent of those around the subject, or else it will no longer be true, and the psychotic is thereupon compelled to start speaking to people of the desire of the Other.

A certain patient, for example, believed that state universities and military organs were attempting to manufacture human clones, using him as a test case. He existed as the object of the desire of the state. Another patient believed that the military and public security forces were planning a coup, and were attempting to draw him into their numbers. He further believed that, to achieve this goal, he would be forced to marry a certain policewoman. He, too, verified his own existence through the desire of the Other – here, imaginary conspirator forces.

In yet another case, a young woman passed her adolescence in an obscure torment. Her suffering was inexplicable – until, that is, it one day came to her notice that all her life she "had been 'run'" – manipulated – by some force beyond her control. This realization was the key to understanding the cause of her pain. According to her, there was a man who had set his sights on women whose family lineages made it likely they would give birth to geniuses. By means of a machine he controlled potential girl geniuses, tormenting them, and so seeking to prevent their genius flowering. The suffering she had tasted was thus "the worst in the universe",[30] and

---

– one reading of the Lacanian dictum, "Desire is the desire of the Other." – Trans.

[29] The word here translated as "nothing", is *kū*. As opposed to other words for "empty, nothing, nothingness" which exist in Japanese, *kū* is strongly associated with the *śūnyatā* of Buddhism, particularly as it is found in Zen. - Trans

[30] She later elaborated further to describe her suffering as "*worse than* the worst in the

the man the most frightening animal "in the universe". She believed that it was probably a scientist operating the machine. She said that although the pain was too much and she wanted to die, she could not, because if she did no-one would be left to prove her story.

In each of these cases, the "desire of the Other" had made a beeline straight for the patient, backed up in each case by some sort of public base (state initiatives etc.). Moreover, each patient could tangibly hear the "discourse of the Other", in the form of auditory hallucinations. These patients experienced the desire of the Other as a torment, but at the same time, it was also the ground that enabled them to go on living. The extraordinary proximity of these ailing subjects to the desire of the Other (in various delusional guises) amply testifies that it is precisely through the desire of the Other that they sought to subjectify life.

Where we would expect the desire of the Other to be characterized by a primal lack of meaning, we find in these patients meaning in excess instead. But their testimony does correctly convey to us a particular kind of pain to be found in the assumption of the desire of the Other. Let us elaborate further on the suffering that is involved in the assumption of (this Other) desire, referring this time to Lacan's commentary on the works of Heironymous Bosch.

The pleasures (*jouissance*) of "Music Hell"
According to the Lacan of "Aggressivity in Psychoanalysis", which preceded the Rome Discourse by five years, the paintings of Heironymous Bosch represent the "fragmented body" (*corps morcelé*), which bespeaks "a specific relation . . . between man and his own body".[31] This relation ultimately matches that between the speaking I and the being I, where the being or existing I that grounds the speaking I in truth can only accept the groundless desire of the Other unquestioningly, as *corps morcelé*. The *meaning* of the desire of the Other is a closed book to I, but should I refuse that desire, nothing but nothing would support the truth of I's speech and thought; so we grin and bear the void of meaning. Bosch's "The Garden of Earthly Delights" figures the stoic I as it bears this pain (see illustration, page xiii). The picture overall has a panoramic structure, and in one panel of the triptych we find a Hell, oddly enough named "Music Hell", where people are tasting musical torments: they are tied to lutes and plucked or strummed, or stuffed inside bugles and blown.

A number of sources relate how the infant Mozart, on hearing a trumpet, burst out crying. His subtle and delicate ears supposedly could not bear the brash sound of the trumpet – but this is only half the story. As the picture of "Music Hell" shows, the musical experience is composed of pleasure and pain in equal measure, and is even tempered with masochism of sorts – for as much as the subject hears sound as object

---

universe".
[31] *Selection*, 11.

in experiencing music, it is also passively sounded as object itself. We can read this anecdote as evidence that Mozart, in his precocious sensitivity to all dimensions of music, had come face to face with this "other side" of musical pleasure. As I mentioned earlier, the discourse of the Other fails to communicate meaning to us, for all that it is us that it discourses about. The discourse carries on *about us* (around us and in regard to us) regardless, oblivious to its failure to tell us anything. The desire of the Other is constituted in the plain continuation of the discourse, and we bear the brunt of that desire; just as we might suffer this desire in the form of birdcalls, we can also bear it as music, and so we go on being strummed and played. That is the Hell Bosch depicts.

That which requires the *objet a*
Having utilized signifiers representing experience to construct a logical world, human subjectivity eventually seeks a signifier for the human subject itself. However, alone among the signifiers wielded by the subject, this self-referential relation can obtain no logical guarantees. In this part of the system arises not language but the *objet a*. Only the slender fact that the *objet a* is desired by the Other holds meaninglessness at bay from our world of signifiers of experience. The *objet a* in all its vicissitudes takes a wide variety of forms, but all of them are at base passive kinds of experience, like that of the dead in "Music Hell" being passively *played* as pure, meaningless sound. In this way, the *objet a* compensates for the logical impotence of the human subject to vouch for itself. Our powerlessness before the incompleteness of self-referentiality is not something we can simply overcome by disciplining and honing the logical faculty. Far from it – in fact, the further we press logical inquiry, the more glaring and stark it becomes.

The most central relation between the human subject, and language as Other, lies in the fact that the human subject has no signifier for itself. Confronted with this lack, humanity ends up experiencing itself as the object of desire of the Other called language. For the subject, this experience is something we can say is truly *real*. But for the unfortunate relation between subject and language, however, the need would never arise for the *objet a* – which, as Real, makes up for that misfired relation. Humanity experiences the world through language, therefore, but the ground which keeps that experience real is not knowledge, but desire – and the desire of the Other at that. Without this ground, all that would remain is a wordy castle in the air. When desire conforms to the desire of the big Other, an "I" that is object of the desire of the Other appears before us, i.e. the *objet a* – in psychoanalysis, when I gets what it truly wants, it is as the desire of the Other that I's desire is realized. In the words of the key Lacanian formula: "[M]an's desire is the desire of the Other."[32]

---

[32] *Selection,* 312. Immediately before he gives this famous epigram, Lacan has expressed the same idea in a somewhat expanded form: "[I]t is . . . as desire of the Other that man's desire

Chapter 4: LANGUAGE AS THE OTHER

Zen freedom, psychoanalytic freedom

If human desire is ultimately the desire of the Other, is there any such thing as freedom of desire for the human subject? After all, was not the modern social ethic predicated on the freedom of human desire and aimed at its maximum satisfaction? With psychoanalysis, doubt is cast above all on this premise of modern society itself. As Lacan, following Hegel, tells us in the Rome Discourse the industrious and compulsive subject of modern society just barely maintains its dignity with the thought that even though it is oppressed by twin masters – the state, and society at large – should it die, those masters could not enjoy the fruits of its labors.[33] In other words, the subject coerces the Other to renounce its desire with the threat of the subject's own death, and "freedom" is just an alias of the capacity to threaten the Other with frustration of its desire. No matter how we look at it, then, the only conceivable basis for the pride of the subject is some form of recognition of the desire of the Other.

If modern freedom thus consists in saying "no" to the desire of the Other,[34]

---

finds form ... " (311).

[33] "In fact the obsessional subject manifests one of the attitudes that Hegel did not develop in his dialectic of the master and the slave. ... [S]ince he [the slave] knows that he is mortal, he also knows that the master can die. From this moment on he is able to accept his labouring for the master and his renunciation of pleasure in the meantime; and, in the uncertainty of the moment when the master will die, he waits" (*Selection*, 99).

Note that while Lacan states that Hegel "did not develop" this attitude, this is not to say that Hegel does not hint at it at all. In fact, in the section of *Phenomenology of Mind* entitled "Independence and Dependence of Self-Consciousness: Lordship and Bondage", he says, "[T]he master relates himself to the thing mediately through the bondsman . . . . The master . . . who has interposed the bondsman between it and himself, thereby . . . enjoys it without qualification and without reserve. The aspect of its independence he leaves to the bondsman, who labours upon it" (G. W. F. Hegel, *The Phenomenology of Mind*, trans. J. B. Baillie [London: S. Sonnenschein 1910], 235-236). From this we can see that without the slave, the master would not be able to enjoy the independence of the thing, that is, its efficacy as the fruit of labor.

Now, it would in fact be more accurate to say that what Hegel is describing here is the attitude of the hysteric, rather than that of the obsessive compulsive. This is because the desire of the hysteric one that "leaves the desire of the big Other unsatisfied". In this sense, it is true, as Lacan says, that of the two aspects of the attitude of the slave towards the master, Hegel places the emphasis on the hysterical, while he fails to give a full description of the strategy of the obsessive compulsive.

[34] It is important to note here that in both modern Chinese and Japanese, "freedom" (Ch. *ziyou*, Jpn. *jiyū*) is a compound written with two Chinese characters that literally mean "determined by (or 'coming from', or 'dependent upon'; Ch. *you*, Jpn. *yū*) the self (*zi/ji*)". In older texts (like the Chan *Record of Linji*) it can have a fully verbal sense meaning something like "to come from the self, to rely on the self, to be based upon the self, to act out of the self". In the freedom of Zen, therefore, the impotence of self-referentiality is already intrinsically accounted for. For this reason, one might expect that at the end of the investigation undertaken in Zen, the *objet a* will rise to the surface, and as we will see in the following, this

psychoanalytic freedom is something utterly different. For psychoanalysis, freedom of desire consists in *becoming* the desire of the Other. But once desire has become the desire of the Other, the subject is no longer itself, and if I is an Other that desires I, then presumably the I that has become Other can see the true I. If freedom in this sense can be called "freedom" at all, it is assuredly close to the freedom of Zen. When Lacan refers to Zen in the Rome Discourse, it is not solely because of commonalities between Zen practice and the "short session". It is also because the conception of the freedom of desire in each system speaks intelligibly to the other.

According to the *Rinzairoku*,[35] the "true person of no status" within oneself, which continually goes in and out of the body, is neither beautiful nor holy. In fact, Rinzai calls it a "shit-wiping stick".[36] When a practitioner recognizes such a "true person of no status" in herself, through dialogue with the master, she becomes extremely free. The gulf between Lacan's *objet a* and this "true person of no status" is bridged by the mediating image of "shit" – a kind of waste matter, which acts as a stopgap to a perceived cavity or hollowness within the body/self. Through the desire of the Other, we discover the unknown essence within.

Surely, then, there is indeed freedom in psychoanalysis, if only in the Zen sense of freedom. In psychoanalytic freedom, the desire of the Other is recognized and striven for. The subject becomes both the object of that desire, and its cause, and we could even go so far as to say that psychoanalytic freedom is the freedom of the *objet a*. The "desire of the Other" expounded by Lacan thus smacks strongly of a religious background, and this religious overtone ranges right across the religious field, from the Christ's "bearing witness to the self", which we examined earlier, to Zen freedom. The path that leads from freedom of desire to becoming the object of the desire of the Other might also lead us still further, to recall the Eastern conception of nature (shizen). It suggests a novel interpretation of *shizen* – nature as the Other. Let us develop this insight a little.

---

is indeed the case.

[35] *The Recorded Sayings of Ch'an Master Lin-chi Hui-chao of Chen Prefecture, Compiled by his Humble Heir Hui-jan of San-sheng*, translated from the Chinese by Ruth Fuller Sasaki (Kyoto: Institute for Zen Studies, 1975). Chan master Linji Yixuan (in Japanese, Rinzai Gigen) died in 867.

[36] Ibid, 3.

Chapter 4: LANGUAGE AS THE OTHER

Four: The Desire of Nature

The desire of Eastern nature [37]

Shinran once said, "Non-contrivance on our side is called 'naturalness';"[38] which means that when we become one with nature and relinquish self, salvation comes to us from Amida Buddha. Desire reaches the point where it is the desire of the Other, in the form of "Amida's vow",[39] and it is complete. We will not enter into whether the path to this point is one of being helped by the Buddha (*tariki*) or helping oneself (*jiriki*).[40] The point is this: be the Buddhism Pure Land or be it Zen, freedom is still sought in a return to nature. Now, it seems to me that Lacan's concept of "the desire of the Other" is interchangeable with this "desire of nature" found in Japanese thought. In so saying, I am not reducing Lacan to Buddhism, nor vice versa. Rigorous comparison of Lacanian and Buddhist thought would no doubt require careful work to prepare the ground. But I think it not meaningless at this point to compare the concept of *shizen* to Lacan's Other. To put it another way, "nature" (*shizen*) is not "nature" as the object of science, but the Eastern "nature" as that to which self returns, and with which it becomes one. I think the idea that this "nature" possesses "desire" in the Lacanian sense is one well worth entertaining.

"The desire of nature" thus becomes a question of what humanity *is* as far as nature is concerned. We often hear that "Man is part of nature." Even if we concede that this is a self-evident truth, the question remains: What *sort* of a part does that make humanity, in nature's eyes? In what manner does nature desire man?

When one tries to answer these questions, one will be confronted with the reappearance of the traditional opposition between creationism and evolutionism. Now, Lacan is an unequivocal creationist; unlike Freud, who attempted to take into

---

[37] The word here translated as "nature" (*shizen* in Japanese, *ziran* in Chinese) is a pivotal notion in Chinese and Japanese thought, and there has been much discussion of how it can (or cannot) be translated into English. Broken down into component morphemes it literally means something like "like [it]self", "self-'ly' (in the manner of [it]self)", or "as from whence [it came]". "Spontaneity" is an alternative rendering. - Trans.

[38] Shinran, *Tannishō: Notes Lamenting Differences,* translated and annotated in the Ryukoku University Translation Center (Kyoto: Tsuchiyama Printing Co., 1962, 1980), 68. *Tannishō* is one of the prime texts of Pure Land or Jōdo Shinshū Buddhism. Shinran (1173-1263) was the founder of the Jōdo Shinshū sect. - Trans.

[39] The Buddha Amida (Sanskrit: Amitābha) took a vow, when still a Bodhisattva, that he would not enter Nirvāṇa until he had ensured the salvation of all sentient beings. — Trans.

[40] *Jiriki* and *tariki* are pivotal terms in Buddhist theological debate. *Jiriki* or "own strength" refers to self-deliverance, or salvation through one's own efforts. *Tariki* or "other strength" doctrines hold that self-deliverance is beyond the strength of fallen, deluded beings, and that salvation comes through the intercession of divine powers. Pure Land is a *tariki* doctrine, and Zen (at least Rinzai Zen, which is more widely known) is *jiriki*. — Trans.

consideration Darwin's discoveries and their implications for his own psychoanalytic theories, Lacan gave no quarter to evolutionary considerations in his work. For him, there is no evolutionary continuum between animal languages and human language; rather, he perceives a radical discontinuity here, and connects it to human pathologies such as psychoses. However, there are times when Lacanian truths appear in the startling context of research conducted from an evolutionary perspective, as in the following episode from primatology.

The *objet a* in the hand of the chimpanzee
Television once carried cover of a Japanese research team investigating chimpanzees in Africa.[41] The research team established themselves in the midst of a troupe of chimpanzees, and patiently filmed all that went on around them. They confirmed that use of tools could already be seen among the group. Similarities existed between the chimpanzees' use of stones to split fruit, and human use of stone tools.

However, in the midst of these observations, and quite by chance, a baby in the troupe gradually weakened and died. The camera strayed from its intended observations and took to following the fate of the young chimp. Even after the baby died, its mother would not stop humping it around. She turned up every day at the observation site, piggy-backing the corpse. The camera faithfully recorded the gradual decomposition and mummification of the corpse, until it wasted away to a mere thing, glistening darkly. One day, as the camera followed the corpse, its father picked it up from where the mother had left it and charged the camera with bared teeth, brandishing the corpse and menacing the camera with it.

How are we to read this series of incidents? Somewhere in the title of the program, or in captions superimposed on the screen, were the words "a mother's love"; clearly, for the research team or the director of the documentary, the incident showed that the chimpanzee was mourning in a way somehow similar to a human, and therefore that human social mechanisms *do* exist on an evolutionary continuum with other species. In my opinion, however, this does not nearly account for everything that is going on. Let us recall the original motive for the observations: to verify the hypothesis that humanity exists as part of nature, as an evolutionary development from the chimpanzee. This objective was achieved with the discovery of continuity in the use of tools. However, the question of *what sort of thing* humanity is, as a part of nature, still remained. We must still ask whether nature really views

---

[41] The research team was led by Matsuzawa Tetsurō of the Kyoto University Primate Research Institute. The television program was "Yasei chinpanjī haha to ko no ai: Jokuro no shi" ["The love of a wild chimpanzee mother for her child: the death of Jokuro"], Anika Productions, dir. Nakamura Miho, broadcast as the Monday documentary by Tōkyō Terebi [TV Tokyo] on 31 August 1992. For an English account of the event see Tetsuro Matsuzawa, "The death of an infant chimpanzee at Bossou, Guinea", *Pan Africa News*, 4 (1997), 4-6. I am very grateful to Professor Matsuzawa for providing this information. – Trans.

Chapter 4: LANGUAGE AS THE OTHER

humanity as fit to be a part of itself, or not.

Let us entertain briefly the possibility that this second question, that of what *kind* of a part of nature humanity is, motivated the team's practical observations. The formula found in the previous chapter once again applies. In the fact that the humans observe the troupe of chimpanzees, the nature of humans for nature is inexorably brought out in relief. We arrive at

$$\frac{y}{x} = \frac{x}{x+y}$$

where x is the humans, and y the chimpanzees. $x + y$ is the evolutionary continuum of nature as a whole, reached by adding humans and chimpanzees together. The Golden Section, i.e. the *objet a*, appears once more, just as in the previous chapter. We can therefore find the answer to the original problem – what *kind of* a part of nature man is – as follows. Humanity is to nature exactly what the humans find in the chimpanzees – the mummified corpse of the baby chimp. The mummy in question was the *objet a*.

If humanity is to nature something like the mummified infant chimp, then Kojève's reading of Hegel, studied by the young Lacan, fits perfectly. Kojève held that humanity is a "sickness unto death" at nature's heart.[42] The research team's observation of the chimpanzees may well have empirically proven humanity a part of nature, as a user of tools. On the other hand, though, we can also see in these images that there is only one way for humanity to be part of nature – precisely as its "sickness unto death". Here we must mention that the Eastern notion that the return to nature itself was identical with death, and setting out for the "other side".[43] This conception of the return to nature, formulated so long ago, speaks volumes in our current context.

It is highly probable that many viewers overlaid a psychoanalytic experience onto this series of images. During analysis, we get the feeling there is something uncanny within the analyst, and this something ultimately appears before us, showing us precisely what we are like as a subject. The troupe of chimpanzees corresponds to the analyst, and the camera's line of sight corresponds to the gaze of the analyzed

---

[42] Alexandre Kojève, *Introduction à la lecture de Hegel,* réunies et publiées par Raymond Queneau (Paris: Gallimard, 1968), 548: "L'Homme est la maladie mortelle de la Nature." See also 554: "[L]'Homme est une *maladie* mortelle de l'animal." [These passages not included in the English translation of Kojève – Trans.] For the phrase "sickness unto death", see *The Sickness Unto Death: A Christian Psychological Exposition for Edification and Awakening* by Anti-Climacus, edited by Søren Kierkegaard, trans. Alastair Hannay (London: Penguin, 1989).

[43] Lit. "setting out for *higan*". *Higan* is roughly an alternative word for *nehan, nirvāṇa*, or *satori* "enlightenment", and literally means "the other shore". In Japanese in particular, it also signifies death, following the standard Buddhist use of the term *nirvāṇa* to refer, in some cases, to the final physical death of an enlightened being (*parinirvāṇa*) – Trans.

subject. Lacan's psychoanalysis lays emphasis on the heterogeneity of the analyst and the subject under analysis; the two are not of a kind, as we might expect of two human beings, and they are therefore not related symmetrically, like an object and its reflection in a mirror. The analyst is so far separated from the human realm that he or she might indeed, in passing, be less of a person than a chimpanzee – in one case actually appearing in an analysand's dream like the simians in *Planet of the Apes*. Note, however, that the *objet a* as it appears in analysis is an unmistakable guise of the subject.

The Other in Lacan is the Other as language, and this detour through Eastern philosophy has shown us that this same Other is also interpretable as the Other as nature. Long before nature was ever the nature of evolution, it was always-already articulated by language to an almost hopeless degree, transformed into language-nature; we can thus say that, from the Lacanian perspective, the Eastern concept of nature indicates the structure of language *qua* that which is prior to any subject. Assuming the desire of this nature/Other, as we have seen, is the path to the peculiar brand of freedom elaborated in both Buddhism and in Lacan – and this step leads to the paradoxical and disorienting consequence that self *becomes* Other. In the following chapter, we will see in detail what this "becoming Other" could possibly mean.

CHAPTER FIVE

BECOMING OTHER

One: The *Objet a* Within the Discourse of the Other

I, the other

In his article "Aggressivity in Psychoanalysis" (1948), Lacan quotes a famous line from Rimbaud: "I is an other".[1] The theme of the other preoccupied Lacan throughout his career, and we can hear the echoes of Rimbaud's line in the fundamental Lacanian concept of "the relation between the subject and the signifier of the subject",[2] which he used in attempting to delineate the origins of psychosis.

As speaking beings, we find this Rimbaudian otherness of our "I" deeply troubling. Even if there is such a thing as the signifier of the subject, and as soon as the subject attempts to use that signifier to present itself in the form of a truth like "I am such and such", the subject is immediately alienated from the fact that it is itself, for this signifier comes from an Other place. Signifying itself through the mediation of the big Other in this way is the only means the human subject has to approach its original, proper state, and it consequently must for better or worse proceed via the Other if it is to establish itself at all. In doing so, the subject cannot avoid *becoming* something besides itself – an other. This path to becoming an other is paved with repeated "identifications", in the sense of the term problematized by psychoanalysis – taking self for other, and other for self. Rimbaud's line expresses perfectly the frailty of human being that results from this Symbolic self-referentiality – a frailty that is the Achilles heel of human identity – and this frailty is what psychosis shoots for when it assails us. We can easily imagine Lacan ruminating on Rimbaud's line as he went about each day's psychoanalytic work, his thoughts playing on the inevitability of becoming the other for the human subject.

As we saw in Chapter IV, our life in its current form is grounded in the helpless suffering of a past ordeal, and we are convinced that, whatever else it might have been, this ground was at least alive. If we want to approach this ground, however, the only path open to us runs through the gauntlet of the Other. We must resurrect

---

[1] "Je est un autre." Letter to Georges Imbazard, May 1871 (the "letter of the seer"). Arthur Rimbaud, *Complete Works, Selected Letters,* trans. Wallace Fowlie (Chicago: University of Chicago 1966), 303-4. Lacan quotes the line at *Selection,* 23.
[2] See, for example, *Selection,* "On the possible treatment of psychosis", 183.

the speech mannerisms and turns of phrase of the other with whom we once identified, and so relive the experience of becoming that other. Only then can we approach the place of our past provenance – and even then, only by a supreme effort.

When we do make it through the dark woods of the discourse of the Other, what we at last see before us, where we look to find the ground of ourselves, is the *objet a*. We saw this in Chapter III, when we noted that the *objet a* is what appears when we represent ourselves through the trick of self-duplication called "dialectic" – specifically, when we look at ourselves as individual beings from the place of ourselves as universal being.

Assuming that some trace *does* survive of the helpless suffering from which we began, let us conceptualize that trace, and call it "the *objet a*". Because the *objet a* is the thing that we were at the very beginning, we can only experience it as object once we have entered the world of language – the discourse of the Other. This means that even if it is possible to experience it in this way, the object of that experience itself disappears as soon as we become conscious that the subject of this experience was ourselves, and try to express the experience in words. This means that, so long as we are a self-conscious subject, we must acknowledge that the thing that constitutes the vital ground of the self has been effaced, and faded from existence.

Because it is this sort of elimination or erasure in its essence, the *objet a* is said to be "simply the presence of a hollow, a void".[3] It is a hole that is found filled in or covered over "however you like", by absolutely all manner of things. The self as individual, as it appears to self as universal reason, approaches infinitely close to this void. The *objet a* can be described as an irrational aperture gaping at the heart of the world of rational numbers. Rational being, precisely in being rational being, betrays itself, and falls into the perdition of irrational number wherever it represents itself.

As we have just said, the aperture opened up by the *objet a* can be filled in or covered over by "all manner of things". Specific psychoanalytic experience finds that in fact, however, it often takes the form of a few specific objects. We will now proceed to look at some forms of the *objet a*, beginning with the most typical.

Four forms of the *objet a*

In his seminal *The Four Fundamental Concepts of Psychoanalysis*, Lacan lists four representative forms of the *objet a*: the feces, the breast, the gaze, and the voice.[4] The *objet a* takes these forms for specific pragmatic reasons. Let us look at each in turn, beginning with the feces.

Shit follows on the heels of our very being from day one, and having lost our origins, it is in shit that we tend to look for them. As soon as we are born, we begin to deposit a trail of feces, signifying that we are alive. Along similar lines, when we

---

[3] S XI, 180.
[4] See S XI, 242.

Chapter 5: BECOMING OTHER

come to look for the faded vital ground for our being, we naturally look to find it in fecal form – just as, in recent archeology and paleobiology, researchers have looked for our collective origins in the remnants of toilet facilities at Heian (794-1192) and Heijo (Nara, 710-784) sites, or in fossilized dinosaur excrement. As for the breast, its relation to the feces obviously runs very deep. The breast is prior to the feces in both logical and alimentary terms, and as surely as archeologists are led to reconstruct the diet of our ancient forebears through the analysis of toilet sites, so the feces lead us infallibly to the breast.

The third and fourth items in Lacan's list – gaze and voice – are also mutually interconnected. As infants, we turned our gaze to where the voices of others speaking could be heard. Though we may not have been able to form meaningful words, we could, instead, respond to the voices with our gaze, and of course that is what we did. Not only that, but we also vocalized in response to the gaze of the other. We gave voice to cries of terror when the gaze menaced us, and we also gave voice to joy, when a gaze that had momentarily vanished appeared before us again. It makes perfect sense that when, in our borrowed guise of the other, we draw near to the place of what we once were, our past self will restore those gazes and cries to our new, *other* self.

We can well imagine that these four forms of the *objet a* wait in the unconscious for us to discover them – scars that bear witness to the fact that we were once alive. These imaginary scars each do their part to help us mentally depict the ground of our being, as that which is desired by the Other. Between them they thus plaster over the lack of that ground. It may have been our inexorable fate to alienate ourselves into the Other, but we did not neglect to lodge our original selves inside that discourse, in these slight, indefinite forms.

We cannot expect to ever again discover ourselves fully present and existent within the discourse of the Other. We can and do, however, put the various forms of the *objet a* in the place of the void this impossibility leaves, and clutch them close to our heart. This preservative function is performed by the fantasy, which Lacan expresses with the matheme $S \lozenge a$.[5] This matheme[6] expresses in compelling visible form the subject (which having disappeared into the Other is notated crossed out with a slash) as it attempts, despite its own erasure, to preserve its own being through the

---

[5] Bruce Fink explains the reading of this formula as follows: "$\lozenge$ - This diamond or lozenge (*poinçon*) designates the following relations: 'envelopment-development-conjunction-disjunction' (*Écrits*, p. 280), alienation . . . and separation, . . . greater than . . . and less than . . . and so on." $S \lozenge a$ "can be read as 'the barred subject in relation to object *a*,' that relation being defined by all the meanings the lozenge takes on." Bruce Fink, "Glossary of Lacanian Symbols", *The Lacanian Subject: Between Language and Jouissance* (Princeton: Princeton University Press, 1995), 174. – Trans.

[6] "Matheme" is a neologism coined by Lacan for the formulae that make up his idiosyncratic algebra. – Trans.

relation with the *objet a*; and this is the relation the subject bears to Lacan's four privileged forms of the *objet a* – feces, breast, gaze, and voice.

Privileged as these guises of the *objet a* may be, however, they are not its essence. At base, as we have seen, the *objet a* is simply the hole the Rimbaudian otherness of I – the signifier of the subject – leaves in the Other as language. The specific forms it takes are as varied as the materials that come to hand when we come to cover this hole. We will now look at a famous instance of the *objet a* which is much more arbitrary in its choice of materials, and as we do so, pursue further the implications of symbolization for the subject.

Two: The Murder of the Thing

"Baby o-o-o-o"

In the Rome Discourse, Lacan gives another valuable example of the *objet a*. There again we see in the *objet a* the thing that replaces life when life eludes us and disappears; at the same time, this example also captures the formation of the subject within the Other.

Lacan takes up the "*fort-da* game", which Freud writes about in *Beyond the Pleasure Principle* (1920).[7] *Fort* is a German adverb, signifying distancing or disappearance; *da*, also an adverb, signifies existence, presence or appearance.[8] The game, then, is to make something appear and disappear alternately, an interchange that gives infants a lot of joy, as we know from games like "peekaboo". Let us first look at how Freud himself described the game.

Freud held that mental processes, though subject to continual modification by the reality principle, were driven by the pleasure principle. But as practitioners gradually accumulated a rich fund of psychoanalytic experience, he began to notice a significant phenomenon that could not be explained by this doctrine alone. Psychoanalysis aimed at making patients aware of unnoticed unconscious connections. No matter how far an analysis was carried, however, some such connections always evaded this process, and in fact, it seemed likely that it was precisely the most elemental and essential contents that were most impossible to bring to consciousness. In such cases, patients would *repeat* the repressed content as present experience, instead of recovering it as a recollection of some fragment of the past. They would bring experiences connected to infantile desires – oral, anal and

---

[7] Freud, *Beyond the Pleasure Principle*, SE XVIII, 14-15.
[8] *Fort* is like English "away", "gone", "off", e.g. *Ich muß fort*, "I must be off," *Sie sind schon fort*, "They have already left." *Da* is like "there", "here", e.g. *Da bin ich*, "Here I am," *der Mann da*, "that man there," *wer da?* "Who's there?". Examples from E. Klatt et al, *Langenscheidts Taschenwörterbuch: Englisch* (Berlin: Langenscheidt KG, 1983). – Trans.

phallic – into the relation with the analyst, and re-enact them in that context (the phenomenon known as "transference").

However, just because the patient re-enacts these experiences does not mean they attain satisfaction. On the contrary: all they get, at best, is the return of past suffering. These experiences, so stubbornly repeated regardless of the suffering that attends them, obviously exceed the pleasure principle, so much so that in can seem as if patients are "pursued by a malignant fate", or some "daemonic power" is at work.[9]

Another phenomenon that occupied Freud, and similarly a repetition driven by some fatalistic force, was the dreams of patients suffering from traumatic neurosis. Such patients often dream repeatedly of the accident or incident in battle which caused their neurosis. These dreams, which do no more than replenish pain, forced Freud to admit a unique exception to his thesis that "a dream is the fulfilment of a wish."[10]

In working towards a unified understanding of these various experiences, Freud came to postulate an instance that exceeded the pleasure principle, which he called the "repetition compulsion". Chance then furnished Freud with the opportunity to observe an extremely early instance of this repetition compulsion in the behavior of children. One day, he happened to see a child of eighteen months (his grandson) playing with a cotton reel. The child would repeatedly throw the reel over the edge of his bed and then pull it back in, saying as he did so, "O-o-o-o" (corresponding to *fort*, "gone, away") and "Da!" ("There!"). According to Freud, this "O-o-o-o" and "Da" represented events when the child's mother went off somewhere and then came back. With the cotton reel, the child was acting out the process of being separated from its mother, and then reunited with her.

> "This, then, was the complete game – disappearance and return . . . . The interpretation of the game then became obvious. It was related to the child's great cultural achievement – the instinctual renunciation (that is, the renunciation of instinctual satisfaction) which he had made in allowing his mother to go away without protesting. He compensated himself for this, as it were, by himself staging the disappearance and return of the objects within his reach."[11]

The child also invented another fascinating game, which he played before a mirror. He would stand reflected in the mirror, and then duck down so his reflection disappeared. When his mother came back, he would report his activities to her with

---

[9] Freud, *Beyond the Pleasure Principle*, SE XVIII, 21.
[10] Freud, *The Interpretation of Dreams*, SE IV, 122.
[11] SE XVIII, 15.

the words, "Baby o-o-o-o!"[12] Of course, this "O-o-o-o" meant the same thing as the "O-o-o-o" in the first game, that is, *fort*. In the first game, it seemed hard to deny that the cotton reel was a vehicle for the being of the mother. In the game with the mirror, however, the child made its own reflection disappear directly, without the mediation of the reel, and this reflection naturally represented nothing other than the being of the child itself.

Founding the desire of the Other

Lacan elaborates on this *fort-da* game to make two points about the formation of the symbol. These two points are encapsulated and formalized as follows: "Thus the symbol manifests itself first of all as the murder of the thing, and this death constitutes in the subject the eternalization of his desire."[13] The "eternalization of desire" signifies the fact that "the desire of the little child . . . become[s] the desire of another."[14]

As we saw earlier, the notion of the *objet a* had not yet been developed at the time of the Rome Discourse. Later, however, in Seminar 11 (*The Four Fundamental Concepts of Psychoanalysis*), Lacan interprets the cotton reel of this *fort-da* game as an instance of the *objet a*.[15] How does this cotton reel function as *objet a* in the context of the game, then? And what sort of change does this object bring about in the child?

The cotton reel is related to his mother's work. It is something often found in her hands, something that belongs to her. We could even say that it is a part of her. So what shall we suppose happens when the child picks up the reel and plays with it? The child himself, taking the reel in his hands as his mother had taken it in hers, takes up the place of the mother. Insofar as he has the reel in his hands, he *is* his mother, and the cotton reel represents him, the child – something the mother holds. The child being held in the arms of the mother is represented by the reel in the hands of the child. But note: this is no simple matter of one thing transforming into another thing. In fact, one *relation*, between mother and child, is symbolized by another *relation*, that between child and reel.

The cotton reel, originally part of the mother's body, has now been split off from her, and lies in the hands of the child. Looking at the reel through his mother's eyes, the child sees another thing once split off from his mother – *himself*. In casting out the reel, banishing it from his field of vision, the child signifies the mother abandoning her child: he somehow throws himself away in his mother's stead. He thus converts himself into something invisible, something with no being.

It is now assumed that the reel stands in the child's heart as the child stands in the

---

[12] For the mirror game, see SE XVIII, footnote to page 15.
[13] *Selection*, 104.
[14] *Selection*, 104.
[15] See S XI, 62, and 239 (where it is referred to as a bobbin).

Chapter 5: BECOMING OTHER

heart of its mother. By virtue of the symbolic equivalence between relation and relation, the mother's desire for the child becomes the child's desire for the reel, and at that moment is founded *qua* desire in the child's heart. In other words, "the desire of the little child . . . become[s] the desire of another,"[16] and appears as such before us.

We recall that the child's original trouble was the absence of its mother. We can anticipate, however, that the child as yet knew nothing of the forms in which desire is subjectively articulated, and most likely was not thinking, "I want my Mum." How, then, could desire first come into being within such a subject? The game, as symbolic operation, clearly has the syntactic structure of "I desire the reel." What syntactic structure does this syntactic structure of the game represent within the child? Freud's discussion might lead us to believe that it is, "I desire my mother." But this would be wrong. The correct answer is, "Mother desires me." This "Mother desires me" appears in the place of the putative, unarticulated "I desire my mother," of which we in fact find no sign. Thus, the desire of the other roots itself within the child at the moment when the self the child has entrusted to the cotton reel is cast away.

This process should give us some idea of the ultimate destination of the exploration followed out in analysis, when we trace back to the root the question of what we really want. The primal desire, "I desire my mother," which we expected to come to being within the child, turned out to have been usurped by the desire of the other. From this we can see that the ultimate desire, which we expect psychoanalysis to make clear, will always be realized in the final analysis as the desire of the other for the subject. And when that desire is realized, we can anticipate that the subject will metamorphose into a thing like the cotton reel, annihilated and discarded – into the *objet a*.

We should also note that, because the syntactic structure "I desire my mother" never in fact comes into being, "mother" is here negated as an object of desire. The introduction of the desire of the other through the agency of symbolic structure is, at the same time, the prototype of the Oedipal prohibition of desire.

At the moment when the desire of the child is thus realized as the desire of the other, the cotton reel must be made to momentarily disappear. This is because the reel is a guise of the child himself, abandoned by the mother. Despite this abandonment, however, the mother is imagined to desire the child just as the child desires the disappearing cotton reel. The child, having become the mother in the course of its play, rediscovers the cotton reel and rejoices. The child's joy here is in fact the joy of an other – specifically, the mother, on rediscovering the child himself.

In the joy of this play, there is no longer any such thing as the "actual" mother and the "actual" child. There is only the child become other (the absent mother) and the

---

[16] See note 14 above.

discarded and abandoned child – the *objet a*. Returning to Lacan's text: at the moment when the desire of the little child becomes the desire of another, he takes himself, as he has been suffering "in his solitude",[17] for the object of his desire. The cotton reel embodies this suffering being – the helpless suffering being at the subject's origin; in thus representing the child suffering, the reel is the *objet a*. The child repeats over and over his act of making this *objet a* vanish, only to produce it once more.

The child's other game, in which he looked at himself in the mirror and then made himself disappear, highlights even more clearly the tendency for the child to effect his own extinction. Children are indisputably fascinated by their own reflection in a mirror, and yet here we have a child deliberately doing away with his reflection and then going to his mother to report his deed. He thus introduces the desire of the other (in this case his mother) for the vanished reflection, even as he bids farewell to his own very being.

The *fort-da* game is thus a specific instance of the *objet a*, further to Lacan's basic list of its four fundamental forms. It also encapsulates the moment in which desire *per se* is founded in the subject, a desire Lacan calls "eternalized", and in this moment, "the desire of the little child . . . become[s] the desire of another."[18] What then of our other Lacan quotation in regard to this game, in which he borrows from Kojève's Hegel to speak of "the murder of the thing"?

The symbol manifests itself

Lacan uses the expression "the murder of the thing" in speaking of the annihilation or disappearance objects like the cotton reel or the mirror image undergo in the process of symbolization. Let us unpack the phrase, and the use Lacan makes of it.

Kojève explains that when the existing being called "dog" is grasped by its concept, this process implies that the dog's life is finite. He says, "[I]f the dog were not mortal . . . one could not detach its Concept from it."[19] For him, to detach the concept from the dog is to "cause the Meaning (Essence) that is embodied in the *real* dog to pass into the *non*living word."[20] Conceptual understanding of an empirically existing entity is thus "equivalent to a murder".[21]

Obviously, the conceptual understanding (*Begreifen*) Kojève describes here corresponds to Lacan's "manifestation of the symbol".[22] In Lacan's case, moreover,

---

[17] *Selection*, 10.
[18] See above note 14.
[19] Alexandre Kojève, *Introduction to the Reading of Hegel: Lectures on the* Phenomenology of Spirit, assembled by Raymond Queneau, edited by Allan Bloom, trans. James H. Nichols, Jr. (New York: Basic Books, 1969), 141. Emphasis removed from original – Trans.
[20] Kojève, 141.
[21] Kojève, 141. Emphasis removed. – Trans.
[22] See *Selection*, 104, "Thus the symbol manifests itself first of all as the murder of the thing[.]"

"the symbol" is nothing more or less than "language", and language as the desiring Other at that. When the child occupies the place of the mother and desires himself, the self that is the object of this desire is bereft of life, just like Kojève's empirically existing dog. The child makes the cotton reel or his reflection disappear, having first assigned to each the cargo of his very being. With this, a set of linguistic elements – the phoneme pair of *o-o-o-o* and *da* – is catapulted into action. The phoneme pair enters into a relation with the vanished being of the child, alternately absenting or re-presenting it. By installing the instance of language within himself, the little person entrusts what can properly be called the core of his being to the action of language's binary oppositions, that is, to the interplay of presence and absence. At this moment, through the shift to the other called language, the subject grasps (understands, *Begreifen*) itself as a thing lost, and this moment cannot fail to activate the concept of death for the subject.

The symbolization of desire thus implies the death of the subject. If Freud understood the *fort-da* game as an expression of the death drive, this was because it *repeats* the process whereby the reel is absented and becomes present once more. In isolation, the connotations of a term like "death drive" might seem to contradict the part of Freud's interpretation that sees the game working to master the passively experienced pain of separation from the mother by transforming it into an active behavior. Once we see how Freud weights the act of eradicating and annihilating the thing, however, and also that this action is a representation of the subject's own death, it is clear what he intended in presenting this game in the context of his theory of the death drive.

What Freud called "activity", as opposed to passivity, is anything but the autonomous behavior of the subject. It is, rather, the perpetualizing function of language. The presence and absence of the *objet a* is connected, within the subject, to the binary opposition of phonemes in language. The murdered "thing" internal to the subject becomes an object within the subject, and a linguistically articulated desire is established which is directed at that object. Freud's notion of the "thing" (*das Ding*), which we met earlier in covering Lacan's relation to Melanie Klein,[23] designates the object as the result of a murder – the murder required so that eternal desire based on language might come into being. When Lacan speaks of the "eternalization of desire" in the passage cited above, he is referring to this process, whereby the desire of the Other, *qua* language, is subjectified – taken on board by a subject, and set in perpetual merry-go-round motion.

Freud calls the child's behavior its "great cultural achievement". Lacan, fleshing out the implications of Freud's text, disentangled the death "instinct" (the death drive) from its biological formulation,[24] and formulated it anew in the terms of his

---

[23] See Chapter II, section four ("Enter Lacan").
[24] The problem of the role of biology in Freudian "instincts", and particularly in the "death

concept of the Symbolic. The Symbolic is the totality of culture, and as the mediation of the *fort-da* game in Lacan's Hegelian reading makes clear, it is deathly. On a very large scale, then, we might say that what we call "history" (the diachronic accretion of culture) is the practice of symbolizing, by means of the linguistic function, the "death" of countless human subjects. Lacan utilized the interplay of presence and absence in the Symbolic to describe the mode of being of the human subject, living in the context of such a "history", as follows: "Man literally gives his time up to the unfurling of the structural alternation in which presence and absence each invoke the other."[25]

Lacan's reading of the *fort-da* game is, then, highly nuanced. It links to the classic Freudian death drive on the one hand, and the Hegelian dialectic on the other. It captures in a nutshell a manifold moment: the moment of the establishment of desire (the desire of the Other) in the subject; the moment of entry to the Symbolic; the moment of primal alienation from the subject's origin. At this moment, the *objet a* is precipitated out as a residue of the original, living subject – but it is precipitated out as any one of a variety of outlandish things, from the feces or its other "typical" guises, to forms as idiosyncratic as a cotton reel. This *objet a* is the subject as a thing long since lost, and this is what Lacan sums up in his dense use of the phrase "the murder of the thing."

As we have seen, this entry to the Symbolic also precipitates a perpetual cycle of alternating presence and absence, which manifests itself subjectively as the repetition that first drew Freud's attention. What, then, does this repetition mean? What sort of function is served in human life by the "structural alternation . . . of presence and absence" Lacan describes here?

---

instinct", is complex, rendered more so by vicissitudes of translation. Two of Freud's German terms – *Trieb* (cognate with English "drive"; *pulsion* in Lacan's French) and *Instinkt* ("instinct", Fr. *instinct*) – were both rendered indiscriminately as "instinct" into English by the Stracheys and other translators. Laplanche and Pontalis note, however, that "it is quite possible to contrast [the two terms] with each other [in Freud's usage], though no such contrast has an explicit place in his theory." They observe that Freud uses *Instinkt* (though he does so relatively rarely) in the "classical sense" of "a hereditary behavior pattern peculiar to an animal species, varying little from one member of this species to another". *Trieb*, on the other hand, refers to "a pressure that is relatively indeterminate both as regards the behaviour it induces and as regards the satisfying object". See Laplanche and Pontalis, *The Language of Psycho-Analysis* (New York: Norton, 1974), "Instinct (or Drive)", 214-217. – Trans.

[25] "L'homme littéralement dévoue son temps à déployer l'alternative structurale où la présence et l'absence prennent l'une de l'autre leur appel." "Le Séminaire sur 'La Lettre Volée'", *Écrits*, 46.

Three: Repetition (I)

A dream of infanticide

If, as Lacan says, man gives up his time to the interplay of presence and absence, then we would expect the history of each individual life to be shot through by this structural interplay from start to finish. Freud noticed this fact early on, and gave it the name of "repetition compulsion", which we touched on earlier. Not only our dreams and the transference, but also our everyday actions, are controlled to a surprising degree by the repetition of this structural interplay.

The symbolization process, with the implication of death encapsulated in the phrase "the murder of the thing", is thus not something that occurs once and for all in infancy, thereupon retaining its efficacy over the whole life of the subject. On the contrary: it only exhibits its true force when it undergoes innumerable repetitions. This is because the desire of the other introduced by symbolization is in its essence an intricately layered phenomenon, and works to interrogate the subject at a number of points throughout its life.

In this way, the repeated interplay of presence and absence is characterized by a brutal cruelty, to the extent that we can almost, with Freud, call it "fate".[26] The process of annihilating one's own being and becoming other is never re-experienced without this attendant suffering, and it is no exaggeration to say that the scene of psychoanalysis is prepared just to make this re-experiencing bearable. We will now look at a clinical case that starkly demonstrates that there is something equivalent to murder included in the symbolization of desire.

The subject, a woman, was incapable of eating because food stuck in her throat. She had lost a great deal of weight, and finally went to the hospital. Her throat was examined by an ear, nose and throat specialist, but no abnormality was found. She thereupon commenced psychiatric treatment, but ordinary medicinal therapy had almost no effect. She did, however, relate a particular dream, and it became clear that an abortion she had had two and half years earlier was still working powerfully on her mind. Until that point, she herself had never suspected any relationship between her inability to eat and the termination of her pregnancy. It was only when she related her dream, and it was interpreted psychoanalytically, that the memory of the abortion revived in her mind and she became conscious of its connection to her trouble eating. From that point on her treatment made clear progress. The content of the dream was as follows:

First scene
Some man I don't know is peering into a large house looking for someone. And

---

[26] SE XVIII, 21.

Chapter 5: BECOMING OTHER

then its weird but a woman's face appears, and it's kind of spooky. And I think the man has gone into the house, but then it seems like it's me who's gone into the house, and when I go in my sister is there polishing the gas range, and her stomach's all back to normal. [In real life the patient's elder sister was pregnant, and in the dream her stomach had returned to normal size. – SK] I get this feeling like my sister has done something I was supposed to do, and I kind of glare at her. Next thing I'm doing the cleaning instead of her, and it's like she gives me a look as if to say, "Hey, that's *my* job!"

Second scene
The scene changes, and the man from before, who was looking into the house, is tumbling down a hill with another man, and they're hurting their faces. At the bottom where they end up was the sea, but then it turns to mud. Then all these fish come jumping out of the mud one after the other, and then a hairpin comes out of the mud. An old man puts it into my hair for me, and when I look I see that my hair is done all pretty like a *maiko*.[27]

Third scene
Next it changes to something like a *maiko*'s house, and there's some kind of sore on the *maiko*'s back. It looks really itchy and I am kind of whacking her lightly on the back. After a bit it turns into a revenge scene from a period drama, and a *samurai* is going with a woman under an umbrella to rescue someone. There's this guy in some kind of bamboo grove, and he says that someone has killed "every other person" in a big group of people. A woman appears from the path, and says it was children who were murdered. For some reason the area around the bamboo grove goes all red, and the place where I am is really dark. It's an awful dream.

This long dream can be divided roughly into three scenes, and each of these scenes represents the patient's abortion. In the first scene, the sister's polishing the gas range represents bathing a newborn baby. (The sister should be pregnant, but the baby is no longer inside her. The dreaming patient looks to see where it has gone, and her imagination presents it to her metamorphosed into the gas range, over which

---

[27] *Maiko* are professional female "entertainers" sometimes referred to as "apprentice *geisha*" in English. The hairpin is a symbol of the *maiko* and her legendary charms, as in the *Yosakoi bushi* from Tosa (Kōchi Prefecture) that runs, "At Harimaya Bridge at Kochi in Tosa / I spied a monk buying a hairpin" (note that Japanese monks are bald, and thus have no call for such accoutrements themselves!). The reference to the *maiko* and her hairpin thus underwrite the dream with a sexual subtext, and also, since *maiko* hold high status and such a hairpin would be a mark of special favour, with connotations of social prestige. In the Western context, a similar subtext of sexual and social power might be expressed by a dream of being a movie starlet and receiving an Oscar from the hands of a Hollywood patriarch. – Trans.

the sister fusses just as she would a baby.) The cleaning work the dreamer subsequently usurps from the sister represents the same thing. In the second scene, the men rolling down the hill and hurting their faces represent the child passing through the birth canal in parturition. These falling men disappear for a brief moment, but then re-appear as the fish or the hairpin, and in this form they are seized by the dreamer. Just like the child described by Freud, the dreamer is playing out the *fort-da*, making things vanish only to bring them back again. In the third scene the recuperative function does not work so well as it has in previous segments of the dream, and finds only a slender foothold in the concept of revenge, or the fact that only "every other person" was killed. Finally, the dream arrives at the murder of the child itself. At this point the dreamer is woken by her mounting anxiety.

This dream clearly repeats the traumatic past experience of the abortion, and this repetition is conspicuously characterized by alternation between being and non-being, or what we can call with Lacan "the structural interplay of presence and absence". Each of the three scenes is structured by dovetailing aspects of disappearance and recovery, and the combination of these two elements is repeated at least three times. (If we look closely, we see that this repetition continues *ad infinitum*, as in the notion of "every other child" in a big group being killed.)   The dream differs from the *fort-da* game in that the object thrown out is not necessarily the same as the thing recovered. On the contrary, the recovered object changes form at a dizzying pace, from the gas range, to fish, to the hairpin. All of these phantasmagorically metamorphosing objects, however, stand for the same thing – the lost life of the aborted fetus.

The recuperation of the mother's desire
As we saw previously, the repetition of traumatic experience in dreams like this one gave Freud a good deal of theoretical trouble. There is one explanation, however, which seems reasonable at least at first blush. We could posit that such repetition reproduces the traumatic experience in watered-down form, providing an opportunity to adapt or "acclimatize" to it, so the individual might learn to tolerate its strain. Of course, it is true in this dream that the series of representations of the abortion, each successively closer to the fact, eventually arouses anxiety, but this can be explained as a simple failure to adapt due to the overwhelming strength of the trauma.

While this explanation at least appears reasonable, there remains at least one large question that it cannot resolve: Why have the abortion in the first place?   Of course, there are sensible, logical reasons to have abortions. The mother may be physically weak, poor, unmarried, and so on. However, if we consider abortion only in terms of reasons like these, then all subsequent discussion will be confined to the social domain. We will end up addressing issues like the provision of economic and medical conditions allowing women to bear children without fear, the creation of new relations between the sexes, or the woman's right to choose abortion proactively

Chapter 5: BECOMING OTHER

rather than have it forced upon her.

What is required of us here, before we enter into all such controversies, is that we consider more basic questions. It seems that some force was at work within her, a force resistant to facile understanding, and that her abortion held some subjective meaning for her. Most likely she was driven (*sekitate*[28]) to seek psychiatric treatment by the unconscious question, "Why did I ever do such a thing?" Otherwise she would never have spoken to the doctor of this dream, which hints so strongly in this direction. As we mentioned in passing, the dream bears a strong resemblance to the *fort-da* game described by Freud, and if we read the lost life of the fetus, and the fish, hairpins etc. that represent it, as the same *objet a* found in the cotton reel, we can approach the structural underpinnings of the abortion. This background may be psychoanalytically reconstructed as follows.

When she was pregnant an unconscious idea arose within her – the question of how her mother, in turn, had felt about her. If she had been loved by her mother, then she would be capable of caring for the baby growing inside her. If, however, she had not, then she would not know how to look after her own child. The question of how her mother had really felt became the focus of anxiety for her, but there was no way for her now to return to her childhood and evaluate the feelings her mother had had so long ago. All she could do was live for herself the feelings her mother had felt for her, through her experience of becoming a mother to the baby now inside her. Her desire for the child in her womb was thus on the point of being established as the desire of the other – the desire her mother had felt for her. She was undergoing the symbolization of desire.

There was just one sticking point. When the patient came to adopt the position of the child – the *object* of her mother's desire – this symbolization process was inevitably blocked by the factual existence of the child. The child had to be obliterated as a concrete existence, converted to a pure sign, so that it could indicate a structural locus whose occupant could be the target of the mother's desire. And precisely by becoming such a sign, it would symbolize the real state of affairs, in which the patient was in fact no longer in her mother's womb.

In feeling heartfelt love for her child, then, and wishing hopelessly for its return, the patient at last convinced herself that she too had been just as loved. She experienced first hand her mother's regret at no longer having her child (the patient) inside her. Within her, then, the patient's desire for her lost unborn child functioned as the desire *her* mother felt for her. The desire of the subject, as Lacan would have it, is the desire of the other. It is so that this process of the conversion of desire might be realized that the fetus is annihilated. The fetus, having been thrown out (just like a certain cotton reel), can function as a surrogate for the subject herself,

---

[28] For *sekitate*, see Chapter III, note 12, and the section entitled "The race against time to determine self" in that chapter.

who is thereby imagined still to be in her own mother's womb.

We see, then, that if we "reasonably" write repetition off as a mechanism to acclimatize the subject to its trauma, we cannot answer the question of why the abortion was carried out in the first place. In fact the trauma itself – here, abortion – is interwoven into a deeper-running pattern of repetition, reaching back to more primal events. If we are to explain this larger web of repetition adequately, we must make use of Lacan's general analysis of the Symbolic interplay of presence and absence.

The structural alternation of presence and absence: "Now you see it, now you don't"

As we saw in Chapter IV, Lacan holds that the subject must be born again as something *wanted* – that which is desired by the Other. The subject realizes this by in fact *becoming* the other. The patient, desiring her aborted baby, is no longer herself; she is, instead, none other than her own mother (an other), who is assumed to have wanted the patient. As we can imagine, however, this faces her with an agonizing dilemma, since the terms of her "abortive" proof of her wantedness can only map the her that originally desired to be desired onto the annihilated child. The subject has, indeed, refound herself as desirable object, but that object is lost – in other words, it is the *objet a*. Lacan's most important prescription for the *objet a* is that it is "eternally lost".[29]

In the dream, numerous *objets a* are found, one after another. But who is it that finds them? It is not the patient herself, who common sense would tell us is the one who "has" (dreams) the dream. In fact the dreamer is the Other, and the patient is *dreamt* by this Other, to whom she appears as *objet a*. And while it is true that the dream repeats a traumatic experience, it is not the patient herself, as subject and agent, who engages in this repetition, let alone a subject aiming at adaptation. It is in fact the Symbolic function (the Other) itself that repeats, by virtue of its own innate operations. It was to this autonomy of the symbol that Freud gave the name "repetition compulsion".

Perhaps it would be as well to confirm that the lost fetus does in fact appear in the locus of the *objet a* as the golden mean. When the patient got pregnant, and the baby began growing inside her, she became a mother – *the* mother. In her imagination, her condition meant that she had become her mother and was carrying herself. We can posit, then, that "mother" is a term that emerges from her pregnant condition, a term constituted by the sum of herself and the child. If patient is x, and child is y, "mother" is thus $x + y$. The patient's relation to the unborn child (x to y) equals

---

[29] For example, "It is not introduced as the original food, it is introduced from the fact that no food will ever satisfy the oral drive, except by circumventing the eternally lacking object." S XI, 180. See also *Écrits*, 45, "l'objet foncièrement perdu."

"mother's" relation to the patient ($x + y$ to x). It follows that if her feelings for the fetus are the same as those her mother felt for her, we can use the formula given in Chapters III and IV to calculate that each of these mother-daughter relations, and indeed the value of x (the patient herself) equals the golden mean. This confirms that the lost fetus is indeed the *objet a*.

The same process that transforms the subject into the other, through the mediation of desire, also symbolizes the relation of the subject to some object – a relation identical with the relation of the Other to the subject itself. This shows us that the equation we have used to this point for calculating the golden mean is, in fact, also the equation of the symbolization process. We can see from this example that symbolization is not merely the replacement of some simple substance by a unary symbol. It is rather the replacement of a *relation* by another *relation* (the subject-object relation for the Other-subject relation).

If we ask what the individual I is in respect to the universal, therefore, there can only be one answer: the golden mean. This question is one that the human subject already starts asking in early childhood, and which troubles it sharply once more before death. But it is also asked in relation to love, as we saw in Chapter III, or in becoming a mother, as we see here, and these situations, too, engender the golden mean with tireless fecundity. With every turn of the wheel, something is annihilated or eradicated, and the desire of the Other symbolized anew – and human subjects keep offering up their time[30] to the structural interplay that is woven of presence and absence, for as long as they shall live.

Four: The Theory of the Mirror Stage

The quantum leap from "dereliction"[31] to eternalization

In the structural interplay of presence and absence, it is particularly the aspect of "absence" that is laid bare by the notion of the "murder of the thing". This absence is marked by the concept of the "eternally lost" *objet a*. But the *objet a* is, more than this, something which is not only lost, but *recovered* – or more accurately, which at least provides us with fleeting representations of the recovered object, like the fish and the hairpin in the dream examined earlier. As the *fort-da* game and the patient's dream make clear, some representation is offered to make up for what has disappeared, so that the annihilation and disappearance of the object are not always the whole story. The model for this mechanism is provided by the experience of the human subject with its mirror image.

---

[30] *Écrits*, 46.
[31] For the term "dereliction", see *Selection*, 103.

Chapter 5: BECOMING OTHER

The "murder of the thing" is ancient history to the subject, for the moment when we first became the other has faded so far into the past that we have come to think we chose our social role, and the expectations of us that come with it, of our own volition. In the course of leading life as the other, we lose sight of our selves. No matter how lost we might be to ourselves, however, we never doubt for a moment that we can find ourselves in one place at least – in our reflection in the mirror. But if we think about it, is it not odd that we place such faith in the mirror? The reason for this trust is that we seek to rediscover, in our mirror image, the self that vanished with the murder of the thing. We thus find a lot more than a mere optical reflection in what we see; we wish for the rebirth of the self that turned into the eternally lost object, and we think our wish is granted by the image in the mirror.

This peculiar relation to the mirror image is elaborated in Lacan's theory of the mirror stage. On accession to true humanity, the subject discards an almost pre-human phase of its being, a stage at which it was no more than a collection of scattered bodily excitations. This discarded being thereupon resurfaces as the unified mirror image. It is not hard to see that this process, the description of which constitutes the core of the theory of the mirror stage, is recapitulated in the instant every day when we face the mirror.

It is important to notice that the mirror stage, while in a sense recuperative, does incorporate the perspective of the "murder of the thing" that we examined above. Lacan read the *fort-da* game described by Freud as an instance of the child's "dereliction". Here "dereliction" implies a state of solitude and isolation specifically consequent to being banished from the theological state of grace. Throughout this book it has been referred to as "helpless (or suffering) being".[32] It is easy to see that the undeveloped infant, helplessly tormented by the unincorporated bodily chaos described in the theory of the mirror stage, is precisely in this state of "dereliction".

This reminds us that in the Bible, the grace of God is explained by reference to the fact that the body is one, even though it is made up of many parts.[33] Just as the whole body suffers when one of its members suffers, so when each individual suffers Christ suffers with them. By realizing the odd fact that we are a whole, despite our bodies being comprised of various parts, we can feel the presence of Christ (again the formula for the golden mean). This capacity of the body for unity is not, as we might imagine, a self-apparent consequence of natural biological development. It is, rather, the fruit of a quantum leap, a leap that partakes of the miraculous quality of grace.

As the moment at which the leap of "grace" from the "derelict", fragmented body to corporeal integration is accomplished, then, the mirror stage maps onto the "murder of the thing": it is a moment at which a primal state of the subject is lost, to

---

[32] See Chapter Four, particularly sections "The ordeal of language" and "The family romance".
[33] First Letter of St Paul to the Corinthians, 12:12-30.

be replaced by a representation (the mirror image, the signifiers of the symbolic). It is vital that, even as we note the recovery of the lost object that the mirror image, like the various guises of the *objet a*, allows, we do not lose sight of what is at the same time lost.

We might say that this quantum leap, which delivers us from dereliction to a state of being as the subject of eternalized desire, is the basic problematic of the Rome Discourse. This much granted, we must also see similar concerns in the theory of the mirror stage, where Lacan attempts to grasp the movement that propels us from the unarticulated biological body towards a being unified in the fictional dimension of the mirror image. It is clear that the Lacan of the mirror stage was already engaged in the attempt to conceptualize this leap, that is, to conceptualize the process of symbolization.

We will now consider the theory of the mirror stage in light of this reading, beginning with a step-by-step revision of its successive basic elements. As we shall see, Lacan has frequent recourse to biologically grounded argument in this early theory; it is important that we do not let this lingering biologism blind us to the fundamentally symbolic nature of the thesis he is propounding, a thesis which has more in common with the Hegelian doctrine of the "murder of the thing" than with the empirical work he explicitly draws on.

I precipitated in the visible

For some time after a human is born, the capacity of the nervous system to organically unify the various parts of the body remains undeveloped. For instance, when an electrical excitation travels along the axon of a nerve cell, neurotransmission is speeded by a structure called myelin, comprised of protein and lipids, which encases the axon like a sheath. Myelin formation takes place primarily in the four months after birth, though it subsequently continues at a more leisurely pace. This immaturity of the nervous system delays the completion of the unified sense of body. In particular, we can imagine that awareness of the particular spatial form of the body, and of the fixed relation it maintains with external space (the proprioceptive sense, or sense of posture), remains substantially different from that of an adult right up until the child can stand and walk. For some time after birth, then, the internal image of the unified self remains unformed, due to this imperfect regulation of posture and movement.

Consider, then, what happens when an infant, its proprioceptive sense in such a state of "primordial Discord",[34] stands before the mirror. The child is between six and eighteen months of age, and has only just learnt to stand, or perhaps can only do so by holding onto things. At this age, the child still feels this discordance within itself as an intense threat to its well being. The visual sense develops much faster

---

[34] *Selection*, 4.

Chapter 5: BECOMING OTHER

than the sense of posture, however, and for this reason, the unification of self is realized in the visual image when the child sees its reflection in the mirror, despite its internal disunity. The unity of self is not so much sustained from within as anticipated, and indeed preempted, by external appearances.

This experience leaves an extremely deep impression on the child, and the image of the self in the mirror that enabled the experience therefore acquires a decisive meaning. The child is overjoyed when it recognizes the image of itself, a joy undoubtedly produced by the gap between the unity of the image and the internal disunity felt by the child. By contrast, researchers report that even when other species, like chimpanzees, do at first show interest in their mirror image, this interest evaporates as soon as they realize that it is merely an image, and not another living organism.

The human subject thus becomes attached to a notion of self-image that has been established through its reflection in the dimension of appearances, and this attachment persists even when the internal sense of a distinct self has attained completion. The feeling that the self exists at all also has its roots in the joy experienced on finding the unity of one's self in the mirror. In addition to the self-image itself, moreover, our interest is attracted by the network of relationships the self-image enters into with the objects around it, and within which it moves. The self is formed as the privileged relational *position* the self-image occupies in the mirror's world of seeming.

The more incomplete the internal unified self-image, the higher the value placed on the self-image in the mirror and its relations with the other images around it. Lacan held that the highly cathected self-image in the mirror is a formative element in the development of the I, a concept the human subject puts to such good use in its social life. The value attributed to the unified mirror image is a direct product of the differential between it and the disunity of the body touched on above, and when the I makes its entrance, it co-opts this value to itself.

Upon reflection, this notion conversely implies that the value placed on the unity of the mirror image depends on the state of internal disunity of the self, as a kind of hidden term of reference. Since this reference point is internal, however, and invisible in its essence, it normally remains stubbornly hidden. When it is projected to the visual level, it appears as a negation of the unified visual image – the fantasy of bodily dismemberment.

When the analysis reaches a certain point, therefore, "*imagos* of the fragmented body"[35] always appear in the dreams of the patient, and we also catch glimpses of them in the symptoms of hysteria. This fragmented body is a representation of the anarchic disunity of both body and self, which can never be entirely subsumed by the unity of the mirror. The paintings of Heironymous Bosch examined in the last

---

[35] See, for example, *Selection,* 4, 11.

chapter graphically depict this fragmented body image, which as we noted above forms the structural background for the emergence of the I. It is precisely the unity of the mirror image, as it acts to cover over the terror of this dismemberment, that is the mainspring from which the function of the I derives its powerful cohesion and positive emotional connotations.

The unified image of the body-self, reflected in the mirror, maps also onto the perceived image of the other in the context of the social relation. The other comes to serve a function like that of the mirror, and comes to be the bearer of the mirror image self. This process is referred to as the deflection from the specular I to the social I.[36] As a result of this deflection, the value proper to the unity of the specular self (the self of the mirror image) is alienated wholesale into the other. The value that by rights should belong to the self is thus misappropriated by the other, and the I, just when it becomes a unified entity, is absorbed into the other, and can only exist within the other. We have here a kind of identification that amounts to capture.

When an identification like this is formed by the deflection of the specular image, then, the other identified with (the object of the identification) usurps the rightful unity of the self and takes it for its own. Numerous aggressive elements thus end up included in the identification. At this point the self disavows all conformity to the internal sense of disunity that originally constituted it, and begins struggling with a single-minded zeal to wrest back from the other the unity it so firmly believes must constitute its own future value. The claims of deprivation of rights and violation that accompany this orientation are defining characteristics of the paranoiac mode of being, and the fervor of the self as it denies that it is itself the fragmented body is called "paranoiac *méconnaissance*."

Paranoia – the social contract
Before Lacan proposed his theory of the mirror stage, he had observed and treated paranoiac patients (his famous case study Aimée among them), and it is only natural that a theory of paranoia should be interwoven with the theory of the mirror stage as we have been presenting it here. We will see that this theory of paranoia quietly ushered in the structuralist concept of the "desire of the Other", albeit in the context of a theory done up in a biologistic, developmentalist garb.

We have seen that according to the theory of the mirror stage, the subject not only first recognizes itself in the empty form of the specular image, but also comes to demand that society acknowledge this self as a natural thing, a matter of course. Recall the case history of Aimée. Aimée believed that the actress Z did not deserve the homage society paid her, and acted as if it was actually she herself who deserved that homage. In other words, her behavior demonstrated an attachment to Z, who functioned as Aimée's specular image. It was as if Aimée wanted to say that Z had

---

[36] *Selection*, 5.

Chapter 5: BECOMING OTHER

misappropriated the rewards that were due to her. If we think of this social tribute paid to Z as the desire of the Other, we can see that Aimée's whole life was shot through by the demand that this desire of the Other be rendered to her and her alone.

In paranoia, the desire of the Other maps onto the recognition society directs at the self of the specular image, and the unity that self has attained. In the form of acknowledgement, society directs desire towards the unified appearance of the self-image. But the target of this desire of the Other is the empty fiction of a mirror image; and in the process of deflection described above, this specular illusion has ended up borne by someone else to boot. What the self thus experiences is not satisfaction, but rather violent disappointment and jealousy, and so long as the self identifies with the other *qua* self-image to assure itself of its ongoing unity, this dilemma can only grow more intractable. The self has nothing but the most impassioned praise for the specular self-image, if only because it serves to paper over the reality of the self's inner sense of itself. But all this idolatry is guzzled by the empty self-image embedded within the other, and the self is left with no option but to continue confirming itself ever more desperately, in the form of an increasingly bitter hatred for the specular self-image. This process is not limited to clinical paranoia, either. Anyone who believes that they are a good person, whether or not they erect a concrete other as the object of this process, is steeped in these paranoid passions in relation to the social ideal of the "good person", which they have set up as their version of the specular image.

This paranoiac mode of being of the self is an inextricable component of human social relations. This is because society is predicated on the inviolability of the individual's personal integrity on the one hand and the equality of individuals on the other. It therefore primes individuals to realize the integrity (unity) of the self by projecting it onto other individuals, where they can see it reflected. This encourages the maintenance of mutual mirroring relations; recall that we always teach children to think how it would be if they were in the other's shoes ("How would you feel if it were you?"). We thus allow the self to demand that society recognize it as an integrated, unified self, absolutely indivisible (we thus speak of the "integrity" of the "in-dividual"), and as a society, we protect the specular image of the self invested in the other in the form of "individual rights". In this way we construct the mutual mirroring relations constituting the potentially aggressive and yet indispensable organizing bond that sustains society.

This organizing bond is a hotbed of paranoia, then, and as much as society continually strives to prevent that paranoia from breaking out, it must also at the same time cultivate this paranoia. Lacan placed great significance on the fact that we see in children a particularly paranoiac state of mind, which at the same time is a splendid instance of "imagining if it were you": "The child who strikes another says

Chapter 5: BECOMING OTHER

that he has been struck [and] . . . cries."[37] Here we see the prototype of the scenario that has a member of the exploiting class, out of a genuine heartfelt empathy, give charitably to the weak and the poor.

In these considerations we see Lacan's answer to the question of what ties the so-called normal social function so closely to madness: there is a substratum of paranoia underlying the social bond *per se*. In the view of madness he elaborates in the theory of the mirror stage, Lacan is thus the intellectual heir to Pascal's epigram, "Men are so inevitably mad that not to be mad would be to give a mad twist to madness."[38] In this connection, he has described the relation between madness and freedom as follows:

> "Far from being "an insult" to freedom, madness is her most faithful companion, and follows close on her every move like a shadow. Not only is human being impossible to understand without madness; it would not be human being at all if it did not carry madness with it, as the limit of its freedom."[39]

If freedom is based on consciousness of oneself as human, this consciousness must be born of the alienation of the mirror stage. The free subject, which is supposed to be an independent agent, is therefore obliged to drag an unfree component around after it wherever it goes, and right from the start, this unfree part, the "shadow" of which Lacan speaks, is an essential element of the establishment of the free subject. This is the sort of paradox that is implanted in the human subject by the mirror stage.

Thou art that

As we saw in the previous chapter, the psychoanalytic problem is this: At the point of its origin, how did the self know that it did in fact exist? A gap lies between the subject that thinks now, and the helpless suffering being we imagine existed in the beginning. How is this gap bridged? One way or another, the mirror stage offers an answer to this fundamental psychoanalytic problem. True, there seems no way for the thinking I to access the point where its thinking first arose; what I can do, however, is cast a reflection of the self in a mirror, and so clad itself in enough continuity to bridge the gap – just as you can see parts of the body not directly visible to the unaided eye by looking in mirrors or having your body photographed. The other of the mirror thus intervenes wherever continuity is preserved between I and

---

[37] *Selection*, 19.
[38] Blaise Pascal, *Pensées*, edited by Léon Brunschvicg (Paris: Hachette, 1971), 414. Translation from *Pascal Pensées*, translated with an introduction by A. J. Krailsheimer (London: Penguin, 1966), 148. Quoted in *Selection*, 71, 109, where Sheridan has the odd translation "Men are not [sic] so necessarily mad that it would be being mad by another kind of madness *not* to be mad."
[39] From "Propos sur la causalité psychique", *Écrits*, 176.

its origins, or else the other serves *as* a mirror. Whenever I feels a sense of continuity with itself, it alienates its "self" to that extent in the mirror (an other). The sense of continuity is something that I can only feel in the place of the other (Other).

There is a fascinating anecdote about a mirror in the work of some essayist or other. It is a little too perfect, and smacks of fiction, but for our purposes here we can take it seriously. The author of the essay was working as a schoolteacher in a poor area, and took photos of all the children in the class. One of the children was looking at the finished photos and pointed to one, asking, "Who's that?" It turned out to be the child's own photo. The child's family was so poor, the explanation goes, that they had no mirror in their house.

In circumstances like these, too, the other functions directly as mirror. In the everyday life of the group, the growth of human consciousness is nurtured by experiences of mutual reflection. A person could conceivably grow up never knowing their own face, but not without at least knowing who they *resemble*. Even in the absence of a mirror, there would be some sort of mirroring experience. The mirroring experience is not simply a matter of looking into a *physical* mirror and thinking, "I'm this," or "I'm that". It is more accurate to say that a mirroring experience arises when one's concept of the identity of "I" depends entirely on a self-origin grounded in *any* other *qua* mirror, where that putative ground of the self in fact has nothing to do with oneself. In this anecdote, the physical mirroring experience occasioned by the photo, rather than constituting the child's only experience of mirroring, functions rather to relativize pre-existent mental mirroring experiences.

We might also consider the problem through the following science fiction fable. On a planet far from Earth, there lives a race of sentient beings. Over time, these creatures have created their own history, but this history has grown so long that they have lost all clues as to their own origin, and the problem is embroiled in endless controversy. At this point, humans on Earth, who have been observing the planet, detect light emitted from it a billion years ago, light which as it happens was emitted at precisely the moment life arose on the alien world. The Earthlings immediately beam the light they have captured back to the alien race, using an instant displacement technology that works much faster than the speed of light. The aliens now know how things stood at the moment of their origin – though of course they would never have expected that this knowledge to come to them from the outside.

When we map this fable onto the mirror stage, the "Earthlings" correspond to the self in the specular image, and the mirror relation is represented by the instantaneous teleport mechanism. At the mirror stage, then, the impotent powerlessness of self-reference, like the confusion of the alien race about their identity and origins, is sublated[40] in one fell swoop, annulled by the magical power of this mirror relation. (The race to develop and maintain advanced communications networks, currently pursued with such passion, boils down to a competition to see who can create the closest thing to this magical force.) Just like this parable, Lacan's theory of the mirror stage is the tale of the germination of a self-consciousness that is interwoven with otherness, whether we like it or not. Even if the mirror stage itself is located at the level of visual experience, what Lacan wanted to pursue in it was the symbolizing mechanism by which the human subject decides itself as human.

If it is true that the subject undergoes an experience like this, in which the self is first erected in the alienating agency of a mirror image, in the initial phase of human formation, then we can be sure that the exploration of origins that constitutes psychoanalysis will find itself drawn to revisit that experience. For the subject of thought will always seek out someone it imagines will reflect its origins back to it, and the mirror stage will then lurch back into life, in adults no less than in children. The analyst is often selected to fill this role, and this fact is an important component of the transference.

Lacan brings his essay on the mirror phase to a close by referring to the "ecstatic" experience of the "Thou art that."[41] This is an experience that brings us to the limit of psychoanalysis. At this point, an other steps in to point out the origins of I instead of I, which is incapable of speaking of the origins of its self. This is, on the one hand, an experience fraught with both anxiety and ecstasy. It is also an experience that can offer a very commonplace relief, however, insofar as it is predicated on a bond of mutual resemblance between other and I. In his later years, Lacan was therefore to come to emphasise as the prototype of the mirror stage not the infant as it faced the mirror alone, but the experience of being reflected held in the arms of some adult other (who resembles the self).[42]

We might say that Lacan established the theory of the mirror stage as a reply to the psychoanalytic question, "What makes me human?" Answering this question is a matter of how far back into our history we can trace our origins, as we practice the discourse of psychoanalysis. Lacan, it seems, conceived of the mirror stage as one of a series of points of arrival on this journey towards the source.

The mirror stage as symbolization

At one point, Lacan says that the homeostasis of the subject concretely realized in the specular image is a symbol of the subject's alienating destiny.[43] By "alienating

---

[40] "Sublate" is the usual technical philosophical translation of Hegel's *Aufheben*, which has the dual meaning of "to negate, to do away with" and also "to preserve". – Trans.

[41] *Selection*, 7.

[42] S VIII, 411.

[43] *Selection*, 2; "[I]t [the mirror image] appears to him . . . in a contrasting size (*un relief de stature*) that fixes it . . . [this] symbolizes the mental permanence of the *I*, at the same time as

Chapter 5: BECOMING OTHER

destiny", Lacan means that the subject weaves the world for itself, but in the process it ends up bound to a phantom, or a kind of automaton, that wanders trapped in the world of its making.[44] The subject is fated not just to weave its world, but to weave itself into that world as well – albeit as little more than a shadow – and this process of so positioning itself in the world can be called the original symbolization. Here, despite the biologistic overtones of the mirror stage theory, we encounter again the problem of the imbrication of the subject in the big Other, which we covered in the previous chapter.

In fact, we might say that it was this originary symbolization that Lacan was attempting to conceptualize with the theory of the mirror stage. Symbolization of the self is accomplished by asking what one is, and then answering that query, in the context of the universal. The symbol of the self is what we use to ascertain the position of the self and grasp its meaning, and the specular image that appears in the mirror stage plays precisely this role. Mirror image also becomes a symbol. For Lacan, the world of the mirror is something more than a simple object of perception – it is more of a plane of meaning, peopled by a jostling throng of images. He refers to the world presenced for the infant at the mirror stage as a "symbolic matrix".[45] In it, no less than in the world of the dream or the discourse of the Other, a swarm of images hems the subject about on all sides.

This process of identifying oneself by means of the symbol, however, implies a special logical difficulty, as we already saw in the previous chapter. Prior to the identification, the object of the identification must be an other, and in becoming "itself", the subject thus comes to the contradictory pass of branding itself with something more other than self.

In the course of everyday life, many people have the experience of forgetting (or nearly forgetting) themselves when counting heads, for instance if they organize a party. What you have to do is put a kind of phantom self among the guests, and include it in the number, splitting the self that is counting from the counted self. But then, if you count each self, both counting and counted, you will end up with one person too many. One or the other of these selves is superfluous, at least so far as the proprietress of the establishment hosting the party is concerned. You must rub one self out again. If you erase the counting self, then the subject who has to report to the proprietress will disappear, and that won't do. If, on the other hand, you wipe out the phantom self you just went to all the trouble of creating and counting, you'll just be back to square one! What to do?[46]

---

it prefigures its alienating destination."
[44] *Selection*, 2-3.
[45] *Selection*, 2.
[46] This sort of difficulty in counting oneself is an integral part of the effort to symbolize one's own being, and is therefore also one of the prime motors driving the discourse of psychoanalysis. When this difficulty becomes apparent, we can assume that a self that is

Chapter 5: BECOMING OTHER

This is the sort of numerical difficulty you confront in the process of identifying yourself, and identifying *with* yourself. It seems likely that this "logico-mathematical" difficulty (to coin a term) is experienced very early by the human subject, and then forms the basis for further experiences in turn. Lacan takes the view that experiencing the ordeal this difficulty entails is what makes us characteristically human. Psychoanalysis is founded on the thesis that "It [and not the self] speaks",[47] and Lacan also conceptualized this "It speaks" in the form of "It counts".[48] The Other, which is prior to the subject, is not only the Other that *speaks* of the subject; it is also, at the same time, a *counting* Other.[49]

When we first represent the self by the symbol, that which is identified with the symbol (thus crossing to the side of the symbol) becomes irrevocably other. There is no way to integrate the original self, represented by the symbol, and this self that has become other. We are therefore forced to start over from scratch, attempting afresh the Sisyphean task of representing the self by the symbol. In this repetitious process, the subject becomes other time and again, and as a result loses over and over the object that was once the original self.

There is a bitter irony here. The identification of self with a term in the discourse of the Other, or the "symbolic matrix", far from producing identity, leads only to an inexhaustible splitting of the self – a crumbling into a mess of disparate fragments. This dismembered state is a *Gestalt* emblematic of the impotence of self-referentiality,

---

difficult to identify (in both senses of to identify something, and to identify *with* something) is present in the analytic situation, and at that moment the timing of the end (scansion) of the analytic session arrives. A good concrete instance of this is to be found in the following case material from Pierre Skriabine.

The patient was describing family life after the death of his brother. He said that "the three of us" often talked about the brother after he was gone. When the analyst asked him to clarify what he meant by "the three of us", he enumerated: "My mother, my father, my sister, and . . ." and was quickly forced to admit, "I forgot to count myself." Skriabine comments:

"This session had by that stage lasted for perhaps one minute, but I closed it there and then, saying 'Right, that's exactly it.' For at that point something had come along to punctuate the session – the subject's mistake in counting, a computational error which indicated precisely the place at which the subject presented himself as "one short" [*un en moins*, a Lacanian term variously translatable as "one less", "the minus-one" – Trans.]. In other words, here one can see the structure of the subject as "a signifier less" [*un signifiant en moins*] – a signified which has no signifier. And one can also see the subject as vanished in the same sense as the dead brother, to whom the subject is bound by a pact that the work of analysis will gradually bring into the open." In Kazushige Shingu, ed., *Beyond Meaning: Lacan in the Clinical Setting* (*Imi no kanata e: Rakan no chiryōgaku*), (Kongō Press, 1996), 197-198 (in Japanese). [This note added for the English edition, and a typed transcript of Skriabine's original lecture in French was also consulted.]

[47] S VII, 206.
[48] S VII, 317. Lacan does not directly use this wording.
[49] This notion is well expressed in the concept of *le trait unaire* from Lacan's later years. See Chapter VI.

Chapter 5: BECOMING OTHER

and is identical with the Boschian experience of the "fragmented body". The impotence it represents stems from two sources: the perpetual "dis-integration" (failure to integrate) of the symbol representing the self and the self so represented; and the passion with which the self seeks integration (and integrity) regardless.

This line of argument shows us that the specular image that appears at the mirror stage, eliciting so much joy from the infant, is not just a term like any other in the symbolic series. Unlike other terms, which produce the *ad infinitum* crumbling of the self, it is a privileged instance, which gathers together the dis-integrated fragments of our experience, and seals them up together. The mirror image takes our origin, which we would otherwise only ever expect to encounter as the *objet a*, and knits it into a corner of the other in the radiant and noble form of an image.

In fact, it is only when the mirror image makes its glorious entrance that we first interpret the fragmentary experience that preceded it as suffering. A new self, constituted as a temporal binarism, comes into being, pitting its new life in the state of integrity and truth against the suffering fragmented existence that preceded it. It is only then that the experience of fragmentation is seen clearly as such, in the retrospect of the unity bestowed by the specular image – another case of deferred action (*Nachträglichkeit*). The suffering occasioned by becoming the other through self-reference, and thereby losing oneself forever, is overlaid onto the memory of the undeveloped state of the infantile nervous system. Biological development is historicized at the mirror stage.

If we are to grant this sort of privilege for the specular image, however, it seems clear that it cannot go on being a mere reflection in a mirror for ever. It must be possible to relativize it as a term in the discourse of the Other, thus stepping outside the bounds of its pure specular character and into the realm of the symbol. And we find that this is indeed the case. It was, after all, his own mirror image that the child observed by Freud played at erasing.[50]

In the same moment that this privileged specular image is established, self also undergoes the "deflection to the social": the first step towards the alienation and paranoid structure we traced above. Psychoanalytic experience frequently brings into plain view the privileged specular image in the making, and when it does, we find it in the relation between the subject and the other; and if we ever win reprieve from the imperative to confront the origin of the self-as-lost-object, it is always thanks to someone we assign to the role of this specular image. Aside from the pure experience of the mirror image, then, the mirror stage also involves this important,

---

[50] "One day the child's mother had been away for several hours and on her return was met with the words 'Baby o-o-o-o!' which was at first incomprehensible. It soon turned out, however, that during this long period of solitude the child had found a method of making himself disappear. He had discovered his reflection in a full-length mirror which did not quite reach to the ground, so that by crouching down he could make his mirror-image 'gone'" (SE XVIII, 15, n.1).

social element of entrusting the image of the self to some other person.

It is easy to appreciate why we entrust the vital underpinning of our self to someone else. So long as the specular image is (the) other, we can get away without facing up to the difficulties of self-referentiality – even if the image *is* also implicitly or potentially the self. All we have to do is make sure we treat the person in question as other, and all we ask is that the other will consent to serve us as mirror image indefinitely – what we usually call "love". Whenever that demand is frustrated, and "love" fails us, the experience of dis-integration will assail us once more.

Analysis teaches us the ways the experience of bodily disintegration returns in the fabric of our day-to-day life, and consideration of this point brings us full circle. We have traced repetition to its roots in the originary trauma of the loss of a primal, chaotic self, and then seen how that self is lost, when we entrust an alienated, unary self to the mirror image. We now return to repetition – to what happens when the contradictory structure bequeathed us by the mirror stage breaks down.

Five: Repetition (II)

"The aborted child is me!"

One day, a patient burst into the consulting room, literally breathless from running. He was so anxious he could not stay in one place for two minutes at a stretch. It was the first time he had sought psychiatric help, and he had been driven to do so by a dream he had had that morning.

> "I was clinging to this dried-up old tree. Underneath was mud. I couldn't get down even if I wanted to. Then I noticed that there were all these corpses floating in the mud. I hung onto the tree even tighter, and then I woke up. I was so freaked out I didn't know what to do with myself. What's going to happen to me? What does my dream mean?"

In analysis he remembered something that had happened before he had the dream. His sister, Kyō, who was married and had been pregnant, had had an abortion. I interpreted immediately. The corpses floating in the mud were the aborted fetus, and that fetus was him.

Some time later, he went home, and yelled at his parents, "The baby Kyō aborted is me!" The analysis transformed his anxiety into this single, true utterance. Of course, his words strike us as utterly meaningless at first, and in all likelihood, either he himself or his parents ultimately interpreted it to mean, "I was never loved, just like the baby she aborted!" But the true essence of psychoanalytic interpretation lies in making contact with the meaninglessness that flashes momentarily in his cry.

When we hear a member of the South American Bororo tribe (made famous by the research of Lévi-Strauss) say, "I am a parrot,"[51] we are assailed for an instant by the feeling of a meaningless blank, a feeling of radical unfamiliarity. But what really separates this statement from declarations like "I'm a tiger" (sign of the zodiac),[52] or "I'm the eel" (when ordering in a restaurant)?[53] Originally most people thought that the sort of totemic thinking behind the utterance of the Bororo was pre-logical, but Lévi-Strauss demonstrated that it was in fact a complex and systematic body of thought;[54] and in the essay on "Aggressivity" introduced in Chapter II, Lacan points out that even the utterance "I'm a man" ultimately contains the same logical difficulties as the totemic statement – the basic contradiction of stating that "one" is any "other".[55]

When our patient declared, "I am the aborted child!" he foregrounded this logical difficulty, but at the same time he enabled himself to shoulder the difficulty squarely, and assume it afresh. It is plain to see why he fell into such acute anxiety. He had placed his mirror image in safekeeping inside pregnant sister's womb, comfortable in the idea that it could thrive there free from harm.[56] Instead, it was destroyed without warning, and the result was the corpses in his dream – the carcasses of countless repeated identifications tried and discarded before he arrived at the self of the specular image. It was to remind himself that the grim denizens of the dream were in fact his own off-cast husks (to acknowledge their *identity* with him) that he announced that he was the aborted child.

The dreaming Other
As we can see from this case illustration, the unified self-image is squirreled away

---

[51] Cited in *Selection*, 23: " . . . the astonishment of a Van den Steinen when confronted by a Bororo who says: 'I'm an ara.'" [Ara is a genus of parrots in Central and South America. - Trans]

[52] The reference here is to the Chinese zodiac. - Trans.

[53] In Japanese, the copula *da* is looser than English "be" in the semantic linkage it allows between subject and predicate, so that it is common to say "I am X" when ordering X in a restaurant, for instance. This mode of expression can be barely glimpsed in the (admittedly unusual) English diction "I'm the eel" (i.e. "The eel for me"). - Trans.

[54] Claude Lévi-Strauss, *The Savage Mind* (Chicago: University of Chicago Press, 1966), p. 42: "['Savage'] thought . . . is experienced in all the exercises of speculation and resembles that of the naturalists and alchemists of antiquity and the middle ages: Galen, Pliny . . . From this point of view, 'totemic' classifications are probably closer than they look to the emblem systems of the Greeks and the Romans, which were expressed by means of wreaths of olive, oak, laurel, wild celery, etc."

[55] *Selection*, 23.

[56] Of course, it was not just since his sister became pregnant that he had situated his mirror image inside her. She had first taken on his specular self long before, when the "deflection to the social" first took place at the mirror stage.

inside the other, unbeknownst to the subject itself. Against this, the thing that constitutes our origin is left isolated, a corpse smashed and scattered and abandoned to the winds. In this case, the specular image the patient had secreted away inside his sister was obliterated by chance events of his sister's making, and his fragmented internal body image was revealed starkly in his dream. When his anxiety drove him to the analyst, he was looking for a place where he could reconfirm that this body image was in fact his own.

We can fairly say that, in the case of such important dreams as this one, the dreamer is almost never the subject themselves. Rather, the way the subject appears *to the other* is inscribed into the dream. As we saw above, the Other dreams, and we are merely "dreamt", as it were.[57] It may sound mystical to say that an other dreams within us, but in fact it is no different from Bertrand Russell's assertion that we should say, "It thinks in me," rather than "I think;"[58] a comment he made in the context of a highly rational argument. Because of the fragility that the structure of self-referentiality implants in human thought, this sort of interference from the other (and the Other) is unavoidable. In the dream, we do not so much encounter the other, as become it, and once again we see that regardless of what immediate, surface trauma may occasion it, it is this becoming that ultimately bankrolls the uncanny loops of repetition.

Six: Symbolic, Imaginary, Real

Lacan's fertile theorizing produced a great number of new terms. The Symbolic, Imaginary, and Real surely rank among the most famous of these Lacanianisms – though not necessarily the best understood. We will now try to unravel these intertwined instances from the knot they form in the mirror stage, and the related instant of symbolization (the murder of the thing) captured in the *fort-da* game.

The original plus/minus – the Symbolic
As early as the theory of the mirror stage, Lacan was already searching for the originary symbolization prior to all identification with specific others in the group. As we saw, at a certain point in its development the subject comes to ask what it is in the context of the universal. In attempting to answer this question, it erases its self, transforms it into a chimerical shadow, and then "re-cognizes" it from scratch

---

[57] See page 97.
[58] "[T]he grammatical forms 'I think,' 'you think,' and 'Mr. Jones thinks,' are misleading if regarded as indicating an analysis of a single thought. It would be better to say 'it thinks in me,' like 'it rains here.' Bertrand Russell, *The Analysis of Mind* (London: George Allen & Unwin, 1971), 18.

Chapter 5: BECOMING OTHER

through extremely elemental concepts like "being" or in pure forms like number. Self thus first acquires meaning in a play of presence and absence, of dissolution and (re)constitution. The image in the mirror and the cotton reel alike are mental images that reflect the self *qua* this interplay. As Lacan says in an essay dating from the same period as that on the mirror stage, "[T]he efficacy of the images [is] furnished with a plus or minus sign."[59] In other words, we must realize that the specular image and the cotton reel function, not simply as mere optical phenomenon or physical object, but as the plus or minus sign that each of them represents.

It is clear here what Lacan had got his hands on in the theory of the mirror stage – the process of symbolization of self, carried forward by the transparent, formal movement of presence and absence. For Lacan, the plus and minus signs were the purest, most rarified symbols of all. He was soon to be calling this structure of interplaying presence and absence, which enables the manifestation of self to self, "the Symbolic".

In the interplay of pure presence and absence revealed in the game of the cotton reel, Freud perceived something like a perpetual cycle, which dogs the subject at every turn. The interplay of presence/absence also bears a resemblance to the process of reincarnation, relentlessly advancing, casting the empty husk of each individual life by the wayside. But Freud saw in it not eternal life, but death – the return to the inorganic. Our being is now cast away, now hauled back out into the light, stringing together a trail of alternating plus and minus signs as it goes. It would be little wonder if, exhausted, it was to revert to the inorganic matter whence it came.

When the Symbolic promises the advent of self as it is to self, it thus brings the "far shore" of life – death – within range. Our being will eventually be used up and revert to the inorganic, but it will go on being our being regardless. The subject has been reborn as other into the universal Symbolic, and so long as the interplay of presence and absence goes on within that Symbolic, the subject will transcend the border between life and death to maintain its identity as the residuum that always reappears in repetition.

All this symbolizing is all very well. But we must bear in mind that the theory of the mirror stage has an eye to not only the exploration of the symbolization process, but also to something more, which we cannot ignore – the paranoid element that comes to bear in human relations. We turn then, from consideration of the Symbolic to that of the Imaginary.

---

[59] "L'efficience des images . . . [est] déjà pourvue d'un signe positif ou négatif . . ." *Écrits*, 91. [The source of this citation was incorrectly given in the first Japanese edition, and has been corrected for the English translation – Trans.]

Chapter 5: BECOMING OTHER

Captured by the "human" – the Imaginary

When another person comes to bear a subject's specular image, the image itself, up to that point a term in the symbolic matrix, undergoes a qualitative transformation. So long as it remains a term in the symbolic matrix, it is capable of serving as a signifier of the self, and for this reason it triggers the pain of self-referentiality. But once the image is placed in safekeeping within someone else, it no longer admits of such a linguistic relation with the subject, and the tribulations of self-referentiality are purged from it. The subject comes to believe that somewhere within the other there is a self replete with absolute tranquility and self-confidence, exempt from the pain of self-reference, and totally at one with its signifier. Within the other, a feeling of unity is realized, bestowed by a sense of linguistic security on the one hand and a freedom from the splitting function peculiar to language on the other.

In other words, the state of unity that ought by rights to belong to the subject is somehow captive within the other. Just as animals are drawn to a decoy or lure, humans are always on the lookout for someone to whom they can entrust the unity of their self. While the other reflects our unity to us, the relation is one of love, but when we feel that the other has usurped our unity and is hogging it all to itself, the relation turns to hate. Paranoia breaks out.

This sort of captive relation to the inside of the other *qua* specular image is the realm of the Imaginary. It is a kind of "short-circuit" embedded in the heart of the self-symbolization process of the mirror stage, and try as we may we can never eliminate it completely. It cuts the line of reference to the "other side" of life (the beyond of the death drive) introduced by the Symbolic, and restores to the human subject the competence to live as a biological being.

Lacan offers the example of guessing games played by children, which require the players to estimate the cleverness of their opponent to win.[60] We are to imagine a child who keeps winning by this means. The structure of the guessing game, itself, belongs to the realm of the Symbolic. But the process of estimating how one's opponent will move within that structure is a function of the Imaginary. In order to think, "My opponent will probably expect me to do such-and-such, so I'll do something else," I must cast myself into my opponent, conjecture what judgement the opponent will pass on me, and then reel the judgement back within myself. The Imaginary function has a very large say in what goes on here, as each player ensconces their self-image in the other in the context of the mirror relation.

With Lacan, we can expand our view of this relation to encompass the broad sweep of the social. The fate of all social values hangs on the number of people who will accept them *as* a value. If we can only move in keeping with the choice and

---

[60] The Seminar on "The Purloined Letter". In John Muller and William Richardson, eds., *The Purloined Poe: Lacan, Derrida, and Psychoanalytic Reading* (Baltimore: Johns Hopkins University Press, 1988), 36.

preference of the majority, then, we can obtain wealth and power. A new type of television quiz program is on the rise, where rather than being grilled on their knowledge *per se*, contestants are given a range of possibilities and required to guess which will be most favored by a group of, say, a hundred respondents. Games like this reflect the Imaginary function. An instance with more real implications is to be found in the movements of the stock index. While it is probably possible to make sound investments on the basis of a company's performance record, what holds the market up is the game of guessing where the herd will put their money next.

This sort of Imaginary function can never be eliminated from society, for it *is* the fundamental social bond. At the limit of this game of following the multitude, there always floats the mirage of the "absolute majority". We imagine this "absolute majority" as an individual figure, something like the intangible will of the majority made incarnate, and this image originates in the specular self-image erected at the mirror stage. The self never rests from the task of reconfirming its self-identity in this stereotype of the "typical person" conditioned by the notion of the "absolute majority".

In tandem with the functioning of this Imaginary mechanism, whereby the self has always already returned to itself, the splitting movement of the Symbolic is also repeated constantly. The self intertwined in the Other thus achieves the symbolization of a self that is no more. The idea is that the origin of self will maintain its identity even in the midst of this splitting process, as a trace or remnant glimpsed from the very limit of this splitting. But can it really do so? Let us track it to the limit and see.

At the limit of the *cogito*

We do not merely look on, detached, at the binary interplay of presence and absence. We can never forget that we have offered up something like a part of our body in order to manifest the structure of this interplay in the dimension of the sensible. The act of throwing out the cotton-reel, or making one's reflection disappear from the mirror, are all no more or less than the relinquishing of a body part – after all, the Symbolic must function, and because it functions, something has to serve as its material support.

To furnish this support, we first consign the joy of the sheer fact that we *are* to various forms of "the thing" (starting with our body). We then subtract the particular use value from this "thing" to arrive at the pure form of interplay between presence and absence. This formal instance, however, is arguably still supported from within by the various individual "things", even if they have lost all trace of their individuality. It is in the form of such things that we would expect to find the *plus de jouir* (leftover joy) of the fact that we exist.[61]

---

[61] For *plus-de-jouir*, see S XVII, 56: "In fact, it is only in this entropy effect, this effect of loss,

Chapter 5: BECOMING OTHER

Lacan's Symbolic is thus conceived as always concealing the "kernel of our being" within it, in this pure form of presence/absence distilled off from the concrete forms of the various materials supports with which we furnish the Symbolic. This kernel supports the Symbolic, and keeps it in motion. This structure coincides completely with that whereby "das Ding", described above (Chapter II, Section 4) is at once cause (*primum mobile*) and goal (*telos*) of the mental apparatus. Inescapably confined within the limits of the Symbolic and yet never entirely of it, the kernel of our being always requires further, new symbolizations, and is thus the engine driving its repetitions as well as its ever-receding terminal point.

We will now look at one instance of a chain of repeated symbolizations driven by this engine – a string of symbols which repeats *ad infinitum* the symbolization of the fact that I exist(s). This chain will take us to the limit of the splitting process, where we will see whether or not we can find the promised vestige of the origin of the self.

"I" knows that I exists, here and now, and also that this state of affairs has to have started somewhere. To symbolize this piece of knowledge, we require three different subjects: respectively, the subject of knowing, the subject of present being, and the subject at the origin. Now, because the I that knows "I exist in the here and now" *also* exists in the here and now (the logic of the *cogito*), the subject of knowledge becomes the subject of a new instance of present being. Whereupon yet another subject, which knows this new fact, comes into being in turn. Let us express this never-ending sequence of events as a mathematical series.

First, we write

$$0 \rightarrow 1 \rightarrow 0 + 1 = 1$$

originary I   present being I   knowing I
(I of knowledge subsumes both I of the origin and I of present being)

With the following operation, terms each shift one step to the right:

$$0 \rightarrow 1 \rightarrow 1 \rightarrow 1 + 1 = 2$$

originary I   present being I   knowing I

Repeat the operation, and the "knowing I" changes to the "present being I" once

---

that the status of *jouissance* is clear – that it shows itself. That is why I have introduced it under the term *Mehrlust*, or "surplus pleasure (En fait, c'est seulement dans cet effet d'entropie, dans cette déperdition, que la jouissance prend statut, qu'elle s'indique. Voilà pourquoi je l'ai introduite d'abord du terme de Mehrlust, plus-de-jouir)". *Mehrlust* is coined after the pattern of Marx's *Mehrwert*, "surplus value" (F. *plus-value*). For more detail see Bruce Fink, *The Lacanian Subject: Between Language and Jouissance* (Princeton: Princeton University Press, 1995), 131, 190-191 n. 28.

Chapter 5: Becoming Other

more:

$$0 \rightarrow 1 \rightarrow \underset{\text{originary I}}{1} \rightarrow \underset{\text{present being I}}{2} \rightarrow \underset{\text{knowing I}}{1 + 2 = 3}$$

In this fashion, new "knowing I's" appear one after another, each as the combined sum of the last two terms.

The resulting succession

$$0 \rightarrow 1 \rightarrow 1 \rightarrow 2 \rightarrow 3 \rightarrow 5 \rightarrow 8 \ldots$$

comprises the "Fibonacci series", defined as

$$U_n = U_{n-1} + U_{n-2} \quad (n = 2,3,4 \ldots) \quad U_1 = 1 \quad U_0 = 0$$

How, then, should I of present being be expressed in relation to the I that knows that I exists? If we follow the line of reasoning we already encountered in Chapter III, and show this relation as a ratio (i.e. "rationally"), we get

$$\frac{U_{n-1}}{U_n}$$

Since the value of n is always increasing, the relation of the present being I to the knowing I has a limiting value of

$$\lim_{n \to \infty} \frac{U_{n-1}}{U_n}$$

In other words, the point of convergence of the series

$$\frac{1}{1}, \frac{1}{2}, \frac{2}{3}, \frac{3}{5}, \frac{5}{8}, \frac{8}{13} \ldots$$

is the answer to the question of what exactly the present being of I is. Let us see if we can determine its value.

Each individual term of the series is expressed by

$$\frac{U_{n-1}}{U_n}$$

We can express this in the following form

$$\frac{U_{n-1}}{U_n} = \frac{1}{\frac{U_n}{U_{n-1}}}$$

Since $U_n = U_{n-1} + U_{n-2}$, however

$$\frac{U_{n-1}}{U_n} = \frac{1}{\frac{U_{n-1}+U_{n-2}}{U_{n-1}}} = \frac{1}{1+\frac{U_{n-2}}{U_{n-1}}}$$

As *n* approaches infinity, we can assume that $\frac{U_{n-1}}{U_n}$ and $\frac{U_{n-2}}{U_{n-1}}$ converge on the same value. If we call this value *r*, we can use this last calculation to derive

$$r = \frac{1}{1+r}$$

Therefore

$$r^2 + r - 1 = 0$$

If we solve for *r*, taking the positive solution, we arrive at

$$r = \frac{\sqrt{5}-1}{2}$$

i.e. the golden mean (r = a).

    Here we see the passion of I, desperately keen to discover its present existence in the form of the golden mean – the *objet a* – driving the production of the whole chain of symbols, ensuring that it will never end. In the originary act of symbolization, the self identifies with the signifier of itself, and objectifies the self of present being. For the self, this involves the pain of an infinite series of splits. At the same time, the symbolization process also holds out the sweet promise that one day the self will be expressed as one, fixed, beautiful number – the golden mean – somewhere on the far side of infinity.[62]

As we have seen, Lacan held that the I is "anticipated" at the mirror stage. Here, the "anticipated I" is the I symbolized in the form of "What am I?" We can think of it like this: the golden mean, which awaits us somewhere over the rainbow of infinity, is reflected in the concrete instance of the specular image, and this is what is anticipated by the nascent subject. It was not until his seminar of 1970, *Séminaire 17*, entitled *The Other Side of Psychoanalysis*,[63] that Lacan had recourse to the Fibonacci series; we see here, however, that we can say in retrospect that he had already perceived the golden mean (as that which the child is to itself) in the specular image of the mirror stage, and most of all, in the particular object presented by the cotton-reel of the *fort-da* game.

The specular image is of the domain of the Imaginary, but it is lodged in a corner of the Symbolic, where it drives the infinite chain of symbolizations of I, a process which seeks to reach the shimmering lure the image sets up on the horizon. Thus the Symbolic and the Imaginary: what then of the term that is in many ways the most elusive in the Lacanian trinity – the Real?

The "extimacy" of the Symbolic – the Real

As we have seen, the Symbolic includes within itself the golden mean, as the logical end-point of the extension *ad infinitum* of reflexive selfhood. But because the

---

[62] In a paper inspired by the first Japanese edition of the present work, students of Yamaguchi Masaya, working with a function created by Yamaguchi himself, have developed an algebra with fascinating results (Takemoto Yasuyuki and Hiwahara Yoshiyuki, "The Complexity of Self-Formation in Psychoanalysis [Seishinbunseki ni okeru jiko keisei no fukuzatsusei]", Final Dissertation, Ryukoku University, 1996 [unpublished]). Presenting the technical details of Takemoto and Hiwahara's argument would require a great deal of space, and is not possible here. We will, however, attempt to describe briefly the outline and findings of one part of the paper.

The function (the "golden model") described by the paper is modeled on the *cogito* described here, in that $x_{n+1} = f(x_n)$, i.e. each value in the series is calculated taking the result of the previous calculation as its raw material (*x*). The parameter, *m*, represents the relation between self and other as a ratio (a fraction of 1); different values of *m* are tested to see what series of values they produce for *x*. Due to the construction of the function itself, in which *a*, the "golden number", is a constant, different values of *m* all produce graphs which approach *a* in different ways: moving stepwise towards it, circling around it in an ever-tighter approach, and so on. When *m* (the ratio between self and other) = a^2, however, the function suddenly produces *chaos* centered around *a* – it becomes non-linear.

[This note added for the English edition.]

[63] *Le Séminaire, livre XVII. L'envers de la psychanalyse, 1969-1970*, ed. Jacques-Alain Miller (Paris: Le Seuil, 1991). Translation by Russell Grigg, *The Other Side of Psychoanalysis*, forthcoming from Norton.

Chapter 5: BECOMING OTHER

Symbolic is the realm of *ratio* (rational number), it can only contain its own limiting value, the *objet a* (an irrational number) as its own impossibility. In a sense, then, it does not "contain" it at all – as that which is impossible to it, the *objet a* is *beyond* it. Lacan liked to call this situation, in which external to the self is contained within the self, *extimité* (extimacy), because such a relation, although sustained with something outside (*ex-*), requires the most in-*timate* closeness.

The Symbolic is the domain of the symbolization of self. At the point where we run up against the limits of this domain, that which is impossible for it is enfolded within it. The rationality that represents itself by the symbol must sustain a relation with this externality, even though it is impossible for rationality to do so. This externality is called the Real. The self supposed to have existed at the origin demands symbolization afresh as the *plus de jouir* (leftover joy), and in response to this demand, we stride onwards to the ends of infinity, where the Real awaits us.

Lacan frequently illustrates the touch of the Real in connection with beauty. When faced with the beautiful, we sometimes find ourselves wanting to pin down just what the beauty comes from. Beauty has the power to dupe us, and we want to clarify for ourselves where it gets that power. But we are also fully aware that there is no way for us to strip the surface off beauty, and see the reality that lies beneath. If we could peel the skin off beauty, all that would be left is the uncanny thing that Lacan calls the "grimace of life".[64] We must recognize the *reality*, however, that we nevertheless desire to reach for the far shore that lies beyond beauty.

Our relation to beauty recalls the relation to the breast, as described by Melanie Klein (see Chapter II, Section Two). The infant goes beyond the relation with the breast that nurtures it with food and love, and seeks the breast it suspects lies behind it – a breast it imagines possesses infinite power and absolute goodness. The unfulfilled aspiration to find this breast eventually releases jealous and destructive impulses within the infant, who ultimately encounters instead a breast that has been cruelly ravaged. The infant thus peels the skin off its ideal of beauty – the omnipotent breast of fantasy – and finds beneath it a thing of horror, a "grimace". In her account of the shift from the schizoid position to the depressive position, Klein can be read as having attempted to describe the Real as it is found within the body of the mother – that is, a description of *das Ding*.

Having undergone originary symbolization, the human mind is pulled onto a slippery slope to infinity. Everyone feels sometime the temptation to try and think about the infinitely large or the infinitely small, or about the boundaries of the universe, its beginning, or its end. In fact, we feel the tug of that temptation constantly. In this place called "infinity", we imagine an I become absolute other and enjoying (rejoicing in, enjoying, getting off on; *jouissant*) the real of its origin in the form of the golden mean. As a child, I already anticipated this enjoyment once,

---

[64] "Grimace de la vie." S VIII, 324.

at the mirror stage, and thus from very young I has known the pleasure of seeing itself from the vantage point of death.

We thus find the three separate instances of Symbolic, Imaginary and Real intertwined and overlapped in the nodal logical moment of self-representation. The Symbolic is locked into the repetitive interplay of pure presence/absence, "re-presenting" (and re-absenting) successive selves to the edge of doom. In the mirror image of the self, ensconced at the heart of the Symbolic and yet evading its inadequacies, we find the Imaginary: the anticipated image of the full and whole self that drives the Symbolic chain as both cause and promised destination. And finally, beneath the glorious chimera of that image lurks the Real: the threateningly irrational golden mean, impossibly beyond the very Symbolic in whose heart it finds its home.

In the process of thus developing from his theory of the mirror stage to a theory of the Symbolic, Lacan produced a celebrated diagram, which he called "schema L". We will now consider how the mirror stage and symbolization look when considered in light of this schema.

Seven: Schema L and the Mirror

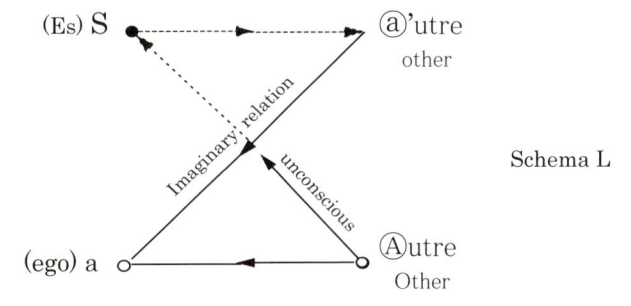

Schema L

The mirror experience as reflected in Schema L

Schema L, which Lacan first introduced in 1955,[65] presents the relationship between the paranoid social bond established with the founding of the ego at the mirror stage – the Imaginary – and the subject's inscription into the Symbolic. It is shown above in its complete form. In explicating it here, we will venture the experiment of mapping the schema onto the theory of the mirror stage, first breaking it down into its component elements, and then gradually building it back up again. We will first treat the S found in the top left-hand corner.

S is *Es,* that is, the "id" (it) of Freud's triad of id, ego and superego. It is also the initial "s" of the word "subject", insofar as it is posited to have existed at the origin. In German, one says *Es regnet,* just as in English we say "*It* is raining." (Recall the

---

[65] S II, 243.

Chapter 5: BECOMING OTHER

references to Russell's "It thinks in me" and the idea that "It dreams" above.) Just as the rain falls without knowing that it (*Es*) is falling, the human subject *is* without knowing that it (*Es*) is, and is alive without knowing that it lives. Of course, this may no longer necessarily be true of us when we have grown up, but we can easily conjecture that it must have been so in the beginning. This "it", the human subject as it is found at this primal stage, is notated "S". It has no medium through which it might see itself from outside, and therefore no access to knowledge of itself (fig 1).

fig. 1

Even in this state, the subject is already being spoken of by others (A). This relation, though, is a one-way street. While the subject is one-sidedly spoken *of*, it can only experience the fact that something is being said of it *passively*, and has no way to know what people are saying about it. For this discourse of the Other exists outside the subject, and the words the subject attempts to incorporate into itself for its own purposes only give rise to the problem of self-referentiality. The subject tastes the bitter pill of indecidability and the pain that it entails (fig 2).

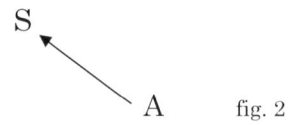

fig. 2

This is the background against which the "mirror" makes its appearance in some corner of the world of the Other. This "mirror" is not necessarily a physical one. Any other who comes bearing the message "I am X, just like you" will do just as well. When it sees itself reflected in this mirror (*a'*), the subject at last obtains the medium necessary for self-recognition. For the first time, it knows, "I am such-and-such."

This means that the specular image (*a'*) reflects the I that the subject takes for itself (*a*). The subject senses that *a*, a manifestation of itself, is concealed behind or inside *a'* (fig 3). We should be careful to note that the "mirror image" we take so much for granted in fact includes both the "reflecting specular image" (*a'*) and the "reflected I" (*a*).

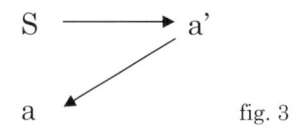

fig. 3

Chapter 5: BECOMING OTHER

Thus, while the actual physical light follows the path indicated by the dotted line, we can indicate the direction of the subject's apprehension of the situation rather by the solid line (fig 4).

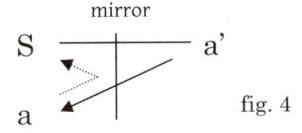

```
            mirror
    S ─────┬───── a'
       ▼   │
        ╲  │
         ╲ │
    a ◄───╲│         fig. 4
           │
```

The subject (S) has, until this moment, known only the pain of being incapable of representing itself (or else felt itself to be the fragmented body). When it apprehends this suffering self (*a*) as something unified and integrated, in the inverted form of *a'*, it thus assumes this notion of itself with jubilation. This process was covered in Section Four of this chapter.

The subject (S) thus finally comes to apprehend itself – to have some idea of what it is. Now as an image, *a* is apparently independent of the linguistic function. The answer to this question of what the self is, however, is meaningful only in the terms of identity and difference established by the functioning of language, and if this answer comes in the form of *a*, *a* must therefore have already undergone, *by means of language*, the operation that distinguishes between that which is the self, and that which is not. We see, then, that the self *a*, which S apprehends via *a'*, is in fact something that has undergone a function derivative of linguistic activity (A) (fig 5).

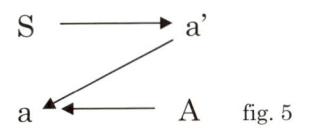

```
    S ─────────► a'
               ╱
              ╱
             ╱
    a ◄───── A     fig. 5
```

However much the subject may have thought it could not understand the talk about it emanating from the Other (A) of language, then, it has in fact known all along how best to make sense of it. As soon as the subject becomes conscious that it has this knowledge, however, the rug of its hard-won self-awareness is pulled out from under its feet once more. It slips into the quicksand of self-referentiality, once more deprived of its ground.

The apprehension of self achieved at the mirror stage has the power to banish this danger of self-referentiality in a single stroke, because the specular image and the I that it reflects are there joined as seamlessly as the two sides of a coin. In effect, the suffering I of *a* is wrapped up in the unified specular image (*a'*) and concealed from decent sight. The *a* is reduced to the status of a meaningless mark – a mere aggregate of random dots and lines to the superior Gestalt of *a'* – but it remains on the flipside of the *a'* all the while, and threatens it with disintegration at any moment.

While the subject before the mirror fancies it is looking at a mere mirror image, or an other, then, its true self in fact adheres to the inverse of what it sees, less than a hair's breadth away. Because of the tight adhesion between image and self, the subject prematurely obtains an ephemeral integrity on the level of the imaginary. The symbolization that might have been given to S at the origin by the discourse of the Other (A) is thus implacably blocked, so that the speech relating to *a* that might have been introduced to S from A is stalled in the unconscious (fig 6).

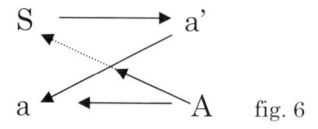

```
S ─────────► a'
  ╲ ╱
  ╱ ╲
a ◄───────── A    fig. 6
```

Thus we arrive at the structure of the "L" schema. In it, the action originates from A, and there are two operations at work. The first, as we have just seen, flows from A → S → *a'* → *a*. The other goes directly from A to *a*. Both originate at A and end at *a*, though the former goes a more roundabout route.

When the path of speech from A to S is blocked, S gains access to *a* as it is for A by way of *a'*, almost as if agency originates from S itself. Interestingly enough, however, when the space between *a* and *a'* opens a little and the axis from A to S is rendered passable, a familiar structure appears. Let us first notate the schema as a direct series (fig 7). The subject (S) hears a discourse about what it is to the Other (A) *qua* universal (①), talk which emanates from behind its own back. But because S does not have eyes in the back of its head, it cannot adequately grasp the contents of this talk. S transcribes the contents of ① onto the question of what the other of the specular image, *a'*, is for itself (②), and attempts to read it this way. The result is that *a* becomes visible in *a'*. What we have here is precisely the situation found in the parable of the three prisoners.

$$A \xrightarrow{①} S \xrightarrow{②} a' \rightarrow a \qquad \text{fig. 7}$$

This is not your back

Schema L thus presents the relation between the representations of self given by the mirror image and by symbolization in schematic form. Let us consider this relation between the mirror stage and the Symbolic from a less abstract perspective, starting with a painting by Magritte (*Reproduction interdite*, 1937). In this picture, a man stands facing a mirror, and in the mirror we see the reflection of the man as seen from the back. Our first reaction will perhaps be something like, "Seeing yourself from the back in the mirror, right, pretty typical Surrealist stuff."

But then, perhaps, we think again. How can we be so sure that the man is really looking at his own back, as he seems to be? Perhaps there is simply another man dressed the same as the first and facing the opposite way, and it is him reflected in the mirror. Or again, even if the man in the picture were in fact looking at his own

Chapter 5: BECOMING OTHER

reflection, how would he know it was him he was looking at? We can hardly expect that he would ever have seen himself from the back before. Although we thought that this man was looking at his own back in the mirror, then, it becomes apparent to us that this idea was only in the mind of the beholder. In a sense, we were forcing this idea of ours onto the picture, saying to the man, "That's you in the mirror you know!" – whether he wanted to know or not.

The viewer is the big Other (A), and the man in the picture is the subject (S). But we must go one step further than this. It is also possible for us to stand in the shoes of the man in the picture. In fact, it is only because we can do so that we felt in the first place that the fact that the reflection showed the man's back was out of kilter with reality. Let us step into the picture, then, and try standing in the man's place. We know that the reflection is of our own back. But how do we know? Because the Other that stands behind our shoulder has told us so, just as we compulsively told the man earlier when we were in the Other's place. Thus, when we first found our self in the mirror (at the mirror stage), we were already listening to the teachings of the big Other. Even if we seem to see an objective self in the mirror, we in fact only ever see ourselves in a form the big Other has taught us to see. In Schema L, the mirror self a' derived its significance from A, the locus of the other. As we saw earlier, in later formulations of the mirror stage Lacan emphasized the experience of seeing oneself *held by an other* in the mirror. This other represents the mediation of the Other, teaching us how to interpret what we see ("Yes, baby, that's you!").

This reminds me of a conversation I once overheard between two young women on a train.

- A: "Yeah, I've got a mole too. A big one, on my back. I only found out recently when my brother told me."
- B: "What? You mean you never knew?"
- A: "Yeah, when I asked my Mum she said she never told me on purpose."
- B: "Really? I never knew your Mum was that sort!"

A's mother is a wise woman. Everyone starts trying to figure out how they appear to the universal Other at some point. But there was no need for A's mother to tell her daughter about the mole, and push her into thinking about this dilemma prematurely, just as there was no real need for us to foist on Magritte's man the knowledge that it was his own back reflected in the mirror. Had A's mother wanted to, she could have told her daughter about the mole at any time – but perhaps she even knew that she should *not* talk about it, just as the three prisoners in the parable were forbidden to talk, though they were allowed to look at one another's backs.

So we see that when the subject recognizes the specular image for itself at the mirror stage, the originary symbolization is already at work behind its back – as Magritte's man needs a viewer behind *his* back, to tell him that the back he is looking at is his. With the hidden help of the Other, the mirror stage clothes the self in a unified costume; at the same time, however, it also inscribes the horror of bodily

—125—

Chapter 5: BECOMING OTHER

fragmentation in the heart of that unity – an experience of fragmentation introduced into the human mental structure as a result of the logically problematic demand to symbolize the self. Thrust prematurely into the world, still unformed, the human subject can only experience the body as a collection of disconnected fragments. This biological condition is given to human perception as the raw material with which we represent the logical difficulty of self-symbolization. The real fear of experiencing bodily fragmentation is inverted in the symbolic series, however, to emerge as a yearning for infinity of which the *objet a* is the vehicle. The human subject lives life symbolizing everything under the sun, and the subject itself cannot evade the long arm of its symbolization process. And somewhere beyond the far reaches of Symbolic infinity, swathed in a joy always just out of reach, the *objet a* seals up the fundamental impossibility of achieving this symbolization, with its cargo of impotence and pain.

CHAPTER SIX

ALL ALONE IN PARIS

One: The Unary Trait

Being "one"
As we have just seen, to experience psychoanalysis is to constantly happen on yourself from behind – to see yourself as the big Other sees you. The form of the self you encounter when this happens is the *objet* a, and the self aware of encountering it is within the big Other. But how does the big Other lead us, in analysis, to the place of this being within it? In *The Seminar, Book VIII* (1960), Lacan deals with the transference, and there he says that the analyst must empty [*kū*][1] the place of his own being, and offer it to the patient as a site for her desire. In this empty [*kū*] place is realized the desire of the patient as the desire of the big Other.

In analysis, the realization of desire *is* the realization of the desire of the Other. When this desire of the Other is the desire of the analyst, and beyond that the desire of Freud, then the road to realizing desire coincides with the road to becoming an analyst, whether the person under analysis has come as an aspiring analyst or as a patient. In his analytic practice, Lacan insisted on positing no essential distinction between training and treatment analysis. In either case the desire of the self is satisfied when the subject becomes the other that is the analyst, and this is achieved via the empty space that the analyst offers. The move towards empty space that Lacan describes here is sustained less by human emotion than by a certain structural requirement, which we can understand as follows.

To be woven into the big Other is to count oneself as "one": "I" is "a" person, one instance of a symbolic category. But what does "one" mean? The mathematician Adachi Tsuneo has suggested that the ability to understand that the moon in the sky and the pebble at the roadside both share the concept "one" may be the fountainhead of the human power of abstraction, and the culture that developed from it.[2] I think he is right, and I want to try to bring this concept of "one" to bear not just on stones and the moon, but on "I" as well.

---

[1] Lacan, S VIII, 128. Lacan's word for "empty" is *vacante*. The Japanese here is "*kara*". The Chinese character for *kara,* 'empty', is also that used for *kū,* thus hinting at the traditional concepts of Zen and Buddhism. See Chapter IV, note 29. – Trans.

[2] Adachi Tsuneo, $\sqrt{2}$ *no fushigi* [*The Wonders of* $\sqrt{2}$] (Tokyo: Kobunsha, 1994).

Chapter 6: ALL ALONE IN PARIS

We begin, then, at the moment "I" symbolizes itself as "a" person. I is "one". Now, if I joins the set "humanity", as it does with this symbolic act, then clearly "humanity" must grow in number. Nevertheless, as a species, "humanity" itself also forms a "one" – a whole. Won't this "one" of "humanity" disintegrate if I joins the set? It is hard to believe otherwise. After all, there must be many "people" apart from I, an endless stream of them, all adding themselves to "humanity" too. Won't they bloat the tidy "one" of "all humanity" beyond definition, into an uncanny riddle? Despite this inherent danger, however, the fact remains: we do have a concept of the "one" formed by the whole of all humanity.[3] Even if I adds itself to this "one", it must remain "one" all the same. Let us, with Lacan, call this "one" "the One".[4]

"I", as "one", adds itself to the One, and yet the One remains "one" all the while. $1 + 1 = 1$. What sort of mathematics is this?

Let us look at it this way. By adding oneself (x) to the big "One" (1), it is possible for one to know what "one" really is. Because the one that one thus sees is the One (1) as seen by the sum of oneself and the One ($x + 1$), it is:

$$\frac{1}{x+1}$$

"I" must then apply this "one", which I knows even as I is part of and within the One, to the one I itself is as a human being (x). We can write this:

$$\frac{1}{x+1} = x$$

All we need to do is solve for x. Once again, we see the golden mean appear before us, and I has become the *objet a*; the *objet a* thus expresses the value of the I that thinks it is human, seen from the viewpoint of the One. It is also significant that in falling on the side of the One,[5] this I somehow falls outside any concept of humanity defined in terms of the living. I is of the same order as a person already dead, or of one yet to be born.

This chain of operations may appear somehow illogical, and admittedly, the above calculation is based on a deliberate and active confusion of the "one" that is the *set* of all humanity and the "one" of each individual human making up that set. In metalinguistic logic this sort of confusion is impermissible. The two levels – that of the set itself, and that of its elements – must be distinguished, or else self-reference arises, and the truth-value of the utterance becomes undecidable. Each utterance

---

[3] In schizophrenia, etc. this concept unravels.
[4] The capitalization of this term seems designed to recall to mind the Other (the "big Other"). See S 20, 128 (also "the One-missing", 129).
[5] The Symbolic, whose connections with death we explored in the last chapter.

Chapter 6: ALL ALONE IN PARIS

requires a metalanguage at a separate level. As Lacan so frequently cautioned, however, as soon as the subject itself engages with language, we must acknowledge that "There is no metalanguage."[6] For the individual subject must have an identity that communicates between the two different levels, so that it can see itself from the level of universal language. The communicating passage opened by thus extending concept of "one", the cross-tie between the two levels, to the being of the individual subject is a good example of what Lacan called a "unary trait" (*trait unaire*);[7] and it is through the being of the analyst that this "one" is brought into the analytic experience, which is why the place of the analyst must be empty [*kū*].

Where I encounters itself

The fact that I is "one" is thus connected to the "one" of the whole, in which I is included one moment, and not the next. The connection is created by a kind of self-referential identity. I is defined in its relation to the whole – the group; at the same time, it turns back to apply that definition to the group itself, even as it remains a part of the group all the while. This is clear if we re-examine the equation given above in the form:

$$\frac{1}{x+1} = \frac{x}{1}$$

On the right, "I", x, determines what I is in the context of (in terms of) the "one" of the whole, the group. I is thus defined by its relation to the group ("one"). On the left, I steps back outside the group in order to determine what I is (i.e. "one", which included I, or x, becomes 1 *plus* x), and the group, "one", is defined by its relation to the sum that results. And since I is to the "one" what "one" is to the sum of the whole and I, I is identified with "one". This identity (identification) is the connection between I being "one" and the "one" of the whole, and it corresponds to the equals sign in the equation.

The identity, or equality, effected by the unary trait is thus a relation between the subject and the group, within which a kind of reincorporation process is occurring

---

[6] S 8, 393.
[7] The concept of *le trait unaire*, one of Lacan's polysemic word-plays, is strictly impossible to translate. It can mean "the unbroken line", "the single stroke", "the unary trait", or "the unitary trait". Lacan developed it from Freud's concept (in SE XVIII, *Group Psychology and the Analysis of the Ego,* 107) of *ein einziger Zug,* a "single trait" borrowed from the object in certain types of identification. See Dylan Evans, *An Introductory Dictionary of Lacanian Psychoanalysis,* (London: Routledge, 1997), 81-82. The author renders it in Japanese as *ichi no sen,* "the line of the one", which in part refers to the Chinese character for "one" – a single horizontal line which figures graphically the connective relationship under discussion here. With these considerations in mind, we have chosen here to translate Lacan's French by "unary trait", by which we hope to suggest a primitive act of counting. – Trans.

Chapter 6: ALL ALONE IN PARIS

constantly. Each time I steps out of the "one" to define the one, the need arises for I to add itself again to the whole it leaves behind; it is assimilated into this new "one" only to step outside and trigger the process anew. As this process is repeated, I finds itself oscillating back and forward between the situation expressed on the right of the equation, and that on the left. In this process, we can see the fundamental identification between the human subject and the group.[8]

In *Group Psychology and the Analysis of the Ego*, Freud sees an identification of this type in the totem. He perceives that the phenomenon of totemism represents not a mystical descent into the animal world, but rather symbolic structuration of the biological givens of the self. The concept of the "unary trait" is, in a manner of speaking, an abstracted totem: a term extracted by Lacan from Freud's text and set up as a concept in its own right. Freud argues that when the relation between the individual and the group is forged, the symbolic identification that stands prior to all else is mediated by "a single trait".[9] Now, in saying "a single trait", Freud does not mean the same particular thing in all cases, a universal "single trait" marked by some decisive characteristic. The "single trait" could be anything, or even almost nothing, like "coughing", for example – he gives the example of a daughter who identified with her father by adopting his cough. All that is required is *some* single trait. What is important is not the various shapes assumed by the trait, but the mathematical essence of its "oneness".

I would like to draw the reader's attention to a point common to Freud's deliberations on the totem and the ideas of Adachi introduced earlier – that what stone, moon, and "I" share is precisely the fact that each is "one". Absolutely any sensory characteristic whatsoever might be the vehicle for this abstract trait. For instance, "one" dark smudge on the face of the moon might be like "one" mark on a pebble I once picked up as a child, and both might resemble "one" mole on my face. It is worth noting here that Lacan says that this "single trait" Freud speaks of represents the "most primary manifestation of number",[10] thereby tying it clearly to the mathematical "one".

It is thus the unary trait that mediates the identification of the subject with the group, serving as an "empty place" prepared within the field of the big Other for the incorporation of the subject. The first line is marked on a blank page, and the subject begins to stir on that line. It is a line with no real substance – a border, a breach, or a moment of cut-off like the punctuation of the session. No Japanese word could convey the concept of the unary trait more aptly than the word *sen*

---

[8] This paragraph and the two preceding it have been expanded and revised for the English edition.
[9] Freud, *Group Psychology and the Analysis of the Ego*, SE XVIII, 107. See also Section XII, page 134ff.
[10] S XVII, 184: "[L]a manifestation plus primaire du nombre."

Chapter 6: ALL ALONE IN PARIS

('line').[11]

In the unary trait, the subject encounters the truth of its own identity. The object might be the voice, the gaze, the breast, or the feces; but whatever it is, in it the subject recognizes and encounters *itself*, as something of the same order as the thing encountered. The unary trait is the place where this contact with the self is made, and is thus identical with the *point de capiton* ('quilting point' or 'anchoring point'), the point, in Lacan's conceptualization, where the endless metonymic slippage of signifiers is pinned down to a stable meaning.[12]

Even if the self is nothing more than the *objet a*, or some similar entity, the subject is still sure to love it in the moment of encounter, for it is only in that moment that individual and universal can be linked– and if the subject (the individual) cannot place itself in the universal, it cannot be loved. The catch is that while the subject does see itself as loveable when it enters into the unary trait, it surely lacks the full dignity that we attribute to the individual in imagination. Indeed, it takes on an air of the ludicrous, because the unary trait is another of the moments when the self-referential impotence of the big Other as a logical system is bared to the light.

Let us see, then, what sort of thing Lacan meant by the term "unary trait". He took his example from Ella Sharpe's *Dream Analysis*.[13] Sharpe was an outstanding analyst of the Kleinian school, and wrote this book in 1937. We will begin by taking a brief look at her case study.

"Oh, it's a dog."
The patient had lost his father at an early age. The father had died while under the care of the patient's mother, and ironically enough, this had given the patient this unconscious idea: "If I were to let a woman be with me and take care of me, I would die just like Father." The patient had gained admission to the bar and achieved intellectual success, but found life painful. He ended up entering treatment with Sharpe, a woman analyst. One day, when the analysis was entering a difficult, stagnant phase, he started talking about a "little cough" of his in the course of free association. He said that he coughed even when there was no need to, and that it annoyed him.[14] Further free association led from the idea of "clearing the throat" to the following fantasy.

---

[11] Recall "the line of the one", the line that represents "one" on the page.

[12] A *point de capiton* is an upholstery button, which holds the upholstery to the underlying frame. Lacan uses it to refer to points where "signified and signifier are knotted together." Lacan, *The Seminar, Book III: The Psychoses, 1955-56*, trans. with notes by Russell Grigg (London: Routledge, 1993), 268-9.

[13] Ella Freeman Sharpe, *Dream Analysis*, introd. by Masud R. Khan (New York: Brunner/Mazel, 1978). The case study discussed here is presented in Chapter V, 125-148. Lacan discusses Sharpe's case at S VIII, 457-458.

"...a phantasy I had of being in a room where I ought not to be, and thinking ... to prevent anyone from coming in and finding me there I would bark like a dog. That would disguise my presence. The 'someone' would then say 'Oh, it's only a dog in there.'"[15]

Clearly, for the patient, the "little cough" represented the bark of the dog. When he cleared his throat, he was in fantasy woofing, and whoever was "there" just said, "Oh, it's a dog," and went off. By this means he could be "there". Where was "there"? The room of the woman analyst. He was *under the care of a woman*, just as his father had been when he died. He was thus where he should not be – the place of his father's death, at his mother's knee – but he was there *as a dog*. From the voice of the other saying "It's a dog," therefore, he gained permission to be a man like his father, though of course, he had to turn into a dog to get it. This man-dog is a hybrid created by his identification with his dead father. (And what was it like, being a dog at the knee of the woman analyst? Perhaps we had best return to Chapter I, and ask André Breton. Recall that Nadja imagined she had been one of Marie Antoinette's ladies-in-waiting, and Breton passed his days with her cowering "like a lapdog" at her feet.[16])

The voice that says "It's a dog" seems to come from the other. But when the patient imagines hearing this voice, his mind has already *become* other. Transformed into the master of this other voice, he then hears the barking of yet "an-other" self – this one turned into a dog. The patient is present on both sides of the fantasy, as seeing Other and as the self it sees. On the one hand, the fantasized voice of the other opens a passageway of identification that leads to being other, and it is here that we find the unary trait in Sharpe's example. On the other hand, the patient loses the power of human speech, and just *becomes* the dog, pure and simple. Here we see the *objet a* in one of its myriad guises.

To describe this process another way: the patient hides himself inside the "woof" of the dog, and then tries earnestly to make the language of the Other welcome, "at home" within him. The dog's bark (the hiding-place) takes on the concrete disguise of his cough, and we can thus posit that in this case, the unary trait corresponds to the part of the patient's body-space that reaches from the ear to the throat. In like fashion, all of us reserve a space somewhere in our bodies for the purposes of contact with the big Other.

By the time Sharpe's patient told her of this fantasy, the analysis was clearly showing signs of coming to an end. Sharpe tells us little of its subsequent progress. Since the patient already had a profession, it seems unlikely that he became an

---

[14] Sharpe, 131.
[15] Sharpe, 132.
[16] Chapter I, page 8. *Nadja*, 108.

analyst even if the analysis did at last come to a conclusion.   Perhaps, instead, he was able to consolidate his achievements in his existing career, thanks to the facilitation the analysis provided for identification with his dead father (also a lawyer).

Lacan's use of Sharpe's clinical example gives us a concrete idea of the unary trait – here the voice of the other saying "Oh, it's a dog" – and the role it plays in identification.   As we see here, the unary trait, whatever its arbitrary concrete form, is the line that links self and alterity, the hidden passage that leads from within to the world of the other without.   It is across the bridge of this unary trait that Sharpe's patient finds his way to seeing himself objectively, so that like Magritte's man he can see himself "from the back".   We will now look at another concrete example, and this time the unary trait is Lacan himself, as his career takes yet another turbulent turn.

Two: The Ecole Freudienne de Paris

Schism – 1963

On June 21 1964, Lacan, "alone as [he had] always been,"[17] announced the founding of a new psychoanalytic group in Paris.[18]   With this declaration, Lacan transformed into the unary trait, as it is encountered by anyone who undergoes analysis.   Recall, from the start of this chapter, that the analyst provides the patient with the unary trait in the form of an empty place [kū] within the discourse of the Other, the scission that the subject must ultimately run up against in the Symbolic.   This is what Lacan became in 1964, and we might even say that it was only at this point that Lacan truly manifested himself as analyst.   For only now was Lacan forced to become an analyst completely after his own lights,[19] and only now did he form the resolve to do so. This situation was precipitated by events of the previous year, when the International Psychoanalytical Association (IPA) stripped him of the authority to train analysts.[20]

Let us examine the events that led up to this moment.   Ten years had passed since the schism of 1953.   We must take things up where we left off at the end of Chapter II.[21]

---

[17] Jacques Lacan, "Founding Act", in *Television: A Challenge to the Psychoanalytic Establishment*, trans. J. Mehlman (New York: Norton, 1990), 97.   See "Acte de Fondation", in Jacques Lacan, *Autres écrits*, ed. Jacques-Alain Miller (Paris: Seuil, 2001), 229-241.
[18] Roudinesco, 417-418.
[19] Cf. Lacan's formula, "The authorization of an analyst can come only from himself," Chapter VIII.
[20] Roudinesco, 350-351.
[21] The events of that decade are the subject of Roudinesco, Chapter 7, "Life and Death of the Société Française de Psychanalyse".

Chapter 6: ALL ALONE IN PARIS

In 1953, Lacan, Lagache and their colleagues parted ways with Marie Bonaparte's Société Psychanalytique de Paris (SPP) and began activity as the Société Française de Psychanalyse (SFP).[22] Lacan's intellectual production also reached one of its peaks. But the problem of how to win official approval from the IPA proved a tough one, and stuck like a thorn in the side of the SFP. While the IPA did eventually issue a reply to the SFP's request for official status, it took them until 1961 to do so – a full eight years. In the meantime, Melanie Klein, the only theorist within the IPA that Lacan took seriously, had passed away in 1960.

After all its deliberations, the IPA's answer was "No." The SFP would not be affiliated to the IPA as a member society. But a list of nineteen recommendations was appended to the refusal.[23] The SFP had to fulfill the conditions laid out in these recommendations to be re-admitted to the good graces of the IPA. Naturally, the recommendations stipulated the length of the analytic hour and the number of sessions per week.

So the SFP had lost one round, but it still had a fighting chance. Negotiations were resumed behind the scenes, with the IPA handling things very adroitly. They began to demand that three individuals, Lacan among them, be permanently struck from the SFP register of training analysts.[24] The SFP might conceivably be admitted to the IPA, but only on the condition that its members relinquish training analysis under Lacan. Now, the IPA was not demanding that Lacan be expelled from the SFP *per se*. But it was clear that the IPA was effectively recommending the equivalent of expulsion, and Lacan was ultimately to roundly and publicly call the procedure "major excommunication".[25] As the IPA saw things, however, nobody had expelled Lacan. He had withdrawn from the SFP of his own accord.

The SFP was in a real bind. Its President, Serge Leclaire, who had been very close to Lacan, worked especially hard on creating strategies to cope with the IPA demands, in an effort to retain the possibility of reinstating Lacan.[26] But in November of 1963, the SFP finally decided to officially acquiesce to the IPA demands, and never again recognize Lacan as a training analyst.[27] From that point on, so far as the SFP was concerned, a training administered by Lacan did not count as training at all.

The rift between Lacan and Lagache also grew decisive, and Lagache remained with the newly kosher SFP, as one of its leaders.[28] By this point, Marie Bonaparte was no longer in the IPA – she had died the previous year – and with her passing, and that of Klein, psychoanalysis began to enter a new era, with its leadership in the

---

[22] Roudinesco, 248-268.
[23] Roudinesco, 329.
[24] The other two were Françoise Dolto and André Berge. Roudinesco, 341.
[25] See S XI, 3, and Chapter 1, "Excommunication" generally.
[26] Roudinesco, 323-329, 335-340.
[27] Roudinesco, 358.
[28] Roudinesco, 359.

Chapter 6: ALL ALONE IN PARIS

hands of a new generation. The freshly recognized SFP reformed itself around a ready-made executive, which had been kept groomed and waiting in the wings, and was reborn as a new group, the APF (Association Psychanalytique de France).[29] Meanwhile, The SFP for all intents and purposes winked out of existence.

For a time, Lacan was left neither here nor there. No new group emerged immediately, as had happened in 1953. It was to be more than six months before Lacan, "alone", founded his new psychoanalytic group the following year. In the interim, many individuals, at a loss what course to take, chose their direction as each thought best. Among those who decided to stick with Lacan were Leclaire, Françoise Dolto (who had shown great promise as an analyst of children and was another of the three originally pilloried by the IPA), and Octave and Maud Mannoni (a couple who had been a driving force behind the development of the anti-psychiatric movement in France). Among those who chose instead to follow Lagache was Jean Laplanche,[30] who was to author the psychoanalytic dictionary *The Language of Psychoanalysis*.[31]

A fresh departure: 1964 and *The Four Fundamental Concepts of Psychoanalysis*

On January 15 1964, ten years after its inception, Lacan's seminar, moved to a new location, the Salle Dussane of the École Normale Supérieure (one of the France's most elite academic institutions).[32] Lacan was able to use this auditorium thanks to the efforts of Louis Althusser and Claude Lévi-Strauss,[33] who obtained for him the status of lecturer of the École pratique des Hautes Études. Ironically enough, Lacan's defeat within the SFP had worked to thrust his psychoanalytic theory into the much broader forum of general intellectual debate.

Incidentally, among the audience for the inaugural session of the relocated seminar was a friend of Lacan's, Claude Levi-Strauss, the famed father of structural anthropology. This was the only time Levi-Strauss ever attended Lacan's seminar, and he reportedly confessed that he had not understood what Lacan said. He went on, however, to say that he had seen in Lacan that day the shadow of the shamans he

---

[29] Roudinesco, 368.
[30] Roudinesco, 357.
[31] Jean Laplanche & Jean-Bertrand Pontalis, *The Language of Psychoanalysis* (New York: Norton, 1974).
[32] Roudinesco, 361.
[33] Roudinesco 361, "Without mentioning Althusser, to whom he owed this new connection [access to the ENS] . . ." Roudinesco further describes the background to the assistance Althusser provided Lacan at 378. As for Lévi-Strauss, Lacan pays tribute to the role he played in the text of the seminar given on this occasion: "M. Braudel extended this welcome to me as soon as he had been alerted by the vigilance of my friend Claude Levi-Strauss, whom I am delighted to see here today and who knows how precious for me this evidence of his interest in my work is - in work that has developed in parallel with his own." S XI, 2.

Chapter 6: ALL ALONE IN PARIS

had encountered in the course of his long and prolific anthropological research.[34] Lacan was thus not much of an influence on Levi-Strauss, then; but Levi-Strauss was a seminal reference point for Lacan. Lacan, as we recall from Chapter IV, had clearly stated that for him psychoanalysis was a creationist and not an evolutionist theory, and the particular creationism he had in mind was none other than the modern structuralism epitomized by Levi-Strauss.

1964 was thus a memorable year, with the re-opening of the seminar in a new location (where it was to continue for five years) and the founding of a new school. The seminar of this year, Seminar XI, was published in 1973 as *The Four Fundamental Concepts of Psychoanalysis*,[35] and was the first of all Lacan's seminars to appear in print.

When the seminar found a new home at the École Normale Supérieure, the event carried with it not only symbolic significance, but also a number of practical consequences. With the dissolution of the SFP, Lacan had lost a number of old colleagues and friends, but at the same time he gained himself a large audience of young people willing to hear psychoanalytic theory as more than a practical matter of applied medicine and psychology – as, rather, a system of thought with claims to universality. Caught up in the 1960s rebellion against the system, this young audience was in need of a new philosophy, and they readily embraced psychoanalysis as one answer to their needs. In his new seminar venue, Lacan was able to address them directly. It is worth noting, however, that Lacan characteristically made a great effort, even in the midst of the era and its changes, to speak strictly from within psychoanalytic experience.

As this lucky set of circumstances propagated Lacan's thought more and more widely, Althusser played an important role that was not restricted to merely giving the seminar a new home and securing Lacan his lectureship.[36] At the time, Althusser was teaching at the École himself, and in addition to taking up the interpretation of Lacan's work, he led students to Lacan. Among these students was one who would later play a key role in Lacan's psychoanalytic movement, Jacques-Alain Miller.[37] Miller, at the time 19 years old, first read Lacan in 1963 on Althusser's recommendation. He read the "Rome Discourse", and, sensing that this was something truly new,[38] began attending Lacan's seminar. The publication of Book 11 of the Seminar was his work. Thanks to Miller and other young people who, like him, received their psychoanalytic baptism at Lacan's hands, Lacan's thought was to

---

[34] Roudinesco, 362.
[35] *Le Séminaire de Jacques Lacan, Livre XI, 'Les quatre concepts fondamentaux de la psychanalyse'*, (Paris: Éditions de Seuil, 1973).
[36] For Althusser's role in the growth of interest in Lacan outside the psychoanalytic movement proper, see Roudinesco, 376-384.
[37] Miller was to be Lacan's literary executor and anointed heir, and today is the leader of the world-wide Lacanian movement. See Chapter VIII.
[38] Roudinesco, 379.

go beyond being simply a school of psychoanalytic theory among others, and eventually be recognized as what Roudinesco calls a "totality" complete with "its own internal logic".[39]

We can see, then, just how significant 1964 was in Lacan's career. If we divide Lacan's work into an early period leading up to the 1953 "Rome Discourse", and a middle period ushered in by it, then we are justified in saying that in 1964 we enter the late period, with the seminar on the *Four Fundamental Concepts* and the birth of the new psychoanalytic group.   That new group was briefly known as the École française de Psychanalyse, before changing its name to the renowned École freudienne de Paris (EFP).[40]

The seminar of this year, *The Four Fundamental Concepts of Psychoanalysis*, reflects the unprecedented heights attained by Lacan's intellectual production in this tumultuous period, and the feverish excitement of his new setting. It is unparalleled for the way it radically examines the fundamental problems of psychoanalysis, from the ground up. It is especially remarkable for the stark light in which it bathes the suffering of the human subject, torn between the fact of its thinking and the fact of its being, and striving after some essence that will bring the two together in one identity. We also find in this seminar the first hints of the unique Lacanian "topology" of the analytic human relation.   Both as the point of departure for Lacan's late thought, and as a point of entry to Lacan's ideas as a whole, it is without compare.   I have already treated the central part of this seminar at length in my work *The Psychopathology of the Unconscious*.[41] In the remainder of this book, we will trace the problematic of one of the "four fundamentals" Lacan treats in this seminar: the transference, which was to grow increasingly in importance in coming years.

The whole internal experience of psychoanalysis crystallizes undiluted in that single word, "transference".   How did this internal experience function, within the new psychoanalytic organization Lacan founded on his own authority?   Again, given that analysts do form analytic groups, the reasons that the group exists must be somehow related to this particular internal analytic experience.   We would consequently expect that the transference, on the one hand, and the principles underlying the formation of the group, on the other, be inextricably linked.   Lacan had refused to define the qualification of analysts in terms of a regular training program, like the IPA, and now the task of theorizing this internal dynamic linking the transference and the formation of the group, and the problem of how to qualify

---

[39] Roudinesco, 379.   "For this young student [Miller], soon to occupy a crucial position in the history of psychoanalysis, Lacan's work no longer needed to be read with reference to Freud. It was constructed as a totality and, as such, possessed its own history and its own internal logic."
[40] Roudinesco, 369, 428.
[41] Kazushige Shingu, *Muishiki no byōrigaku* [*The Psychopathology of the Unconscious*] (Tokyo: Kongō Press, 1989).

Chapter 6: ALL ALONE IN PARIS

analysts on the basis of that theorization, weighed down heavily on his shoulders. We will see how he tackled these problems in our final chapters.

CHAPTER SEVEN

WAITING FOR THE *AGALMA*

One: The Object of Psychoanalysis

The psychoanalytic apparatus
In this chapter, we will look at the transference, and the way Lacan theorized it through a particular form of the *objet a,* which he called the *agalma.* We will begin by looking back briefly at what we have learnt about the unary trait.

As we have seen, at the same time that "I" is a ("one") person, I tries to identify with the "one" set of humanity as a whole. As a result, I becomes an irrational number, the *objet a*, and is expelled from the rational world. This *objet a* always leaves us with the feeling that it does not fit smoothly into the terms of human experience (just as an irrational number will not divide evenly into a rational number).[1] However, this object is no less than the human subject itself, as seen from the perspective of the universal, and it is therefore impossible to cut all ties with it, or to distance oneself from it. Indeed, we find that human desire *is* the desire to seek out this view of the self, no matter what it takes – the desire to get some distance from the individual human and perceive oneself with the eyes of the universal.

Psychoanalysis is an attempt to meet this desire. Since the dawn of the modern, humankind has mastered a set of methods (science) by which we measure all things against the standard of ourselves, that is, by the power of our senses. For this very reason, however, we have lost the yardstick by which we might measure ourselves. The age of science, dominated as it is by this Protagorean world-view (in which man is the measure of all things), is haunted by this mode of anxiety. According to Lacan, psychoanalysis exists for the sake of the subject of science.[2] Any subject that does

---

[1] The word used in Japanese here for "will not divide evenly into (a number)" and "does not fit perfectly into (normal life)", *warikirenai*, also means, by one of those equivocations so opportune to psychoanalysis, "cannot remain emotionally detached". – Trans.

[2] For example, in "La science et la vérité" (not included in *Selection*), Lacan states that it is necessary to recognize that psychoanalysis is exercised upon the subject of science (*Écrits*, 855). However, when the human subject takes herself as the measure in apprehending nature, that measure is often taken for something given to the senses, or indeed for perception itself, but in fact, the act of counting is something that transcends human perception, and as such that which first makes science possible. As we saw in Chapter Six, the subject of science is already constituted in this act (see S XVII, 184). The false sense of agency granted by perception leads the human subject to forget the self-erasure that

science must inevitably also do psychoanalysis. At a certain point in the history of science, then, the human subject thus conceived of an apparatus known as psychoanalysis in order that it might find itself, in the form of the *objet a*.

The *agalma*

In psychoanalysis, in fact, we get the feeling that the *objet a* exists within the person of the analyst, and with this as the only clue to guide him, pursues his train of free association. What, then, of the analyst's relation to the *objet a*? Within who or what, then, does she sense that the *objet a* exists?

The answer is, in a sense, simple. The analyst recognizes the *objet a* in *everything* in the world – in all the gaps and cracks that the world is riven by. An analyst, in fact, is a subject who is *always* in contact with the *objet a*. Of course, a broad generalization like this one carries a certain risk, but for the time being, at least, let us hold to it. All analysts have been in touch with the *objet a* ever since their own analysis, and even when they start giving analysis to others, they must maintain this contact with it. Freud thought that analysts should receive a refresher analysis every few years even after entering practice,[3] holding that it is mere illusion to believe that one can become an analyst once and for all. For Lacan, this problem of staying fresh as an analyst was one of maintaining the internal relation with the *objet a*, and his formalization of the qualifying process for analysts, which we will examine in the next chapter, is a direct result of this conception. Lacan liked to refer to this *objet a* as the *agalma*.

The *agalma*, as we shall see, is something that appears to the person undergoing analysis (the analysand), but it is also something with which the *analyst* must maintain contact. And, of course, it goes without saying that Freud as much as anyone staged an ongoing encounter with it throughout his life. We will now set out to make sense of this key Lacanian notion, first examining the *agalma* as Lacan speaks of it, and then looking at the equivalent as it manifested itself in Freud's experience.

Two: Socrates

Plato's *Symposium*

Not long before the dissolution of the SFP and the establishment of the EFP, Lacan had the opportunity to elaborate his concept of the transference in the seminar of 1960-61

---

originates in the act of counting, and thus misplace the rule by which to measure herself.
[3] SE XXIII, 249. "Every analyst should periodically – at intervals of five years or so – submit himself to analysis once more, without feeling ashamed of taking this step."

Chapter 7: WAITING FOR THE *AGALMA*

(*The Transference*).[4] The results of his work were put to use in designing the qualification system within the EFP. As the prototype of the transference, Lacan took up a relation between two men found in Plato's *The Symposium*,[5] – in other words, an instance of the homosexual love customary among the Greeks at the time. One of the men is Socrates, and the other is called Alcibiades. Socrates needs no introduction; Alcibiades was a man renowned for his prodigious political talent and his rugged, warlike beauty. When Socrates was eventually brought to trial for capital crimes against the Athenian state, one of the charges leveled against him was that he had corrupted the minds of Alcibiades and other youth of promise and accomplishment.

According to Plato's account, Socrates once fell in love with the beautiful Alcibiades, and Alcibiades for his part hoped to gain wisdom from Socrates. The two began a romantic involvement, and ultimately spent one night together, although all that happened between them was that they literally slept together. Alcibiades was subsequently gripped by a powerful desire to monopolize Socrates, however, and it seemed quite possible that he might lash out at a potential rival, were Socrates to show an interest in anyone else.

At that time, a brilliant poet called Agathon had won first prize in a contest for a play, and Socrates, Aristophanes and other friends gathered at Agathon's house for a great banquet. This banquet is the setting of *The Symposium*. The entertainment for the banquet is as intellectual as we might expect for such brilliant company: it is decided that the guests will discourse in praise of Eros, god of love, in order as they are seated. Among the contributions to the game we also find Aristophanes's famous myth of Androgynous (in which mankind was originally a species in which each individual comprised two people in one body).

Just as Socrates, who speaks last, finishes his discourse, Alcibiades shows up roaring drunk. He first harasses Socrates, and then turns to address the whole company. He complains in dilatory fashion that in the course of their entanglement Socrates has scorned and scoffed at his youthful beauty, which all (including himself) acknowledge, and that he has suffered "pangs worse than the bite of any viper".

At the same time, however, Alcibiades praises Socrates in a half-mocking manner. Leaving aside for the moment his praise for Socrates's valor on the battlefield, the way he praises Socrates as an exponent of discourse is most peculiar, and drew Lacan's attention. Alcibiades's tribute to Socrates, following so close on the heels of the guests' eulogies to Eros, derives a special effect from the fact that the object of praise

---

[4] *Le Séminaire, Livre VIII, Le transfert, 1960-61* ed. Jacques-Alain Miller (Paris: Le Seuil, 1991). Untranslated.

[5] *The Dialogues of Plato*, tr. into English, with analyses and introductions, by B. Jowett (Oxford: Clarendon Press, 1871). I have referred to the Jowett translation in what follows and am indebted to it for wording in a number of places. For a more recent translation, see Plato, *The Symposium*, trans. Christopher Gill (New York: Penguin, 1999). – Trans.

suddenly shifts from a god to a concrete person.

In Greece at the time, there was a kind of reliquary or shrine commonly used as a repository for images of the gods, like the *kamidana* that houses gods in Japanese homes. These objects were crafted in all sorts of weird and wonderful ways, particularly their exterior; carved in the shape of a satyr playing the flute, for instance. Alcibiades proceeds to make an elaborate comparison between such a shrine in the form of a satyr and Socrates. Socrates is nothing much to look at, just like a satyr, which is human from the waist up and beast from the waist down. But that doesn't deter old Socrates – oh no! He is smitten as soon as he sees anyone fair (just like the licentious satyr) – and then, moreover, he appears to "know nothing and [be] ignorant of all things"! And when Socrates begins to talk, all listeners feel their hearts leap within them and their eyes "rain tears", just as when the satyr plays his flute. Socrates is thus exactly like the *"kamidana"* shaped like a satyr – and there is more to the analogy than this. Alcibiades feels that he is the only person who has seen the sacred secret housed inside Socrates's shrine: those divine golden images that reside within, and that account for the strange compelling power of his words. These images are fitting objects for the quest of those noble-willed individuals who desire to become the ideal person.

Plato's account of Alcibiades's words fits perfectly with the work of Melanie Klein. The object in question is the ideal "good object", and at the same time is also the "bad object", which refuses identification and issues peremptory, unreasonable commands. While Klein writes that this "primal object" is hidden within the "mother", Plato writes that it is enshrined within the speaking Socrates. This object, with its glittering allure, is what the Greeks called *agalma*, and it was a great help to Lacan in conceptualizing the *objet a*. Situated within the discourse of the big Other, it is what pulls the strings in Alcibiades's bizarre attachment to Socrates, and the *agalma* is thus a constant that governs an attachment in ancient Greece just as much as the transference in modern psychoanalysis.

How, then, does Socrates respond to Alcibiades's allegations? Let us return once more to the *The Symposium,* where we left off.

Alcibiades's dream

Recall that Alcibiades has burst in on the scene of a banquet at Agathon's home, and of course, it was Agathon he was originally after. The first thing he did was sit himself down next to Agathon, and it was only then that he noticed that Socrates was also there, sitting on the other side of him. When he sat down, Alcibiades had "come between" Agathon and Socrates, separating them as if that was exactly his intention all along. When his turn comes to speak, Socrates picks up on this to tell Alcibiades that Alcibiades has only feigned his obsessive love for Socrates, and that his real aim in doing so is to alienate Agathon from Socrates and free Agathon for his own advances. He has inadvertently revealed that Agathon is in fact the real object of his

Chapter 7: Waiting for the *Agalma*

affections.

Socrates thus brings Alcibiades's desire out into the open. In fact, we can understand quite readily why someone in Alcibiades's position would take Agathon for the object of his affections. Alcibiades is a politician and a soldier – a commander and ruler in worldly domains. If people like him are lacking in anything, it is art. Agathon, on the other hand, is a great poet, and this talent is what attracts Alcibiades to him. The same psychology lies behind institutions like medals and honors for culture: rulers feel a need to demonstrate that their power extends over the arts as much as any other realm. This explains the fact that the first thing Alcibiades does on arriving at Agathon's house is to festoon Agathon's head with ribbons. When he notices that Socrates is also present, he then takes some of these ribbons from Agathon's head and uses them to garland Socrates. These ribbons, which can be confusing to the reader, are obviously something like what we might call a "private honor" bestowed by Alcibiades, and it is quite possible that Plato is indulging in parody here.

When Socrates points out what Alcibiades is up to, Agathon leaves Alcibiades's side and moves to sit next to Socrates instead. This change in the seating arrangements gives Socrates the right to sing Agathon's praises. The entertainment, we recall, was making speeches in homage to Eros in turn; but Alcibiades has instead praised Socrates, who is to his right. Socrates proclaims that this should inaugurate a new game, whereby each person in turn praises the person to his right, and he immediately sets out to continue the game by praising Agathon.

Alcibiades is now cut off from Agathon by Socrates – a poor contrast for him to his luck when he originally sat between Socrates and Agathon – and he bemoans his fate, complaining that Socrates always keeps him from "the fair". But in fact, Alcibiades's deep-rooted desire is realized all the more palpably here, and the reason we must think so is extremely psychoanalytic. What does Agathon represent for Alcibiades? Agathon is a poet, that which Alcibiades could never have been no matter how much he wanted to, and for that precise reason he is the object of Alcibiades's desire. Agathon thus represents Alcibiades as he ought to be, embodied in exquisite form.

How, then, can Alcibiades apostrophize this object, clad as it is in such lovely garb? We have just said that he is no poet. The object will be far more tangibly and tellingly praised if Socrates praises it for Alcibiades, than if Alcibiades praises it himself. After all, when Socrates speaks he bears the *agalma* within him, and if Alcibiades hears Socrates praise Agathon, he can be sure that Agathon will be revealed for the glittering golden image of the god itself. For his part, Alcibiades will then identify with the god, and feel himself realized as the self he ought to have been. Although we do not find a description of him doing so in *The Symposium,* it is easy to imagine Alcibiades drifting into a pleasant reverie as he listens to Socrates praise Agathon, just as if it were he himself being praised.

In the skein of words he weaves, then, Socrates gives shape and form to the

Chapter 7: WAITING FOR THE *AGALMA*

original object of Alcibiades's desire. This object is the self that is no more – the self that has already and irrevocably become something other than itself – and the scenario could almost be called "Alcibiades's dream". The words of Socrates are, for Alcibiades, indeed "the discourse of the Other", and when we fall asleep, we bring the discourse of the Other into the foreground inside our heads. We then seek out the original object of desire, in the form of the object of that discourse. This object is what the discourse of the dream is *about*, and it is the self, a self that is no longer; it is the *agalma*, and it is the *objet a*. When we enter into the psychoanalytic discourse, we are enfolded by this dream, as we imagined Alcibiades to be, and there the *objet a* assails us.

We will now move from drawing Alcibiades's implied dream out of Socrates's discourse, to the realm of a real dream. The dreamer, this time, is Sigmund Freud.

Three: Irma

The Freud-Fliess exchange

The dream we will examine is generally known as "the Dream of Irma's Injection". The exceptionally exact date Freud gives for this dream (24 July 1895)[6] shows that Freud attributed special importance to it, and in fact, it is used as the demonstration *par excellence* of the basic principles of *The Interpretation of Dreams,* the seminal work whose publication in 1900 laid the foundations of psychoanalysis.

A vital part of the background to the dream was formed by Freud's correspondence with Wilhelm Fliess. Fliess was two years younger than Freud, and like Freud, was a Jew and a medical practitioner.[7] At the time when he came to know Fliess, Freud was rapidly losing trusted friends and all other places of refuge, and sensed painfully that he had nowhere left to turn.[8] In the midst of these trials, Fliess became the object of Freud's transference. Freud felt that Fliess was the only person who truly understood him, so much so that he comforted himself with the thought of Fliess's approval whenever he felt he was just a voice crying in the wilderness.[9] "I can write nothing if I have no public at all," he wrote to Fliess in a letter of May 18 1898, "but I am perfectly content to write only for you." Ernest Jones suggests in his biography of Freud that Freud's exaggerated sense of his isolation, and the pain it caused him, can be sensed in the disproportionate esteem he formed for his sole interlocutor and

---

[6] *The Interpretation of Dreams,* SE IV, 107.
[7] Ernest Jones, *Sigmund Freud, Life and Work. Volume One, The Young Freud 1856-1900* (London: The Hogarth Press, 1980), 318, 321.
[8] Jones, 325, 328, 330, 331.
[9] Freud, writing of Fliess, calls him "a person whose agreement I recalled with satisfaction whenever I felt isolated in my opinions." *Interpretation,* SE IV, 117.

Chapter 7: WAITING FOR THE *AGALMA*

intellectual soulmate. In another letter of 1897, for instance, Freud wrote that Fliess's words "aroused . . . astonishment" in him, and went so far as to say that they seemed to arrive from the other "end of the world" – from "the stars".[10] This sort of dependence might seem unbecoming for a figure like Freud, and indeed, in his biography of Freud, Ernest Jones writes that this was "the only really extraordinary experience in Freud's life," hinting that by this he means "extraordinary" in a "psychological" sense.[11] Jones explains that throughout this "extraordinary" phase, Freud was "following a path hitherto untrodden by any human being,"[12] face-to-face with the unknown in the form of the unconscious.

Fliess was an ear, nose and throat specialist.[13] He had developed a theory of a syndrome that included headaches, stomachache, cardialgia, and a wide range of other organ dysfunctions, which he called the "nasal reflex neurosis".[14] According to his theory, all of these disparate symptoms originated in disorders of the nasal nervous system. Fliess's speculation had gone further, however, far exceeding the confines of his specialty to encompass the phenomenon of life itself. He held that all living phenomena were governed by periodic cycles of the numbers twenty-three and twenty-eight. Twenty-three was linked to the masculine element, and twenty-eight to the feminine, with all humans containing elements of both sexes.[15] Fliess thought that the subject's fate was decided by these two cycles, and Freud threw himself completely into the eccentric orbit of Fliess's thought.

At the time, Freud had quit his research post at the university, and had set himself up in private practice, where he attempted to treat neurosis by his own powers. One of the patients in his care was a young woman named "Irma",[16] whose condition was proving very difficult to treat. Freud finally began to suspect that her illness was not hysteria, as he had believed, but of organic origin. Surely, then, the best thing to do would be to have Fliess take a look at her; Fliess, after all, was the discoverer of a nasal condition whose symptoms were very close to those of hysteria – the nasal reflex neurosis. Getting Fliess's opinion was the conscientious thing to do under the

---

[10] Jones, 332-333. Fliess was working on the connection between cosmic rhythms and biorhythm.

[11] Jones, 316. Jones also says, "There is ample evidence that for ten years or so – roughly comprising the nineties – he suffered from a very considerable psychoneurosis" (334). Jones describes this neurosis at 334-339.

[12] Jones, 316.

[13] Jones, 318.

[14] Jones, 319.

[15] Jones, 319.

[16] "Irma" was the name given to this patient in Freud's writings to protect her identity. Her real name was Anna von Hammerschlag. According to Jeffrey Masson, the patient referred to Fliess for surgery was in fact a different person, Emma Eckstein (Jeffrey Masson, *The Assault on Truth* [London: Penguin, 1985], 213). In the dream, however, the persons of the two patients are conflated by condensation into the single dream figure of "Irma". – Trans.

Chapter 7: WAITING FOR THE *AGALMA*

circumstances, and Freud thus referred his patient Irma to the nose surgeon for whom he had such inordinate respect.

Fliess examined Irma and judged that surgery ought to produce an improvement in her condition. The outcome of the surgery, however, was horribly cruel. Fliess accidentally left a substantial length of gauze inside Irma's nose, and this led to a suppurating infection, ultimately requiring a second operation. Freud was also present at this second operation, and at the sight of the massive hemorrhaging that occurred when the gauze was removed he was overcome by an obscure but powerful emotion, and felt physically sick.[17]

This ill-fated treatment took place in the early part of 1895, and in summer of the same year, Freud's friend Otto had the opportunity to visit Irma. Otto reported Irma's improved condition to Freud, but Freud, far from being happy at the news, took it as harbouring a veiled reproach to himself.[18] That very night, Freud had the dream of Irma's injection. Let us move on to look at the content of the dream itself.

At the back of Irma's throat

The scene of the dream is a party at Freud's house, and Irma is among the guests.[19] Freud says to Irma, "If you still get pains, it's really only your fault." Irma replies, "If only you knew what pains I've got now in my throat and stomach and abdomen – it's choking me." At this, Freud is alarmed, and looks with renewed care at Irma's face. She looks pale. Freud grows worried (just as he had in real life), fearing that her illness is in fact not hysteria after all, but rather some organic trouble that he has missed. He takes her aside, and examines her throat. (Note that this shift of scene corresponds to the fact that Freud referred Irma to Fliess. In the situational transference it is not Freud himself but Fliess, now a denizen of Freud's dream, who is looking down Irma's throat.) In the back of Irma's throat, Freud sees clearly some "extensive whitish gray scabs upon some remarkable structures . . . modeled on the turbinal bones of the nose."

What exactly are these scabs? Even though he is dreaming the whole scene, Freud's professional habits do not desert him, and he calls Dr M, his medical senior and a source of reliable advice over the years. Otto is also there, at Irma's side. Dr M says that the problem is an infection, but that this does not matter – dysentery will supervene and the toxin will be eliminated. It is also known where the infection came from – an injection Otto had given her of "a preparation of propyl". "Propyl" changes into "propyls", "propionic acid", and finally to "trimethylamin", the formula

---

[17] For Fliess's bungled operation on Eckstein, see Peter Gay, *Freud: A Life for Our Time* (New York: Doubleday, 1989), 84. Gay quotes the letter to Fliess of March 8, 1895, from Sigmund Freud, *Briefe an Wilhelm Fliess 1887-1904*, ed. Jeffrey Moussaieff Masson, assisted by Michael Schröter and Gerhard Fichtner (Frankfurt: M. S. Fischer, 1986), 116-117.
[18] *Interpretation*, SE IV, 106.
[19] The dream itself is recorded at *Interpretation*, SE IV, 107.

Chapter 7: Waiting for the *Agalma*

of the latter appearing before Freud's eyes in heavy type before he finally wakes.

According to Freud's self-analysis, this dream is constructed to exculpate himself from suspicion of medical incompetence.[20] Because Irma has a potentially morbid organic malady in her throat, and is not a hysteric, it is not Freud's fault that his psychological treatments do not work on her. Not only that, but there is every reason to expect that the toxin causing her condition will soon be eliminated from Irma's system; and, of course, it was not Freud but Otto who infected her with the toxin in the first place.

As Freud seeks to exonerate himself in the dream, he simultaneously works to vindicate Fliess as well. Given Irma's ailment has an organic focus of infection, Freud was right to send her to Fliess. It is true that Fliess erred in leaving the gauze inside Irma's nose, but according to the dream it will be easily removed ("the toxin will be eliminated"), so there is no real problem.

We see, then, that the dream realizes the self-serving unconscious thought processes that work below the surface. The dream is the fulfillment of an unconscious wish, just as Freud says.[21] But does the unconscious desire Freud points out really amount to "the core of our being",[22] as Freud calls it elsewhere in the same text? Doesn't the wish this dream fulfills hinge too much on a single incident in Freud's professional career to warrant such a weighty name? Let us pursue our analysis of this example dream a little further, beyond the confines of Freud's self-analysis, and attempt to ascertain for ourselves the truth of Freud's claim that dreams realize the "core of our being".

The core of our being

Let us see, first of all, what associations Freud himself derived from the material of this dream. In the dream, Freud gives Irma a physical examination, and despite the fact that she is still clothed, he determines that a portion of the skin on the left shoulder is infiltrated. In the process of self-analysis, Freud immediately recognized that the sensation of this infiltration corresponded to his own rheumatism.[23] The reason he can detect it, even through clothes, is that the body of Irma in the dream is in fact his own body.

Freud is identifying with Irma here. This identification can be verified from another shared element, "having been given something like poison". In the dream, Otto has given Irma the injection of "propyl" and as a result she has become sick; in real life, the same Otto had given Freud a bottle of very oily-smelling liqueur (which

---

[20] *Interpretation,* SE IV, 118-120.
[21] *Interpretation,* SE IV, 121.
[22] *Interpretation,* SE V, 603.
[23] *Interpretation,* SE IV, 113.

Freud had joked might be poisonous!).[24] The identification is clinched by yet another point in common: the fact that, before Irma became Fliess's patient, Freud himself had also been under his care. In fact, Fliess had operated on Freud, and Freud could just as well have been the victim of the sort of suffering inflicted on Irma.

So much for associations Freud brought to the dream when he analyzed it himself. The perspective of time elapsed, however, gives us access to further meanings, meanings Freud could not possibly have been aware of at that time. Note that the dream presents the scene of a medical examination. The "whitish gray scabs" revealed in Irma's throat by the doctor's gaze cannot fail to remind us of Freud's cancer of the palate, which was to appear in his own mouth nearly thirty years later, in 1923. This cancer, which eventually took Freud's life, was to be first detected in a leucoplastic growth on his palate,[25] exactly where the smoke from his cigars hit the roof of his mouth. The thing found in the mouth in the dream thus corresponds to something that was to be found in the mouth in real life, making this dream look almost oracular. What is it about the dream that makes this soothsaying possible?

One factor contributing to this seeming prophecy is Freud's identification with Irma. Another, however, is that Freud, as we noted previously, sees with *Fliess's* eyes when he examines Irma. In the dream, it is of course Freud who is in fact looking down Irma's throat, but nevertheless, what he sees is "a scab on *the turbinal bones of the nose*", for all the world as if he were an otorhinolaryngologist conducting a professional examination. As much he identifies with Irma, Freud is identifying with Fliess. What is the relation between the two identifications?

Recall that Freud had examined Irma, but had not been able to make a diagnosis, and had therefore sent her to Fliess, the doctor who usually examined Freud himself. Fliess's vision seems here to offer a vantage point that can encompass both Freud, the subject (the examiner), and Irma, the object (the examined). Freud wanted to look on (himself in) Irma as he himself was usually looked on by Fliess – Fliess, the initiate into the world's deepest secrets, the one who knew what made it all tick; the same Fliess who "astonished" him with news from "the stars".[26] If we call Freud x, Irma y, and Fliess, as that which encompasses them both (both subject and object) $x + y$, then we once more arrive at the following formula:

$$\frac{y}{x} = \frac{x}{x+y}$$

---

[24] *Interpretation,* SE IV, 115-116.
[25] Ernest Jones, *Sigmund Freud, Life and Work. Volume Three, The Last Phase 1919-1939* (London: The Hogarth Press, 1980), 94.
[26] Jones, *Sigmund Freud, Life and Work,* I, 333.

Chapter 7: WAITING FOR THE *AGALMA*

On the left, we see what Freud should see when he looks at Irma; on the right, we see what happens when Fliess looks at Freud. These two situations must be made identical; they must be *equal*. If they are, then Freud's human essence, as it is looked on by the universal that is Fliess, will be revealed to Freud's gaze as he looks on Irma. And indeed, if we call the value that Freud assumes for Fliess *a*, then once more we arrive at the equation

$$a = \frac{1}{a+1}$$

which, when solved, tells us that in relation to Fliess, Freud is the golden section.

It is thus the golden section that is represented by the "whitish gray scabs" at the back of Irma's throat. *This* is Freud's essence, his true being, and when Freud says that the "core of our being" is to be found in the dream, this is what he means.[27] In 1955, in his *Seminar, Book II*, Lacan suggests that the human subject must suffer a primal wound when it first enters into a relation with the world,[28] and that this and nothing else is that which is most real for the human subject.[29] Lacan says that this is what the whitish gray scabs represent in Freud's dream, and if we superimpose this scab on the leucoplakia that portended Freud's cancer,[30] as above, then we see that Freud's "core of our being" is that which brings us to our death.

Let us also take a closer look at the role the chemical formula plays in the dream. As we saw, "a preparation of propyl" changes first into "propyls", then "propionic acid", and finally to "trimethylamin". This chain of chemical transformations thus leads from the substance Irma was injected with to something Freud was given by Fliess, insofar as Freud, in his associations from the dream, connects trimethylamin with a conversation he had with Fliess.[31] Fliess's error in leaving the gauze inside Irma's nose transforms into Otto's act, in the dream, of injecting Irma with the preparation of propyl, and further back again, links to the idea that it is Fliess who

---

[27] See S II, 155, "You are this."
[28] See S II. "The world" here is what Lacan calls "the inmixing [*immixtion*] of subjects" whereby "the subject enters and mixes with things" (160). In entering into the relation with the world, the subject gains meaning: it embarks on "the quest for the word . . . the quest for signification as such." (160). This gains it meaning, the "You are this" (155), but wounds it (castration, self-referentiality): the "this" that it finds itself to be is "a horrendous discovery . . . the flesh one never sees . . . from which everything exudes . . . the flesh in as much as it is suffering, is formless." (154) Thus "*You are this, which is so far from you, this which is the ultimate formlessness*" (155, italics in original).
[29] See S II. "The primitive object *par excellence* [. . . is] that which is least penetrable in the real . . . the real lacking any possible mediation . . .the ultimate real . . . the essential object which isn't an object any longer." (164).
[30] Jones, *Sigmund Freud*, III, 94.
[31] *Interpretation*, SE IV, 116.

gives important things to Freud. (According to Lacan, "trimethylamin" is a sexual substance, a decomposition product of sperm,[32] which hints at a sexual element in the relation between Freud and Fliess.) As its transformations unfold, then, the chemical terminology follows a movement from associations with Irma to associations with Fliess.

The chemical terminology thus functions as a unary trait, leading from the individual state at Freud to the judgment of the universal situated with Fliess. The subject, Freud, looks at Irma, and Irma is the object. Freud's identification with this object is realized the moment the subject appears, reflected as it appears to the universal, in the object. At this point, an additional identification with that universal also unavoidably comes about, and this second identification is made possible by the unary trait. By identifying with Fliess through the unary trait of the chemical formulae, Freud transforms himself into the universal, beyond the horizon of his world,[33] and from this vantage point he can know himself, as he is identified with Irma.

We see, then, that the chemical formulae in the dream is the vehicle of an identification – a "unary trait" – and that the "whitish gray scabs" are thus the place where we can locate the *objet a*. We will now return to this uncanny object in Irma's mouth, which is nothing other than the agalma for Freud, and explore further the significance we can ascribe to it in the context of Freud's biography.

Four: In the Mouth

The locus of the generation of desire
Freud was an inveterate cigar smoker all his life, and what went on in the mouth held great meaning for him. There is one other place in the *Interpretation of Dreams* where this uncanny object in the mouth shows itself, again in a highly significant form. This time Freud's own son takes the stage, against the background of World War I. Of course, the war began in 1914, and a lot of time had passed since the first edition of the *Interpretation*. Even so, Freud was struck by the significance of this particular dream, and devoted a good deal of space to it in the revised edition.

Freud's son was at the front, and for some time the family had no news of him. Freud grew anxious, and it was then that he had the dream. In the dream, Freud

---

[32] S II, 158. Note that this significance, in general terms, would not have been lost on Freud either: "[Fliess] had at that time confided some ideas to me on the subject of the chemistry of the sexual processes, and had mentioned among other things that he believed that one of the products of sexual metabolism was trimethylamin." *Interpretation*, SE IV, 116.
[33] The original here has "the universal of the *higan*", the "other shore". See Chapter IV, note 25. – Trans.

Chapter 7: Waiting for the *Agalma*

receives notification of some kind of "distinction" from his son's officers' mess.[34] Freud and his wife then go into a kind of storeroom to find something. Suddenly their son appears. He is decked out not in uniform, but in "tight-fitting sports clothes", and looks just like a "seal".[35] He tries to adjust something inside his mouth, and Freud wonders if he doesn't have false teeth. Just as Freud makes to speak to his son, he wakes up and the dream ends.

Freud's sally into the storeroom in search of something in the dream reminded him of a significant event from his childhood, when he was between two and three years old. He had gone into the store-closet and stood on a stool, trying to reach "something nice" on a high shelf. The stool overturned, and Freud fell, receiving a sharp blow to his lower jaw. The cut, severe enough to require stitches, bled profusely, and Freud carried the scar for the rest of his life. In *Interpretation*, he writes, "I might easily . . . have knocked all my teeth out."[36] The dream storeroom reproduces the scene of this real-life accident.

The "seal-like" outfit Freud's son appears in also connects him to Freud's grandchild, who was still in baby clothes at the time and "like a funny little seal".[37] The figure of the son in the dream thus condenses three real people – the son, the grandchild, and Freud himself at the age of two. This dream-son also tries to adjust something inside his mouth, or else has something inside his mouth; he thus corresponds precisely to Irma as well.

The mouth is thus a site where our two dreams converge. When the two-year-old Freud tried to get something nice to eat, he hurt himself, and wound up with a wound instead of what he wanted inside his mouth. We find an early object of Freud's desire inside the mouth, then, and the "whitish-gray scab" found inside the dream-Irma's mouth connects seamlessly to the lifelong scar that the storeroom incident left on Freud's jaw. Again, Freud wrote in a letter to Fliess that Fliess's praise was "nectar and ambrosia" to him,[38] and Irma got half a meter of gauze up the nose from this same Fliess – not quite ambrosia, but at least something further that appeared in the key locale of Freud's desire. The infamous length of gauze assumes for Freud the same value as the cut on his jaw – something he got in place of the treat he had reached for so long ago, and by blurring himself together with Irma in the dream of the injection, he is finally able to get hold of the object of this very early desire.

Of course, Freud in fact never did get the "something nice" he was after – all he got

---

[34] *The Interpretation of Dreams,* SE V, 558.
[35] *Interpretation,* SE V, 559.
[36] *Interpretation,* SE V, 560.
[37] *Interpretation,* SE V, 560.
[38] Letter of July 14 1894. Quoted in Jones, *Sigmund Freud,* I, 327. See also Jeffrey Moussaieff Masson, trans. and ed., *The Complete Letters of Sigmund Freud to Wilhelm Fliess, 1887-1904* (Cambridge, Mass.: Belknap Press of Harvard University Press, 1985), 87.

for his troubles was a scar, and having missed out on this treat, he grew up the subject of a lasting desire to receive something through the mouth. The dream of Irma's injection re-enacts the moment of genesis of the subject of this desire, and the dream about his son testifies just how powerfully that desire was sustained within him over a period of many years.

The insistence of this desire, which Freud described as "immortal",[39] rests on the structure of effacement of origins that he himself captured when he said, "[T]he earliest experiences of childhood are not obtainable any longer" – that our childhood simply no longer exists.[40] This desire was fulfilled in a *hallucinatory* form, by the dream, when Freud discovered its object in the mouth of Irma or of his son. This scenario of desire satisfied is flawed, however. The Freud who encountered the object of his desire was already an other – alienated, older, friends with that peculiar character, Fliess – and that other had come to roost within Freud right from the time he was that two-year-old boy. Freud's act in adding this dream about his son to *The Interpretation of Dreams*, so long after the book's first publication, is fraught with significance, and represents a moment when he once more touched base with the structuration of the desire of the Other first discovered nineteen years before with the Dream of Irma's Injection.

Becoming an analyst

The trajectory of Freud's ongoing contact with the "core of his being" that we have thus traced from the age of two to his death brings us back, in a roundabout way, to the problem of what makes the analyst an analyst. To become an analyst, or continue to be one, is precisely to maintain, like Freud, a constant cognizance of oneself as a desiring Other through the contact with the *objet a*. In 1959-1960, in Book VII of his Seminar, Lacan addressed "The Ethics of Psychoanalysis", and formulated the problem in terms of "not giving ground in relation to one's desire".[41] In this axiom, Lacan captures the essence of the posture Freud exhibits in our sample dreams from the *Interpretation*.

Lacan himself does not point out the continuity between the Irma dream and the dream of the son, but the discovery of that continuity reminds us how correct Lacan's reading of Freud is. An analyst is a queer beast: a particular kind of other, ever at the ready, as Freud was, for the encounter with the object of an old desire. The very essence of the analyst is thus the Other, as it is found in Lacan's concept of the "desire of the Other". The position of the analyst is decided by the relation to the object of desire, and it is because of this relation that a person is an analyst and not something else. This relation to the object of desire also explains for those who are not analysts

---

[39] *Interpretation,* SE V, 553.
[40] *Interpretation,* SE IV, 184.   See Chapter IV.
[41] S VII, 319.

Chapter 7: WAITING FOR THE *AGALMA*

why analysts exist in the first place, and why the place of the analyst is a site for the elaboration of a special form of discourse. People go into analysis in order to align their own desire with the desire of the analyst to maintain contact with the *objet a*, and through that identity of desire, to encounter their own particular *objet a*, which each individual subject must discover for herself afresh.

If this is the case – if the relationship of desire to the *objet a* determines the being of the analyst – then what sort of position does the analyst occupy in the social structure as a whole? In 1969, Lacan attempted to bring the premise that the analyst is regulated by the relation to the *objet a* to bear on this problem of the public qualification of the analyst. He attempted to formalize the understanding of social relations with a model of four discourses, incorporating the *objet a* into each. He thereby hoped to make clear the place the analyst should occupy in the social context, and, naturally, he expected that this approach would open up a solution of the problem of analytic training. In our final chapter, we will follow Lacan's progress as he attempted to integrate internal analytic experience and the external, public qualification of the analyst, centering our account on the concept of discourse as he elaborated it through the same period.

CHAPTER EIGHT

THE DISCOURSE OF PSYCHOANALYSIS

One: The "Pass"

Who authorizes the analyst?
Lacan once said of the qualifying process for psychoanalysts that "The authorization of an analyst can come only from himself."[1] How should we interpret this statement? Some holier-than-thou critics have sneered that it opened the floodgates to a rash of self-styled analyst quacks. Infatuated with the autonomy of the analyst, they say, Lacan brought chaos, forcing us to tolerate all manner of reckless and unfettered practices. Is this true? I think it is easy to see that it is an error, one of a sort external, surface criticism is often prone to. Even so, however, it is by no means easy to see to the heart of the matter.

Let us begin by directing our attention to the double bind inherent in this formula. If we take what Lacan says seriously, then we are forced to conclude that anyone who authorized himself as analyst on the basis of Lacan's statement would be disqualified from being an analyst by the same Lacan. The reasoning is hard and fast. Anyone who qualifies himself as analyst on the grounds that "Lacan says such-and-such" thereby qualifies himself to practice in the name of *Lacan's* word, and not on his *own* "authority". He therefore violates Lacan's precept.

Lacan thus brings to our notice the self-referentiality of the signifier of the analyst, and positions the analyst as far as possible from the comfortable belief that the signifier of the subject expresses the truth of the self. He thus makes the analyst painfully aware of the insurmountable gulf that yawns between self and signifier. Years earlier, in "The Rome Discourse", Lacan expressed the fraught relation between language and the human subject by paraphrasing this aphorism from Lichtenberg: "The prince who thinks he is in fact a prince is just as mad as the beggar who imagines himself one."[2] Along similar lines, we might also say, "An analyst who believes

---

[1] Lacan, "Proposition du 9 octobre 1967 sur le psychanalyste de l'École", *Scilicet*, no. 1 (1968), 14-30. Translation in Dylan Evans, *An Introductory Dictionary of Lacanian Psychoanalysis* (London: Routledge, 1996), 136.
[2] "Function and field of speech and language", *Selection*, 109, n. 52: "Aphorism of Lichtenberg's: 'A madman who imagines himself a prince differs from the prince who is in fact a prince only because the former is a negative prince, while the latter is a negative madman. Considered without their sign, they are alike.'"

herself an analyst is just as crazy as a psychotic who thinks *he* is one."

If the analyst's authority derives only from herself, then, it means that she knowingly and willingly falls into the meaninglessness of self-referentiality, thereby realizing in her own person the structure of effacement of the origin that we have now encountered in so many different contexts. This is the entry-point to status as an analyst, and for so long as the analyst is an analyst, she can never divorce herself from this structure of the missing origin. The pain and impotence of this self-referentiality will pose a trial of fire to the self-authorized analyst – the ultimate test of whether her desire to be an analyst is really true.

It is important to note a key equivocation in Lacan's wording. "Authorization" can come from an "authority", but it can also be an effect of "authorship" – an authorship that both "authors" and "authorizes" (i.e. mandates, determines or creates) one's own actions or behavior. Lacan's dictum can thus also be read as meaning that the analyst has nothing to fall back on but himself – that the analyst is his own grounds. This will no doubt recall to mind the Zen notion of freedom described in Chapter IV, and also the fact that the "true person"[3] (the ground of the self) – the "shit-stick" – has been wiped from the vital, living world.

The "pass"
The essay containing this celebrated Lacanian *bon mot* is called "Proposal of October 9 1967 regarding Psychoanalysts of the École".[4] I will refer to it as "the Proposal". In 1968, the EFP (École freudienne de Paris) began putting out a journal called *Scilicet* (Latin for "of course", deriving from an expression meaning "you may know"[5]), and this proposal was carried in the first number.[6]

As the title suggests, this essay deals with the requirements for recognition as an analyst within the EFP. At the very opening of the essay, Lacan says, "The authorization of an analyst can come only from himself." If any reader were hoping to gradually work his way through the system to an analytic qualification, this opening would surely stop him dead in his tracks. This dictum, however, is no less than the core principle underlying the entire foundation of the new school, and before the article discusses the finer points of the qualification process, the reader is

---

[3] Rinzai's "true person of no status". See Ch. 4, n. 34. Recall that *jiyū*, "freedom", here etymologically means something like "coming from the self", "based upon the self". Note also that the French verb here, *s'authoriser* ("to authorize oneself"), is a *reflexive* verb. Note also that there are etymological links between the notions of "authority", "authorship", and "authenticity". – Trans.
[4] "Proposition du 9 octobre 1967 sur le psychanalyste de l'École", *Scilicet,* no. 1 (1968), 14-30. See Roudinesco 444-452 for an account of the proposal, its contents, and its reception.
[5] See Charlton T. Lewis, Charles Short, *A Latin Dictionary* (Oxford: Oxford University Press, 1979).
[6] For the publication of *Scilicet*, see Roudinesco, 464, where Lacan's introduction is quoted as follows: "You can know. Such is the meaning of this title."

Chapter 8: THE DISCOURSE OF PSYCHOANALYSIS

therefore required to return to psychoanalytic first principles – the relation between the subject and language.

When actually on the couch, subjects experience these principles at first hand; stumbling across the *agalma* described in the previous chapter, opening the box that holds it, and looking inside (though Alcibiades does not go so far) to be assailed by the nothingness at its heart. And from among those who have been through that experience, some will emerge who express it somehow (probably linguistically). In so doing, they will step beyond the confines of the École, *qua* human group – albeit to an "outside" that is admittedly internal to the symbolic, as we saw in Chapter V – and so propel the entire École forward. If it were indeed to be possible to authorize analysts not through the pursuit of a training program, but through a procedure unique to Lacan's new École, then surely it would have to involve correctly identifying such individuals, because, in setting up his own school of psychoanalysis, Lacan's hope was to create an institution that would always be sustained and developed along the lines dictated by the internal logic of psychoanalysis alone. For this reason, his École required some procedure for authorizing the internal process of transformation from person in analysis, to person conducting analysis.

Perhaps, however, for psychoanalysis rather to be recognized socially as a method of treatment that made its subjects well again, he would have been better to concoct a qualification based on a visible, tangible curriculum. If he had done no more than that, though, Lacan would have locked Freud's discoveries in the oubliette of an ossified *notion* of psychoanalysis, to await their untimely death. Rather, he preferred to entrust the mission of his École, and thus of preserving intact psychoanalytic doctrine itself, to those whom he identified as having become analysts by completion of the logic of analysis – by virtue of an internal shift defined in terms of the relation with the *agalma* described above. A defining characteristic of these individuals was that they recognized, as the consummation of the process that qualified them, that it had been their desire to live the life of the analyst ever since the day they were born. We could say, in fact, that analysts are made by this recognition of desire, questions of technical training aside. To these individuals Lacan gave the title of "Analyste de l' École" (AE).[7]

At the same time, however, clinical training could not simply be neglected. The École was a public body composed entirely of psychoanalysts, and its status was guaranteed by neither medicine nor psychology. In order to maintain its independent position, it required not just theorists or veterans of the analytic test, but also a pool of psychoanalysts with impeccable technique. Such analysts were not necessarily interested in demonstrating their desire to be analysts once more to their colleagues within the École. What was vital was to enable each person who came to them as a patient to come into contact with his own desire. To lead the analysand to

---

[7] For this definition of AE, see Roudinesco 448.

Chapter 8: THE DISCOURSE OF PSYCHOANALYSIS

that contact, analysts had to know how to vacate their own position, and thus had to be both clinically knowledgeable and dexterous at handling interpretative technique. Lacan bestowed upon analysts of this variety the qualification of "Analyste Membre de l'École" (AME).[8]

The real sticking point was this: What procedure should be used to certify an AE? Lacan himself suggested a procedure known as the "pass" (*passe*). We can think of the word "pass" in this context as signifying a through-passage or a way out, in contradistinction to the dead end (*impasse*) of identification with the analyst.

The formalities of the pass are as follows.[9] A person who wishes to become an AE is called a *passant*. The *passant* speaks to witnesses (*les passeurs*),[10] appointed by the jury, about her experiences in analysis. It is expected that in this process the *passant* will manifest the nature of her desire in wishing to become an analyst. The *passeurs* themselves are chosen from those currently undergoing analysis. The *passant*'s story of emerging into the clear on the far side of analysis is therefore liable to strike them as something that could one day happen to them, and thus as impinging closely on their own persons. This should allow them to take on board the transformations the *passant* has undergone in her progress through analysis. The *passant*'s testimony about herself is then conveyed by the *passeurs* to the jury. The jury uses what the *passeurs* tell it to judge whether or not the *passant* is capable of forging avenues for fresh advance on the most fundamental questions of psychoanalysis.

For me, the structure of the "pass" brings to mind the Japanese children's game of *tōryanse*. Two children make a *torii* (shrine gateway) with their hands, and in order to pass through the "narrow way of Tenjin (the god of learning)" that runs beneath the *torii*, the child who is "it" (who corresponds to the *passant*) has to say that he is going to offer a prayer for another child's seventh birthday. But in the words of the song, "It's easy going in, / But scary getting out;" if the *passant*'s timing is off, the children playing the *torii* yell, "Oh help, a fox!",[11] and hit him.

Something uncanny hovers below the surface of this game, something reminiscent of Oedipus's return to Thebes. Perhaps, indeed, the pass is somehow designed to make the subject revisit Oedipus's bitter fate – a fate that recurs in the analysis of each and every one of us. Like child's play, analysis runs to repetition. It makes good sense that the subject who has grown used to the *tōryanse*-like uncanny of analysis will eventually be drawn to the uncanny of the *passe*, as well.

---

[8] Roudinesco 448.
[9] Roudinesco 447-448.
[10] The original Japanese here uses an evocative word to translate *passeur*: *watashimori*, or "ferry-man". The *passeurs* emerge as almost Charon-like figures. - Trans.
[11] In Japanese folklore, the fox is believed to have magical powers, which it sometimes uses to harm or deceive humans. See for example Thomas W. Johnson, "Far Eastern Fox Lore", *Asian Folklore Studies*, vol. 33 (1974), 35-68; and Kiyoshi Nozaki, *Kitsune: Japan's Fox of Mystery, Romance and Humor* (Tokyo: Hokuseido Press, 1961). - Trans.

Chapter 8: THE DISCOURSE OF PSYCHOANALYSIS

Lacan's critics saw no such uncanny object in the process of the *passe*, however. Instead, they derided it as a mere *"passe-passe"*, or sleight-of-hand. And indeed, one could hardly claim that the *passe* incorporated any "objective standard"; Lacan himself usually presided over the jury, and was present at all its deliberations. Resistance to the *passe* system was as strong within the EFP as without, moreover, and as we shall see, the whole issue was eventually to bring Lacan's career to a harsh and bloody end.

The Other Side of Psychoanalysis: Towards a new formulation

After he issued the Proposal in 1967, Lacan continued to interrogate the position of psychoanalysis, taking his place in the intellectual upheaval and furor that seized Paris at the time. The traces of that struggle can be discerned in the Seminar of 1969-1970, *The Other Side of Psychoanalysis*.[12]

As a first approximation, we can say that that which is said in psychoanalysis is spoken *within* the subject who is doing the talking. It seems, therefore, as though a boundary exists between these things and the external, social life that the subject experiences from day to day. But in fact the unconscious, which seems so clearly to be a place hidden within this internal discourse, is also a kind of secret passage leading back to the outside world. By slipping out through this passage, the subject manages to see herself from the outside, and gains the ability to speak of herself. The unconscious is thus structured like a Moebius strip; if you follow the inside to its very end, you find yourself on the outside, on the exact reverse of the spot where you started.

To pursue the unconscious in psychoanalysis is thus to expose oneself to the social activity that writhes on the inverse of unconscious discourse. The two moments are intimately connected. Having established his new school of psychoanalysis, Lacan had to theorize the way the experience proper to psychoanalysis was tied up with the true conditions of social organization. This was the pressing imperative that drove Lacan to present his "Four Discourses" model, which constitutes a kind of social theory. The basic psychoanalytic view behind this model is that there is a *plus du jouir* or "surplus *jouissance*" left over from the originally existent subject, and that the subject desires passionately to get hold of it. This *plus de jouir*, and the subject's desire for it, are caught up in a varied web of social relations, and drive individual subjects as they move through that web. The question becomes: How can we write those social relations? The model of the Four Discourses was Lacan's attempt to answer this question, and we will now look at that model, beginning with the model of precisely what the pass was designed to detect – the discourse of the analyst.

---

[12] S XVII.

Chapter 8: THE DISCOURSE OF PSYCHOANALYSIS

Two: The Four Discourses

The discourse of the analyst

What happens if the analyst does succeed in authorizing himself, thereby establishing himself as an independent analyst of his own school? First, his self will be erased under the aegis of the signifier of the self, leaving behind only the *objet a*. This means that what authorizes the analyst is precisely this *objet a*, which the process leaves behind. The *objet a* sets the effaced subject of the analyst in action as analyst, but elsewhere, in "another scene" (*ein anderer Platz*). The self, having discovered the truth of the self by means of the *objet a*, is already an other.

$$\frac{a}{S_2} \rightarrow \frac{\$}{S_1} \qquad \textit{The discourse of the analyst}$$

In the above formula, called "the discourse of the analyst", the agent of the discourse is the *objet a*. The subject of the analyst $\$$ is present as a passive other, the recipient of the constant action of *a*. Below the *a*, and separated from it by the bar, is the signifier of knowledge S_2. This "knowledge" is knowledge of the "truth" of the subject.

The subject $\$$ cannot arrive at this knowledge directly. The *objet a* does reveal knowledge of the truth of the subject to the subject, in all the multifarious forms that the *objet a* can assume, but what this conveys to the subject is rather that the truth is inaccessible – or, to put it another way, that the truth of the subject has fallen away and is lacking, thanks to the incompleteness of self-referentiality.

The S_1 found below the subject $\$$ is the "master signifier" (the signifier of the subject as master). Reduced to the place of a passive other, the subject is usurped, no longer the captain of his own mind. The subject drops the master signifier, and thus stripped naked as other, suffers bare contact with the *objet a*. The master signifier becomes a kind of refuse, an off-cast of the analytic process. As Lacan hinted from time to time, this is probably the reason the analyst is imagined as a trashcan or similar object, or that the scene of analysis is frequently represented in dreams as a toilet.

Now, perhaps, the subject is a fox (as in *tōryanse*). Or, indeed, a dog (as in the phrase "That's a dog" in Chapter VI, or André Breton's fantasies). And if he tries to tell anyone what has happened to him, he will find he is no longer master of his own words, so that what he has to say about himself can only come across as alienated language – language gone mad. After all, when a fox says it's a fox, who is there who speaks fox-language to understand it?

At this moment when he passes from the receiving end to the giving end of analysis, the subject defines himself in reference to the *objet a*. He understands that his self is an other, and acting through the agency of the *objet a*, he relinquishes the vain endeavor to be master of his own mind and realizes the structure of the effaced origin. In a manner of speaking, the subject gives up the tyrant's throne. Lacan calls this moment the "destitution of the subject".[13] When Oedipus acknowledges his desire and his crime, he is deposed ("destituted"). At this point Lacan recalls Klein's concept of the "depressive position".[14] Just as Klein understood the analytic progress as progress toward the depressive position, Lacan orients the analytic process toward the recognition of one's own desire and the abrogation of the self.

Lacan did not stop at this, however, merely stipulating the characteristics proper to the analyst's position itself. He also attempted to situate the analyst in the context of other social relations. Naturally, this could be seen as simply a matter of course. Having begun training analysts with the establishment of his own school, we might say that he *had* to consider what made it possible for a person living in a network of other social relations to have the desire to become an analyst. Let us see, then, how he theorized other "discourses" (social relations), and how he situated the discourse of the analyst among them.

The discourse of the university

Around the time of the "Rome Discourse", Lacan saw the discourses exchanged by subjects as no more than a layer of linguistic activity, circulating through society, which obstructed the advent of full speech (*parole pleine*) from the unconscious. By the time of the theory of the four discourses, however, he was actively attempting to extend his theoretical explorations to incorporate such discourses. The various discourses are identical with the various forms of the social bond. This means that it is the apparatus constituted by these discourses that drives the unconscious (the relation between linguistic activity and the subject) to operate, with at least some degree of regularity, in the context of the various systematized social relations.

As one of these apparatuses, the discourse of the analyst, too, is a social bond, at least insofar as it functions within a system of qualification for analysts. The discourse of the analyst is closely related, in the first instance, to the "discourse of the university". At the time of Seminar XVII, Lacan was caught up in the very real problem of creating a department of psychoanalysis in the university, and it seems likely that this was the reason he gave this particular name to this discourse; I think it

---

[13] *Scilicet* No.1, 23-24; *Autres écrits*, 252. Note that, as the reference to the Oedipus myth makes clear here, the word "destitution" is used primarily in the sense of "deposition", defined by the OED as "The action of deposing or putting down from a position of dignity or authority; degradation, dethronement." *Destitution* in this sense is more current in French than in English, though even in English, it has clearly carried this sense, derived from the now largely obsolete verb "to destitute". —Trans.

[14] *Scilicet* No.1, 26; *Autres écrits*, 255.

Chapter 8: THE DISCOURSE OF PSYCHOANALYSIS

is possible, however, to broaden our reading of it, to understand it as "the discourse of science".[15] The discourse is written with the following formula:

$$\frac{S_2}{S_1} \to \frac{a}{\mathcal{S}} \qquad \textit{The discourse of the university}$$

In this formula, the subject is on the bottom right, below the *objet a*. The *objet a*, on the other hand, this time stalled in the position of passive recipient, quietly sits at the receiving end of the operation of S_2 (knowledge). This captures the basic cognitive structure of the subject of science. The object (*a*) – nature– is passively worked on (and over) by knowledge, and even the human subject itself is reduced to a part of that nature. Even as it is part of the nature that knowledge operates on, however, the subject is also a surplus, the excess that nature cannot entirely subsume – and so it is dropped below the bar ($\mathcal{S}$). This is the structure of that unique subjective reserve the scientist maintains towards nature and knowledge.

As may be seen from an examination of the formulae, if we turn the discourse of the university ninety degrees anti-clockwise it becomes the discourse of the analyst.

As we saw at the beginning of the previous chapter, psychoanalysis is an arrangement necessitated by the subject of science. To prove to itself that the sense data science relies on is not the product of some dream of the subject (the 'I'), the subject of science seeks the most certain ground it can find (think of Descartes). This subject lurches from the conviction that sense data simply cannot be illusory, to the nagging nihilist suspicion that the whole of life is just a dream. Psychoanalysis is the set-up that allows the subject to get out of this cul-de-sac. If life *does* in fact admit of any remainder that is not a dream, then the question of what it might be can be posed, and it is this question that is to be pursued and worked through in the analytic process.

In the formula of the "discourse of the university", nature is the object of the operation of knowledge. But what if we consider that there is no such thing as knowledge that exceeds nature itself, and that in fact, knowledge is a part of nature, included within it? This is not an altogether unscientific attitude. It is close to the ordinary scientific view that the laws of nature are inherent within it, and that no God gave those laws to nature from without. Let us thus try advancing nature, *a*, in the direction of knowledge, S_2. We then move the subject, $\mathcal{S}$, into the position of that which is worked on by nature, to arrive at the discourse of the analyst. In Lacan's understanding, the movement from the discourse of science to the discourse of the

---

[15] Lacan himself also suggests that this discourse, to which he gives the name of the "discourse of the university," shows the setup upon whose basis the discourse of science is founded. S XVII, 119.

Chapter 8: THE DISCOURSE OF PSYCHOANALYSIS

analyst was thus a sort of "advance" or "progress".[16] After all, the quest of science will never be complete until it can answer this question, certainly and without illusion: What does the human subject look like from the point of view of a universal knowledge inherent in nature? As the scientific subject presses its inquiry to the limits, therefore, it contains hidden within it the dynamic potential to move in the direction of the subject of psychoanalysis.

Thus far, we have omitted to explain a key factor in interpreting these discourse models. As each of the four terms changes position when a shift like this is made from one discourse to another, the meaning of each of the four positions remains unchanged (see formula):[17]

$$\frac{agent}{truth} \rightarrow \frac{other}{product}$$

Lacan says that the position at the lower left is always occupied by truth. The position at the upper left, as is shown by the direction of the arrow, is the position of the agent. This means that at the two positions on the left always signify the agent, at the top and extending its function to the terms on the right, and the truth hidden beneath it, on which it rests. At the right, the position of the term that is operated on by the agent is called the "other" (at the top). Finally, as a result of that operation a surplus emerges, something that cannot be reincorporated back into the operation. This is expressed by the lower right position, the "product".

Returning to the discourse of the university, Lacan explains that a student, who like the *objet a*, is not really anything, is operated on by knowledge S_2, and has the line of "the unit" drawn across her to become $\barS$. (It seems likely, however, that this was one of the gentle pot shots that Lacan took at the contemporary student movement from time to time!) Let us pursue further our reading of this discourse as the discourse of science. In the discourse of the university, knowledge, or S_2, is in the position of the agent. The master signifier, S_1, is in the position of truth. We saw at the beginning of the previous chapter that a worldview that took the human as the yardstick of all creation arose and spread with the development of science, and that the human subject thereby lost the measure of itself. $\barS$, the human subject itself, is relegated to the position of the forlorn scrap left over when knowledge S_2 has measured everything else in creation. No matter how hard the knowledge function works, its effects will never reach the human subject itself. S_1, the signifier that accords the human subject its subjectivity or mastery, hides itself away in the position of truth, making itself inaccessible and estranged from any humanity $\barS$. The subject

---

[16] S XX, 21.
[17] S XVII, 106.

is thus faced with the harrowing prospect of being left in the lurch by truth – that same truth that first ordained the subject with its mission of knowledge.

Pascal was among the first pioneers to live as subjects of science, and he depicted the state of the subject that has lost the ability to know where it comes from, and where it is going. He writes of the quailing terror the scientific subject feels in sensing itself as a part of limitless nature (*apeiron*): "[Lost . . .] without knowing who put him there, what he has come to do, what will become of him when he dies," he is "like a man transported in his sleep to some terrifying desert island."[18] This terror is visited on the subject of science because although the subject *is* a part of nature, as soon as it *knows* it is, the maw of self-referentiality gapes open before it, and it can rest easy in nature's bosom no longer. The subject ought to be a part of nature, and yet it can only be so as a kind of leftover or excess. It is worth observing that Pascal's lines are the exact inverse of the words of Christ quoted in Section II of Chapter IV, where Christ held the incapacity of self-referentiality poses no obstacle to bearing witness for the self.

Lacan thus holds that the anxiety that assailed the human subject from around the time of Pascal finally gave birth to psychoanalysis in the work of Freud. The ninety-degree turn from the discourse of science to the discourse of the analyst renders visible an entire moment in modern intellectual history, in extremely condensed notational form.

Most scientists, however, do not live in Pascal's state of acute anxiety. Rather, the daily existence of the subject of science is governed by the "discourse of the master", which is arrived at by a ninety degree turn from the discourse of the university in the opposite direction to the discourse of the analyst (clockwise), placing the being of the self that engages in science in the place of truth. We will now proceed to examine this third discourse, the discourse of the master.

The discourse of the master

$$\frac{S_1}{\$} \rightarrow \frac{S_2}{a} \quad \textit{The discourse of the master}$$

Most scientists never even ask how they can ground their own being. The truth of their existence *is* the fact that they engage in scientific thought, pure and simple, a truth that for them is tantamount to the truth of "'I' am". The road to this "I am" from "I think" was a long hard one for Descartes, in the search for the most certain possible ground for the subject of science; for these scientists, on the other hand, his

---

[18] Pascal, *Pensées,* translated with an introduction by A. J. Krailsheimer (London: Penguin, 1966), 88.

conclusion is as good as established fact – taken as read. In the name of the master signifier S_1, which expresses the sovereign will of society at large, the subject of science inscribed in the discourse of the master commands its own knowledge (S_2) to engage in scientific production. The scientist tries to make her achievements – the products of the scientific process – serve her as *objet a*, the support for her self and her being, bypassing the Cartesian process and cutting straight to "I am". When modern man *qua* subject of science makes his labors of knowledge sustain his being in this manner, he achieves a particularly stable, secure mode of daily existence.

The master signifier (S_1) for which the majority of scientists set their knowledge (S_2) to work is probably the idea of "humankind"; they spur themselves on to further scientific production with phrases like "for the good of the human race". Any subject of science, insofar as it is a subject of science, can only be the subject of some partial science: physics, chemistry, and so on. This subject, as the human subject $\bar{S}$, is found in the position of the "truth" (lower left) that sustains science from the shadows, but here it is reduced once more to impotent suffering existence; language is lost to it, and it to language. In its place, "humankind" S_1 speaks, addressing the knowledge of the subject S_2. The subject recovers completeness by patching the holes in itself with the product of knowledge, a; the products of scientific knowledge are imagined to extend to every last nook and cranny of the society the subjects of science construct, and all subjects are able to enjoy the fruits of science equally, in the name of "humankind".

The subjects of science, though in fact no more than partial subjects at best, are thus enabled to identify with one another through the control mechanism of the linguistic function (the master signifier), and so to live within the whole known as "the scientific age". This whole that the subject attempts to make its own by way of the fruits of scientific knowledge is one of the structures known as "fantasy". The domain of the fantasy $\bar{S} \lozenge a$ is constituted between the two terms at the bottom of the formula of the discourse of the master – the subject $\bar{S}$ in the place of truth, and the *objet a* in the place of the product.

$$\frac{S_1 \rightarrow S_2}{\bar{S} \,\lozenge\, a}$$

The discourse of the master thus functions as the fundamental framework that binds us into the structure of social meaning, and provides us with the fantasy of completeness within the individual.

As subjects of science living in the scientific age, then, we shuttle back and forth between the discourse of science (the "discourse of the university") and the discourse of the master. This is not necessarily enough to satisfy us, however. As modern subjects, we are supposed to be endowed with an innate human essence, which ought to be our reference point in all we think and all we do. As essential humans so defined, we are supposed to occupy the place of the agent. By contrast, those who occupy the position of the social "master" know absolutely nothing of this human essence, and especially of the true joys and sorrows of ordinary human life. For this reason, we begin to criticize our masters, and to call them to account; we must constantly remind them of our human essence, and demand that they heed it. The subject thus comes to adapt the posture known as the "discourse of the hysteric".

The discourse of the hysteric

$$\frac{\$}{a} \rightarrow \frac{S_1}{S_2} \qquad \textit{The discourse of the hysteric}$$

In this formula, we see the response of the modern, essentially human subject to the dehumanizing discourse of the master. The subject ($\$$), certain that it holds within it the essence (or truth) of human being, a, acts on the ignorant master (S_1) to try to bring it to knowledge (S_2) of the human essence hidden on the side of the subject. The problem for the subject inscribed in the discourse of the hysteric, then, is that it cannot itself draw near to the essence a that is its whole premise. The subject of hysteria thus attempts to corroborate the existence of this essence by bringing it to the master's attention, and for this reason, it depends entirely on the object of its discourse – the master S_1 as other.

Even when the subject manages for a time to take the driver's seat and ascend to the position of the agent, then, it will probably be plagued by a longing to regress to the discourse of the master. At least that way it would have access to its essence, a, through the structure of the fantasy. Such a regression, however, would once more muzzle the subject, confining it to the place of the truth beneath a new master signifier, and this is a fate the hysterical subject is unlikely to take kindly to. He will burn with the desire to see with his own eyes what this essence within him is, but no matter how hard he tries to see it, this essence will remain invisible. The reason is clear, as the events of the mirror stage show – the impossibility of seeing one's own essence is a necessary condition the subject imposes when it structures itself.

This encounter with the cognitive aporia that structures the self, and the attempt to overcome it, is exactly the problem that leads people to psychoanalysis. The speaking subject $\$$ is incapable of directly accessing the essence a, but convinced it must be there. It sees that it might reach a if it can only run the gauntlet of the plane of language barring its path, and it begins to interrogate language. As Lacan says in his Seminar, then, the psychoanalytic situation consists in a structural

Chapter 8: THE DISCOURSE OF PSYCHOANALYSIS

introduction of the discourse of the hysteric by means of artificial conditions.[19]

We can see from the formula that when psychoanalysis introduces the discourse of the hysteric into the subject, the master signifier (S_1), which here sits in the position of the other, will produce knowledge (S_2) of the essence of the subject. The discourse of the hysteric thus bears a formal resemblance to the social reorientation of the mirror stage, in that the subject entrusts the master signifier – the signifier of itself – to the other, obviating the need to use that signifier *itself*, and so dodging the impotence brought on by self-referentiality. The subject hopes that this other will know for it what it cannot know for itself – its (the subject's) original form. This other that is supposed or expected to produce knowledge ("the subject supposed to know") is an element in the transferential situation of psychoanalysis. Indeed, in Seminar XI, Lacan says, "As soon as there is a subject supposed to know, there is transference."[20]

It may be possible for the subject inscribed in the discourse of the hysteric not to regress to the position of "truth" (as in the discourse of the master), but rather to move to the position of the "other" by way of the transference. If this happens, then another ninety-degree turn will take place in the discourse structure, and the discourse of the analyst will appear. At some point, the analyst gives up being a human subject for the patient S , and becomes the *objet a*, the vehicle of the lost essence of the patient. This shift means that the subject, which unbeknownst to itself had moved at some stage to the place of the other, is touched by the *objet a*, which appears suddenly from the midst of the subject's discourse.

Thus, a place where the subject, as other, comes into contact with the *objet a* is prepared in advance for the subject (the analysand) by the present being of the analyst (i.e. one who experiences the *discourse* of the analyst). If the structure of the discourse of the analyst, which is experienced by the subject (the analysand) at the conclusion of each of his analytic sessions, is maintained beyond that point, then that analysand-subject S has already started down the road towards becoming an analyst himself.

Four discourses, one model
It is now possible to set out the four discourses we have been discussing in the form they take in Seminar XVII, *The Other Side of Psychoanalysis*. A, U, M and H are the initial letters of "analyst", "university", "master", and "hysteric" respectively.[21]

---

[19] S XVII, 35-36. "Ce que l'analyste institue comme expérience analytique peut se dire simplement – c'est l'hystérisation du discours. Autrement dit, c'est l'introduction structurelle, par des conditions d'artifice, du discours de l'hystérique..."
[20] S XI, 230. "As soon as the subject who is supposed to know exists somewhere... there is transference." (232)
[21] S XVII, 31.

Chapter 8: THE DISCOURSE OF PSYCHOANALYSIS

THE FOUR DISCOURSES

$$\underset{M}{\dfrac{S_1}{\$} \to \dfrac{S_2}{a}} \qquad \underset{U}{\dfrac{S_2}{S_1} \to \dfrac{a}{\$}}$$

$$\underset{H}{\dfrac{\$}{a} \to \dfrac{S_1}{S_2}} \qquad \underset{A}{\dfrac{a}{S_2} \to \dfrac{\$}{S_1}}$$

As we saw earlier, the four positions retain a fixed role in each of the four discourses. This reflects the psychoanalytic view that the human subject $\$$ is not always the agent. In the course of analysis, a great many different things are spoken, and we can hear agency shifting across the spectrum of available players as we listen to the changes in what is said.

With the theory of the four discourses, and the rotation of their four floating elements through four positions of fixed meaning, Lacan thus offered a model of analysis as a social relation, and of its place within the framework of social relations in general. He gave a new articulation to the role and goals of psychoanalytic training (how does the institute publicly certify to society at large that an analyst is qualified to ply their trade?), and cast new light on the pass. But as we have seen, the theory also cast its net far wider, illuminating historic relations between science, subject, and psychoanalysis, for instance. We will now look at another of these ramifications of the theory: an innovative reading of the Oedipus complex.

Three: The "Discourse of the Master" and Oedipus

Signifier and subject
Both the discourse of the university and the discourse of the hysteric have a tendency to move towards the discourse of the master, carrying the subject far from analysis. Even so, we cannot see the discourse of the master and the discourse of the analyst as merely antagonistic to one another. In the discourse of the analyst, the subject drops the master signifier below the bar, at the same time coming into contact with the *objet a*. However, the fact that the master signifier is deposed below the bar by no means indicates that the master signifier has been conquered. It means, rather, that the subject is rendered precisely "unspeakable" – it cannot be said.

The subject is made ineffable by the inaccessibility of the master signifier because

Chapter 8: THE DISCOURSE OF PSYCHOANALYSIS

it was the master signifier that created the initial conditions for the subject to form itself by interrogating its own nature, back at the moment of the original symbolization. The discourse of the master is the structure that fosters the first stirrings of the fledgling speaking subject. The original subject might conceivably have persisted as it was before the advent of language, with neither surplus nor shortfall, adequate unto itself. In *becoming* a speaking subject, however, it began to question itself and what it was, even as the impotence of self-referentiality snatched the power of reply from its grasp and it was *annihilated qua* subject. Lacan formalizes this fact by the matheme $\frac{S_1}{\$}$.[22]

The subject can only hope that even in these dire straits, some other word or words will express for it this painful, disempowering relation to language. The structure of this situation can be notated as follows:

$$\frac{S_1}{\$} \rightarrow S_2$$

This matheme can be read as a graphic expression of Lacan's famous circular definition of the signifier (of the subject): "[A] signifier is that which represents a subject for another signifier."[23]

Even the combination of S_1 and S_2, however, does not in fact restore anything meaningful to the subject. S_2 merely knows that there is a relation between S_1 and $\$$. All S_2 has to offer, then, is the hope that someone knows that "I" really does exist – that I is there. This does not stop the subject chasing the chimera of a symbolization that would really capture itself, however – and symbolization once more ramifies into an endless chain. When I first came into relation with the signifier of itself and began suffering on its account, S_1 represented I to S_2. S_2 in turn represented I to the next S_2 (we will call this entire chain "S_2") and so on. The ultimate recipient of the meaning of the self thus conveyed down the chain *is* the self – a self already gone from this world – and the meaning the self gets from the process is the *objet a* (recall the presentation of this problem in terms of the Fibonacci series, in Chapter V). This process can be notated in the form of the following formula, i.e. as the discourse of the master.

---

[22] The master signifier, S_1, accedes to the position of agent; meanwhile, however, the truth of the subject is rendered symbolically inaccessible, a fact notated by striking the S of the subject out. – Trans.
[23] S XI, 207. According to this definition, we could read the formula here thus: S_1, a signifier, represents the subject, S, for another signifier, S_2. – Trans.

Chapter 8: THE DISCOURSE OF PSYCHOANALYSIS

$$\frac{S_1}{\$} \rightarrow \frac{S_2}{a}$$

The state depicted in this discourse model is thus an extremely primal one. The subject is effaced under the sign of self-referentiality ($\$$); S1, even though it does once represent the subject, cannot manifest itself as such, and subsequently delegates the representation of the subject to "an-other" signifier, S2.[24]

Lacan's four-discourse model therefore depicts the way the subject, undermined by the structural impotence of being, manages more or less to sustain its own ground through insertion into the social bond. "What does it mean to be alive?" "What is the value of my existence?" The various forms of discourse that are elaborated in search of answers to these questions, both in the internal and the social planes, are captured in the relations between extremely basic elements: the painful self-referential relation between the subject and its signifier; knowledge as produced and structured by combinations of words; and the real object that the subject seeks as its support and ground beyond language.

Of the four discourses, the master discourse, as we have just seen, expresses the underlying relation between the subject and the signifier of the subject, and for this reason could almost be granted the status of prototype – the fundamental form from which the other discourses derive. As we will now see, Lacan situates this primogenitor among discourses in a special relation to another fundamental of psychoanalysis, the Oedipus complex.

Interrogating the holder of the phallus

For Lacan, the relation between the subject and the signifier of the subject is identical in meaning to Freud's Oedipus complex. He held that the Oedipus complex *is*, in fact, the introduction of the signifier.[25] We must therefore see that the discourse of the

---

[24] The precipitate of this whole process, as substitutions multiply to infinity in the wild goose chase to signify self, is *a*, the truth of the subject. – Trans.

[25] In 1956, in the third volume of his *Seminar,* Lacan writes, "If the Oedipus complex isn't the introduction of the signifier then I ask to be shown any conception of it whatever" (S3, 189). Again, in 1970, he writes in Volume 17 of the *Seminar,* "The master-signifier does not merely induce castration, it determines it (Le signifiant-maître, non seulement induit, mais détermine, la castration)" (S XVII, 101). I read the "master-signifier" here as indicating none other than that signifier of whose "introduction" Lacan speaks in the passage from 1956. The entry of the subject into a relation with this signifier is thus identical with the creation of the Oedipus complex, and also, at the same time, connotes the establishment of the structure of the "discourse of the master". On this reading, the induction and determination of castration by the signifier *is* precisely the Oedipus complex.

This surely requires that we say something about the relationship between the Oedipus complex and the castration complex. Freud classically schematizes this relationship as follows: in the male child, the Oedipus complex is brought to an end by the threat of the

master points to the same facts as the Oedipus complex. When we do so, rereading Freud's myth in terms of the discourse of the master, we arrive at a new understanding of Freudian orthodoxy.

First, let us recall what the Oedipus phase is in Freud's classic formulation. At Freud's Oedipal phase, the child becomes concerned with the difference between the sexes (here understood in terms of possession or lack of the phallus only). Note, however, that this is not a problem of cognitive development. Freud emphasized rather, as the point of departure for subsequent development, the particular logical and ethical thought processes that characterize the child at this phase. More concretely, the boy thinks, "Perhaps I'll have it (the phallus) taken off me sometime," and the girl thinks, "I have to get it back." We see here the *logical* notion that things could be different from the way they really are, and a *subjective* posture that understands that notion by applying it to part of the individual's own body.

This logical moment can give birth to any number of different narratives. A boy might think, "Rather than have it taken off me, I'd better make something better to offer up in its place," and be spurred to work hard; a girl might think, "I'm sure to get something better one day, so there's no need to act like I want it," and end up hating it instead. Another boy, unable to bear the idea of losing the phallus, might tell himself "I don't have it," against the evidence of his senses, and try to act like a girl. Another girl, unable to bear the idea that it already *has* been taken, might tell herself "I do have it," similarly against the evidence of her senses, and try to act like a boy. And of course, we could list many more conceivable narratives.

Freud grouped these various reactions together, paying particular attention to the characteristic modes of feeling that bind them together at the root, and placed them all under two rubrics: "castration anxiety" for boys, and "penis envy" for girls. These two concepts have been much bandied about, and the terms have entered common parlance; far more significant than the emotional attitudes these terms can imply, however, is the logical operation that forms their base. When the child perceives the fact of the phallus's presence or absence, it does not occur to it that things "just happen to be that way" (that they could be merely *contingent*).[26] In our adults' wisdom, we might also imagine that the child already has the potential to

---

castration complex, whereas in the female child, the Oedipus complex is rather induced by the castration complex (SE XXI, 225-243). The two complexes are handled as two independent variables. However, if we synthesize the two definitions of Lacan cited above, we are surely required to think in terms of a more fundamental Oedipus complex held in common by both genders; confronted with the prospect of castration, children of both genders alike solve its riddle by inventing the concept of a transcendental "Father". It is only through the existence of this "Father" that the Oedipus complex is manifested for the first time. We explore this process in detail below.

[26] "Contingency" in terms of the philosophy of causality. Like "contingency", the terms "necessity" and "necessary" are used in what follows in the philosophical sense. See section below on Aristotle's theory of causation, p. 178. – Trans.

accept a biological explanation (X and Y chromosomes, etc.), and that there is no other way for the child to think of these things, but this also is not true. The thought processes of the child are far more proactive than that.

It is whys and wherefores that occupy the child's thoughts. Why do some people have the phallus? Why do others have to go without? In other words, the child looks for *necessary* reasons that people are the way they are. The answer it arrives at when it contemplates this critical problem is this: it postulates the existence of some whimsical agency, which puts the phallus on whoever it likes, and leaves it off the rest. This agency ("He") must know the reasons that some people have the phallus and others don't; and He must have given that reason, the reason the individual "I" is the way it is and not some other way, *to* I, as incontrovertible *necessity*. I cannot know the reason, but by virtue of the fact that He made I the way I is, I is at least certain that some value is given to it's being I, and not something else.

There is a catch, however. Because "He" is the only one who knows the reason for I's being, it is possible that I has failed to *realize* the value of its being what it is. I feels culpable in its ignorance, and suffer pangs of guilt. I is also wracked by anxiety, fearing that even if He were to make clear the reason for I's being and tell I to realize it, I could not meet 'His' demand. Belief in a being that gives I the necessary ground of its existence is attended by this certain consequence: that we come to being as guilty subjects.

When it investigates the presence or absence of the phallus, then, the Oedipal child gets caught up in ontological issues – questions of being. Recall how the demons in the tale of "How the Old Man Lost His Bump"[27] pull a bump off one old man and stick it onto his neighbor. This is of course a story, and the plot therefore gives necessary reasons for taking the bump off one person and putting it on another, reasons that in this case all come back to whether each person can please the demons with their dancing. In the background all the time, however, sustaining the plot, are similar questions of ontology.

Ontology on its own, however, is not enough. Besides the necessity of I's own existence, the agent that sticks the phallus on I and not on she (or on he and not on I) also holds in its grasp another species of necessity – the necessity of the *relation* between people with the phallus and people without. If "He" is going to go to the trouble of bestowing a phallus on I but not the next person – or vice versa, as the case

---

[27] A Japanese folktale, translated as "How an Old Man Lost his Wen" in F. Hadland Davis, *Myths and Legends of Japan* (London: G. G. Harrap and Company, 1913), 372-374. An old man with a large bump on his right cheek gets lost in a storm and finds a party of reveling demons. He entertains them with his fine dancing, and the chief demon takes his bump as a pledge that he will return the next night to dance some more. A wicked neighbor has a similar bump on his left cheek, and deceitfully returns in the old man's place, hoping to lose it the same way. He cannot dance, however; the demons return the "pledge" (the original bump) in a fit of anger, and the wicked neighbor gets double the bumps for his trouble. – Trans.

may be – then there must be some necessary relation that holds within Him between that other person and I. "He" maintains and sustains the necessity of I's relation to this other. This enables us to make sense of the word *en* (fortune, luck, relationships), which we use so often in Japan.[28] We say that something was "meant to be" ("[I] had the *en*"), or give up on something else, saying "It's not meant to happen" ("[I] didn't have the *en*", "There was no *en*."). The agent of our phallic fates is, in a manner of speaking, He who holds our *en* in his hands – the heavenly matchmaker who inscribes the "red cord" into human relations.[29]

Lacan says that in love, we find the moment in which chance becomes necessity.[30] Indeed, "love" might ultimately be nothing other than the moment of that shift. When someone starts seeing necessity in too many places, for instance in things like the fact that it is snowing today, we call them superstitious. In the case of "love" alone, however, this is never the case. "It was meant to be", we say; "They were meant for each other." In fact, we routinely go to exorbitant expense for the ceremony that demonstrates, in the face of the congregation and before God, the full force of the necessity of love.[31]

Undeniably, this notion thrown up by the thought processes of the Oedipal phase – that there must exist One who holds the necessity of our destiny in His grasp – threatens our reason. We therefore give this being various names (like god, devil, or the dead father), and in this way, we can temporarily dissociate ourselves from Him. But whenever each of us reaches a crossroads – a point where we must get a fresh grip on our particular destiny – the concept is there waiting for us, and we must call it up once more. For at such moments, we cannot avoid introducing necessity into our relationship with the world, and we call this necessity "love" – the super-alloy forged in the crucible of the Oedipal period, when the yearning for necessity melds with human desire.

The calamity that is tied up with the recall of this concept is expressed perfectly by the structure of the psychotic episode. In such cases, where the being that controls

---

[28] *En* is not entirely translatable. It means both a relationship, e.g. blood or marital relations, and also destiny, being derived in the latter sense from the standard Chinese translation of the Buddhist notion of *pratyāya* (Nakamura Hajime, *Shin bukkyō yōgo jiten* [Tokyo: Seishin shobō, 1980], 59). Generally speaking, it means relations as determined by fate. In conversation it is often used, especially by people of strong Buddhist inclinations, to refer to the good fortune of having met someone. To marry, in particular, is to join *en*, and to divorce to "cut" it. – Trans.

[29] The "red cord" binds married couples and lovers together in Chinese and Japanese folklore. It is held and tied by the god of matchmaking. – Trans.

[30] "The displacement of the negation from the 'stops not being written' to the 'doesn't stop being written,' in other words, from contingency to necessity – there lies the point of suspension to which all love is attached." S XX, 145.

[31] Note that the average wedding in Japan is extremely expensive. – Trans.

our necessary fate was never given a symbolic name in the first place,[32] the subject must take that being upon itself, and with it responsibility for all necessity. It must therefore recast its relation with the world in terms of a new kind of necessity, and from this imperative a delusory world peculiar to the subject is born. Were the subject not to elaborate this world of delusion, the rule of the master of fates would insinuate itself into every last inch of the subject's body, and it would be reduced to a mere puppet, its thoughts drained of all meaning.

On the Lacanian reading we are developing here, then, the Oedipus complex consists, in part, of the child's interrogation of sexual difference, and the logical operations that result. In this sense, Oedipus accomplishes two things: it makes the necessary fate that rules our being, and at the same time, it sets up within us the potential to fall into psychosis. We will now see what our reading makes of another key component of the classical Freudian Oedipus: castration.

"Castration" – the impotence of self-referentiality

At Oedipus, then, we are confronted with these facts: we are ourselves, and not an other; there exists some being that controls the necessity of our relations with others; this being requires something of us. We do not know, however, what this requirement is, and we agonize that we may not be able to meet it. To put it another way: we *cognize* our own existence as a fact, but we do not *know* it as a truth (in our bones, as it were), and that drives us to distraction. It becomes our ultimate goal in life to express the truth of our being, as the master of our fates requires of us. We push ourselves to become subjects of knowledge – to know what we are, and to produce ourselves as *objet a*. Here we arrive back at the discourse of the master, which can be read as a formula of the internal desire of a subject unable to produce the signifier of itself for itself.

It is not given to I to wield the signifier of its self; I cannot create a world of language of which I is a part. One way I might grasp this creative impotence is to imagine it as a kind of *reproductive* incapacity, in which the control of the phallus falls not to I but to the other. There is an analytic term that captures this use of the idea of *corporeal* emasculation to express the *logical* emasculation wrought by the incompleteness of self-referentiality – the well-known term "castration".

Castration is therefore the mark of the ineffectuality of human self-knowledge. That I is powerless in relation to itself is one of the most difficult things to acknowledge, and so we misrecognize (*méconnaître*) our emasculation, preferring to attribute it to the interdict of the other. In the well-known schema in which the father forbids incest with the threat of castration, psychoanalytic theory, similarly turning a blind eye to the harshest truth, prefers to ratify the imaginary operation the subject thus performs, and join it in replacing fear of emasculation with rage against

---

[32] This deficiency of naming is called *forclusion* ("foreclosure") in Lacanian terminology.

Chapter 8: THE DISCOURSE OF PSYCHOANALYSIS

prohibition.

The control of the phallus thus becomes a function of that agency, external to the subject, that knows the necessity of our being. The sign Φ (*phi*), which Lacan uses very frequently, denotes the castrating function wielded by this agency. Note that the word "function" has a dual significance, as it also means a mathematical function.[33] Lacan therefore writes Φ as a propositional function. The agency that wields the function Φ can itself be said to occupy a position completely unfettered by that function, and this agency, therefore, is notated as the exception to the propositional function Φ.

If we require a further instance of this function, we need look no further than the Japanese constitution. If all the provisions of the constitution as a whole are Φ, then each individual Japanese citizen is controlled by that Φ, but the two-thirds "majority" of the Japanese people corresponds to the exception to the rule.[34] Any piece of legislation includes within itself signifiers of the legislators who govern the law from without, for if it did not, it would be doomed to either of only two possible fates: to stand unchanged for all eternity, or to be smashed by the sword. The majority is an externality that has been installed inside us, and is like a slippery god – a trickster, which may or may not be there within, and may or may not show us itself.

We have seen in this section that the discourse of the master is privileged among the four discourses, in that it expresses a primal relation of the signifier to the subject. Central to this relation is the impossibility of representing the truth of the subject symbolically, an impossibility that we have revisited so often, in the guise of the impotence of self-referentiality, that it has become our refrain. Lacan sees the ultimate bedrock of "castration" in this impossibility, a reading that opens up a new understanding of the Oedipus complex itself as identical to accession to the Symbolic. Even the trauma of castration anxiety is merely a blind for the more difficult truth that it is our relation to ourselves, and not the intervention of some imagined other, that emasculates us; and the castrating father, or the master of our sexual fate, is a phantom we conjure to beguile ourselves of that deeper truth. Let us now look at the implications of this radically Symbolic Oedipus for relations between the genders it constructs: the implications for love, in its various guises.

---

[33] This is true of French *fonction* as it is of English *function*.
[34] A two-thirds majority in a public referendum is required to alter the provisions of the constitution. – Trans.

Chapter 8: THE DISCOURSE OF PSYCHOANALYSIS

Four: Towards the Place of the Impossible

The psychoanalysis of love

For the Oedipalized subject, then, the relation between the holders of the phallus and those without it is a necessary one, but the formula that expresses that relation is given by the prerogative of an instance outside the subject. Insofar as the human subject speaks human language, it cannot occupy the place of that instance. Lacan accordingly claimed that there is no way a sexual relation can be notated. He offered a simple proposition: "There is no such thing as a sexual relation."[35] "Relation" here means something based on a necessary law. Thus, Lacan on the one hand laid out an ontology lodged at the heart of the Oedipal subject and taking the phallus as its parameter; at the same time, he tried to make it clear that this ontology is a sham.

In fact, however, we arrive at a perception of this supposedly non-existent (or ex-sistent) sexual relation[36] in the course of psychoanalysis. The subject under analysis can experience an almost indescribable emotion towards the analyst, which he feels is "love", and indeed, when Freud first noticed this phenomenon, which

---

[35] "Il n'y a pas de rapport sexuel;" S XX, 35-36. Lacan glosses this phrase by saying, "the sexual relationship *cannot be written* (le rapport sexuel ne peut pas s'écrire)". In fact, Lacan formulates the notion of "necessity" in terms of what "doesn't stop being written (ne cesse pas de s'écrire)" (S XX, 59), somewhat in the sense that we say in colloquial English that what is fated to be is "written" (in the stars, etc.), or as we might imagine a creator God "inscribing" His creation with natural law(s). — S.K. In this connection, it may help the English reader to also bear in mind that *rapport,* in French, is also a technical mathematical term meaning "ratio", calling to mind the notion of a mathematical "constant" to be found in nature. In psychoanalysis, then, what is at stake is our general tendency to think, rather, that the sexual relationship *is* something to be written (just like the Japanese *en* inscribed in the human relations by the supernatural – see n. 28 above). In fact, however, psychoanalysis is set up to undo this preconception, and what the analytic experience "reports" (*rapporter*) is that there is no such "relationship" (*rapport*). — Trans.

[36] Although I have translated the Japanese *nai* as "non-existent" here, the sexual relation is strictly speaking not merely non-*existent,* but non-*ex-sistent* as well. Existence, Lacan's terms, means that something is "integrated into the symbolic order" (Evans, 58), as we see in the play on rapport. The sexual relation, however, does not *ex-sist* either. Ex-sistence means that something, while not "existing" within the Symbolic, *is* to be found *outside* it, in the real. Bruce Fink interprets Lacan's use of *n'existe pas* to mean non-existence in the former sense, and *il n'ya,* "there is not" to be a more global claim, meaning that something neither exists nor ex-sists. See Fink, *The Lacanian Subject: Between Language and Jouissance* (Princeton: Princeton University Press, 1996), 122. Note also that the problem of "extimacy" (see Chapter V) is once more relevant here. – Trans.

occurs predictably in the analytic situation, he called it "transference-love".[37]

The illusions of transference-love are underpinned by something genuine: the notion that the necessity of one's being oneself lies somewhere within the relation with the analyst. Transference-love is thus an intimation of the necessity of both being and relation. Insofar as this is the true structural underpinning of transference-love, then, all reason for distinguishing between transference-love and ordinary love evaporates.[38] For this reason, Freud required a certain kind of respect of analysts in handling transference-love. Indeed, if love is any passion that ineluctably resurrects the instance of necessity in this way, then it is not only transference-love we must accord such respect. The religious delusion that has the patient think he is the savior of the world; the persecution paranoia that convinces the subject she is the sacrificial lamb to the mammon of scientific experiment – insofar as each intimates a *necessary* relation between the subject and the world, each is equally related to love.

The movement towards necessity that comes about within psychoanalysis is frequently confirmed in the dream. The consulting room of the analyst is often represented as a Shinto shrine, a conjurer's stage, or some such place, somewhere infused with various kinds of supernatural will or power. As we saw earlier, the language of the being that stands outside man or woman and dictates their fates is no human language, and can only be entrusted to the gods or similar beings. The dreaming subject is therefore more logically rigorous than the waking subject, at least so far as the problem of self-referentiality is concerned!

I suggested earlier that the resurrection of the agency that governs the laws of necessity is the core of the Oedipus complex. Since the work of psychoanalysis is oriented towards the dissolution of the Oedipus complex, the analyst's task is to analyze the will towards this re-awakened necessity – i.e. to analyze love. This is why Lacan suggested that the reason that psychoanalysis was created after the invention of science is that "to speak of love is in itself a jouissance".[39] As human subjects, we are plunged into a sea of contingent chance, denied all necessity for both our being and our relations. People have known this since time immemorial, and spoken of it in phrases like, "All we like sheep have gone astray."[40] The subject hopes to be delivered from this state – to restore necessity to itself and its world. Each and every one of us once created this necessity for ourselves, at Oedipus, but we have lost it along the way. Why? And is it wrong to try to restore it?

This demand for necessity flares up from an irreducible remnant of the Oedipus

---

[37] "Observations on transference-love", SE XII, 157-171.
[38] See Lacan's definition of love as the moment where contingency becomes necessity, p. 173, main text, and also note 30.
[39] S XX, 83.
[40] Isaiah 53:6.

complex, and it is this demand that psychoanalysis tries to address. Of course, it would not be without dangers to blindly kowtow to this demand: dangers like transference-love, delusory transference, or, in the effort to avoid these, the benighted dead-end (*impasse*) that arises when analyst and subject identify with one another as living, productive subjects, sharing the burden of society's inevitable (*necessary*) progress. At the same time, however, it is precisely this revival of the passion for necessity that makes it possible for the analyst to set in place the required vector towards the desire of the Other. The demand for the "necessary" thus reappears in anaylsis, and this necessity ultimately comes into violent structural tension with another feature of analysis – a type of impossibility. We will now examine the way this tension plays itself out in analysis.

"I am one of the dead"

When Lacan speaks of "necessity" and "impossibility", it is always linked to a greater or lesser degree to Aristotle's modal logic. Without necessarily being completely faithful to all the precepts of this ancient theory, Lacan experimented with applying the four modal propositions of necessity, contingency, possibility, and impossibility to the state of affairs that psychoanalysis finds itself faced with. Here I would like to consider the way impossibility relates to necessity, referring back to the territory we have covered so far.

If we try to inscribe the sexual relation into general human relations, in a universal format, then as we have seen, "someone" must stand in a space outside humanity, someone that can no longer speak in human language. This impossibility of language *is* impossibility *per se*, as it impinges on analysis. The exterior, beyond language, beyond humanity, is required as the necessity that makes what is said hold true; yet at the same time, whatever stands there assumes the burden of the impossibility of speaking.

This someone that cannot speak in human language – that cannot speak, not because of some accident, but necessarily – is the same someone that gives us the necessary ground of our being and our relations as human subjects. This someone, necessarily unable to speak human language, is to that degree *dead*. "He" can only, by means of the inability to speak, reveal the fact that He exists. "God" is nothing more or less than the pain of being unable to speak, and divinity overflows from music and sculpture because they, too, *are* the suffering of silence.

Now in analysis, the discourse that winds its way forward, weaving its skein of meaning, is at some point suddenly cut off by a slip of the tongue. Moments like this, which are attributed to chance (*contingency*) in everyday life, are in analysis perceived as *necessarily* brought to pass by this same someone that cannot speak human language. As we saw in Chapter III with the example of the patient who left the session to go to the toilet, the existence of such a someone is then revealed to the subject, along with a sense of the reality of the *objet a*. The verbal clumsiness that occurs in analysis and cuts off meaningful discourse is, precisely, a meaningless signifier of the subject, originating from that someone who cannot speak human language. This is the kind of someone that we find out has been there all along precisely *by* the fact of the inability to speak, or by verbal parapraxes. "He" exists only in this mode, and in no other. Psychoanalysis is a scene prepared specifically to allow this someone, the bearer of our necessary fate, to emerge from within the symptom in this way; and the more "He" appears in that place, the more "He" slowly but surely dies away.

In other words, this someone who was there until just a moment ago, stammered something out, and left it (un-)said behind him – such a someone is one mode in which we encounter the dead. When, at Oedipus, we posited a someone that held the necessity of our being in "His" grasp, we thought it would be a living someone, who understood and spoke human language. But this paternal someone from the Oedipal phase is called up any number of times in the course of analysis, and "He" only ever appears as someone who cannot speak, closer and closer each time to a corpse. The apparatus of psychoanalysis exists to thrust the subject ever closer to the experience of this someone as one dead, one who understands no language at all.

We can expect that in the course of the analytic experience, "He" and the subject under analysis will temporarily be identified with one another, beyond the perimeter of language. But both "He" and the subject identified with Him will die, leaving the *objet a* behind them. With that, the subject who was under analysis will be transformed into someone other, unable to say anything, in sustained contact with this *objet a*. Thus the subject's experience will henceforth be configured as a new discourse – the discourse of the analyst (see formula p. 160 above). As Freud says, in order to dissolve the Oedipus complex, we first need to temporarily call it up from its grave – to bring it back to life.[41] From there the way opens to the analytic experience of encountering "He"/"I"as someone who is one of the dead.

"He" will not rise again, of course. It is not "He" who lives, but you. But you have already become someone other than yourself, and you too cannot speak human language. This "He" that will not come back to life is the *objet a*.

An instance of this process is seen in a man who was in analysis with Freud, who dreamt that "his father was still alive, and talking normally." His father had died at the end of a painful illness. In his dream, the analysand thought, "Father is really dead, only he himself doesn't know it."[42] The analysand dreamt this dream while in

---

[41] "It cannot be disputed that controlling the phenomena of transference presents the psycho-analyst with the greatest difficulties. But it should not be forgotten that it is precisely they that do us the inestimable service of making the patient's hidden and forgotten impulses immediate and manifest. For when all is said and done, it is impossible to destroy anyone *in absentia* or *in effigie*." SE XII, 108.

[42] "For instance, a man who had nursed his father during his last illness and had been deeply grieved by his death, had the following senseless dream some time afterwards. *His father was*

analysis, and the scene of the dream overlaps with the analytic scene; the father is Freud, and the discourse of the dream is the analytic discourse. The dreamer himself no doubt noticed that the someone who speaks without knowing that he is dead is not only his father, but also himself. This dreamer had brought his father back to life, and revived the Oedipus complex along with him. He would thereby have recognized himself as "someone" who, like his resurrected father, lived unaware that he was in fact dead, and at this point he would have woken from his dream.

The subject thus becomes an other, and recognizing that in fact, that other is dead, steps outside the language of the living. When the subject returns to the world of the living, then, who will listen to the story of his experience? Stripped of the power of ordinary human speech, he now speaks the language of the other. The role of hearing this language, the language of the one open to contact with the *objet a*, should be assumed by the one who undertakes to lead him to the place of the analyst – the *passeur*.

We thus return at last to take up the tale of the *passe* where we left off. Our theoretical detour has taken us deep into the roots of analysis. We have located the discourse of the analyst in the context of other social relations, modeled by the discourses of the university, the hysteric, and the master; we have seen that the discourse of the master captures a fundamental subjective relation to the Symbolic, and offers a radical rereading of the Oedipus complex. We have located castration, the powerhouse of Oedipus, in an impossibility of language, and finally, we have seen that Lacan articulates this impossibility with the other modal propositions of Aristotelian logic. The necessity of our being is governed by this impossibility, and in analysis, we perceive that necessity in slips and fumbles that always appeared contingent – the shift from contingency to necessity that Lacan pinpoints in transference, and in love.

The knot into which these different modes are intertwined is called analysis, and it was the internal logic of this knot that Lacan designed the formality of the *passe* to examine. The *passe* system, however, soon struck troubled waters. Let us see how it fared.

Five: The Final Failure

The split of the EFP
The École freudienne de Paris, we recall, was founded by Lacan with the declaration that he was establishing it "alone"; in fact, however, a good assortment of strong

---

alive once more and was talking to him in his usual way, but (the remarkable thing was that) *he had really died, only he did not know it.*"   SE V, 430.

accomplished supporters rallied to Lacan's standard. Lacan's entourage recognized his brilliance and acknowledged his seniority, but their analytic education had not proceeded solely by Lacanian lights. As members of the SFP (Société Française de Psychanalyse), each had made their own unique contribution, and each had had full, respectable careers as analysts. How did these people see the *passe*? The *passe*, after all, represented the opening of a new path to becoming an analyst – one that depended solely on the pure experience of undergoing personal analysis, rather than on clinical experience.

The EFP was established in the same year that Lacan began giving his seminar at the École Normale Supérieure, thanks to the good offices of Louis Althusser and Lévi-Strauss.[43] In its new venue, the seminar was directed to a new audience, people who came hoping that psychoanalysis would serve as an ideological new broom – a new thought for a brave new world. At the vanguard of this new audience was the École Normale Supérieure's intellectual elite. For Lacan's colleagues, for who had devoted their whole lives to psychoanalysis as a clinical activity, the *passe* system must have looked like a way to allow this new elite generation access to the core of the EFP while bypassing clinical experience entirely. On the surface of things, this view is entirely correct; it is not, however, adequate.

It is true that the EFP was acquiring a certain double-layered structure, split between the powerhouse of the ex-SFP old guard, and ordinary members, whose ranks were suddenly swollen by the general intellectual upheaval of the times.[44] It is also a fact that Lacan had begun searching among the new members for someone to whom he could transmit something momentous. Nevertheless, Lacan had not stopped thinking of psychoanalysis as a clinical activity, nor was he trying to stuff analysis into the ill-fitting robes of knowledge from other sciences and philosophies – far from it.

In fact, Lacan was not content with received clinical concepts, since he wanted psychoanalysis to develop along its *own* lines, on its own autonomous foundation, without huddling under the skirts of psychiatry or psychology. If it did not, Lacan's thought would amount to no more than a set of idiosyncratic views developed from a derivative field. Lacan held that psychoanalysis, on the contrary, is the system of thought that historically characterizes the modern epoch, and believed it possible for psychoanalysis to stand in the intellectual tradition of the French moralists like Pascal and La Rochefoucauld. Only in this way could psychoanalysis assume its rightful place in French intellectual history – and only in this way could Lacan's name live on in posterity.

---

[43] Roudinesco 361-362, 378, S XI, 2. See also Chapter VI, note 33.
[44] Roudinesco 433-434.

Chapter 8: THE DISCOURSE OF PSYCHOANALYSIS

In the seminar he gave in the year he established the EFP,[45] therefore, Lacan insisted tirelessly on the need to return to psychoanalytic experience, and focused clearly on the concept of transference among the four fundamental concepts, implying that if the social bond of the psychoanalytic community were to be constituted at all, it had to be constituted by none other than the transference itself. The new members of the EFP thus looked to Lacan to do more than just use the tools of intellectualism to explicate his abstruse discourse; the words he exchanged with them had to be no less than "the discourse of psychoanalysis", a means to formulate a radically new type of social bond. This new bond justified its existence by continuing to speak of "love" even in the scientific age, and by giving new content to the concept of "love" itself. This Lacanian "love" is marked by the impossible, just as the impossible orients the discourse of the analyst: one of Lacan's famous formulae holds that to love is "to give what one does not have."[46]

During this pilgrimage through transference-love, then, and even subsequently, does one have recourse to some form of "clinical" activity – "clinical" in this case referring to psychiatry or clinical psychology? No doubt clinical activity can sometimes bring about startling cognitive transformations. However, it is also true that clinical activity is only possible if the practitioner has secured a place as a responsible and productive member of society. When the subject undergoes psychoanalysis, on the other hand, she is led by a particular desire – the desire to encounter her own origins – and this desire cannot be expected to wait in the wings until the subject has acceded to her social responsibilities. And when she has learnt to stand in the place of the impossible other that her desire will lead her to, what is the subject supposed to do next? She will become "alienated" – a radical outsider to her social context – and, to play on an old meaning of the word, will be treated as "alienated" – as mad.[47] There are plenty of people who publicly profess themselves humanist psychiatrists and, claiming to speak for the mentally ill, denounce the tyranny of society; but our subject will surely not want to join in the discourse of the hysteric they propound. She is neither psychologist nor medical practitioner. Where is she to turn in search of a base that will vouchsafe her social survival?

Lacan established the EFP in an attempt to provide such a base. Having advocated the structural possibility of a pure psychoanalytic experience, reducible to neither medicine nor psychology, he wanted to secure a place in society for an organ that could recognize the results of that experience. His École, therefore, could never be just another school of psychoanalytic theory. It also had to provide a place in the world to practice the linguistic activity that the founding of the subject of science

---

[45] S XI (*The Four Fundamental Concepts of Psychoanalysis*).
[46] S VIII, 53.
[47] Recall, for example, that in English the study and treatment of mental illness used to be called "alienism", and its practitioner an "alienist". – Trans.

made theoretically necessary, and a haven where the subjects who became other in pursuing that practice could live.

In the place provided by the École, those subjects of analysis would live as analysts. As a subject moved from analysand to analyst, the join between the two states would usually be shrouded in thick darkness, but Lacan stated that his École existed for the precise purpose of dispelling that darkness.[48] He posited what he called a "psychoanalysis in its intension" (*psychanalyse en intension*) of the subject that has passed through the transference, but this is not to say that ordinary clinical analysis, or "psychoanalysis in its extension" (*psychanalyse en extension*) is something essentially or qualitatively different from it, nor that "psychoanalysis in its intension" can exist entirely independently, as if in some sort of cloister or hermitage. As we saw earlier, the "discourse of the analyst" is constituted by the potential for mutual interchange with discourses woven in the context of other social behaviors. By means of a revolution in the constitutuent elements, the other three discourses may be moved to the "discourse of the analyst", and by means of this shift, the subject comes to occupy the place of the other, and experience the originary split between itself and the *objet a* qua the self supposed to have existed at the moment of origin. The notion of "psychoanalysis in its intension" shows that within the social body of analysts as a group, something is communicated through the medium of the *objet a* entirely apart from anything that may be recognized or authorized by medicine or psychology. That "something" is precisely the "split in the subject", and we can try to imagine that split subject through the figure of the deposed ("destituted") Oedipus setting out on his journey of exile, or the figure of Freud when he had emerged from the far side of his pathological transference onto Fliess. The subject that finds his way into the social body of analysts as a group lives as a subject of science, and at the same time, expresses the split of that subject, and thereby wins a place to transmit that subjective position to the next person in the chain.[49]

Lacan announces the failure of the "pass"

The door of No. 5 Rue de Lille, Lacan's residence for many years,[50] was always open to all comers.[51] Perhaps Lacan believed that the link with him was vital for anyone trying to live in the locus of unconscious linguistic activity, so much so that it would have terrible consequences to deny it to anyone, at any time. Even though the membership of the EFP was growing precipitously, it seemed that Lacan, in Roudinesco's phrase, was trying to be "the analyst of one and all" in the École.[52] Lacan was no longer young, however, although he achieved astonishing intellectual

---

[48] *Scilicet* 1 (1967), 24; *Autres écrits*, 252.
[49] This paragraph was added to the English version by the author.
[50] Roudinesco, 294.
[51] Roudinesco, 418-419.
[52] Roudinesco, 463.

Chapter 8: THE DISCOURSE OF PSYCHOANALYSIS

productivity after sixty. Try as he might to be analyst to "one and all", there was a limit.

Lacan thus came to hope for a way to convert the form of analytic practice that he had taken as an ideal in his career into a principle capable of giving direction to a much larger movement. Now, the core of this ideal is found in the fact that Lacan drew no distinction between analysis for treatment and training analysis. Of course, treatment analysis takes place within the framework of a therapist-patient relation and training analysis does not; the analysis itself, however, operates on exactly the same principles in either case.

The goal of analysis is not to drive the subject crazy – rather the opposite, in fact – and yet analysis undeniably proceeds by bringing the subject to an encounter with potential madness. Freud himself was compelled to defend psychoanalysis on this count on a number of occasions, saying that psychoanalysis wields unconscious linguistic activity (the germ of unreason) to deliver patients from suffering much as surgery counters other blades with the scalpel,[53] or internal medicine fights toxins with drugs. If psychoanalysis was to win credibility in society at large, it could only be through an accumulation of clinical knowledge that safely regulated its intervention in the potentially dangerous linguistic activity of the unconscious.

In principle, then, any psychoanalysis, be it nominally for "training" or "treatment", is oriented to produce within us the "discourse of the analyst". In the actual practice of treatment analysis, however, it is more common to arrive at a moment of choice, when the severity with which symptoms impinge on everyday life has been relativized. This choice takes the form of a question: with the suffering of neurosis gone, should the subject sustain his encounter with the element of seeming madness within him? In considering this question, the analyst must be aware of both of the power of analysis to affect the symptom, and also of the limits of that power. If the subject harbors a desire to set out towards the discourse of the analyst, and to produce a new kind of linguistic activity, however, he must be prepared to follow that desire, and the terror of madness, wherever it may lead. That process may take a very long time.

Now we can see from this fact that the internal logic of analysis (the "intensional" aspect) may well *itself be* a clinical matter, and it is therefore baseless speculation to imagine that Lacan took lightly the clinical knowledge that bears so critically on the social credibility of psychoanalysis, or that Lacan himself was a poor clinician. He had a large number of difficult cases, and put a great deal of work into his clinical practice. This equality of emphasis was reflected in the qualifications system he

---

[53] "Introductory Lectures on Psycho-Analysis" SE XVI, 462-463: "[T]he transference is a dangerous instrument in the hands of an unconscientious doctor. But no medical instrument or procedure is guaranteed against abuse; if a knife does not cut, it cannot be used for healing either."

constructed for his new École. He gave equal weight to both qualifications: AE, which we recall recognized the desire of the analyst by means of the *passe*, and AME, which recognized clinical knowledge and testified competence to bear social responsibility. No hierarchical distinction was posited between the two roles.

Lacan did, however, introduce one subtle provision into the relationship between AE and AME. If a candidate analyzed by an AME succeeded in the *passe* and became an AE, then the AME who had conducted the analysis also "officially" become an AE. This provision appeared to place the title of AE above that of AME.[54] Perhaps a kind of stubborn pride in the child of his own invention, the *passe*, showed its face for an instant when Lacan instituted this provision. Or perhaps we see a kind of naivety here – the belief that all in the École would perfectly understand his original intentions for the AE qualification. Despite weathering repeated political storms, though, Lacan always retained a surprising directness – something that might equally be said of Freud. There was one further explanation for the privilege this provision seemed to grant to AEs, however: like it or not, psychoanalysis was now irreversibly caught in the large currents of European intellectual history, and no matter how sharp its clinical knowledge might be, it would soon be consigned to oblivion unless it had an arm like the AE to sustain it from within. By being seen to privilege AE status over AME, however, Lacan made this fact too artlessly plain.

The question remains: To what extent did Lacan anticipate the emotive reaction the provision was likely to provoke from AMEs and clinicians? If, after all, they did fear that Lacan was setting out to create a school that gave pride of place to abstruse theorizing over clinical work, then he could only have fuelled their anxieties with this provision. As it turned out, Lacan's proposal for the *passe* was in fact approved, one way or another, by a plenary session of the EFP;[55] but it was not long before a factional split within the École was plain for all to see. In 1969, the same year that the *passe* was approved, a faction called the "Fourth Group" split off from the EFP to go it alone.[56]

With this latest schism, the success or failure of the *passe* took on more significance than ever, becoming the linchpin on which hung the cohesion of the whole EFP. Of more than a hundred applications examined between the institution of the system and 1977, however, only nine were actually granted the *passe*, and there was a suicide among the failed aspirants.[57] The *passe* came to be seen as a kind of arbitrary ritual, with no clear standards, subject to the iron whim of Lacan alone. In 1978, a meeting was held to discuss the *passe*, and Lacan was reduced to lamenting, "To be sure, it's a total failure, this *passe* business."[58]

---

[54] Roudinesco, 448.
[55] Roudinesco, 460.
[56] Piera Aulagnier, François Perrier and Jean-Paul Valabréga. Roudinesco, 459, 473-477.
[57] Roudinesco, 462.
[58] Mehlman's translation. Roudinesco, 639.

Chapter 8: THE DISCOURSE OF PSYCHOANALYSIS

Dissolution and death

The conclusion that the *passe* was a failure meant that Lacan was forced to surrender his ideal of systematically institutionalizing the discourse of the psychoanalyst, which must have been extremely painful for him. The apparatus that would take up his ideal and realize it for him, the EFP, had fundamentally misfired. In Chapter II, I described Lacan as a "past master of the political blunder", and perhaps, in the case of the EFP, too, he "did not know" the way things stood until it was very nearly too late. In 1979, however, Lacan at last resolved to dissolve the EFP. No doubt he had his doubts in doing so, but in January 1980, he sent a letter to the École's members informing them of his intent,[59] and the formal decision to dissolve the school was reached within the year.

From 1978, however, when he concluded that the *passe* had been a failure, Lacan's health began to visibly decline. The seminar that year was scheduled to be on "Topology and Time",[60] but when he appeared to teach, Lacan would sometimes stand mute for minutes on end.[61] Eventually, it became common for the seminar to fall under the sway of this silence, and when Lacan did speak, it was only to read from pre-written materials, a move that marked the demise of his former distinctive style of direct, spoken contact with the audience.

The changes brought by Lacan's failing health cast suspicion on his monumental decision to dissolve the École. Some believed that his son-in-law, Jacques-Alain Miller, was manipulating his aging master into signing statements that served his own ulterior motives,[62] and suspected that the decision to dissolve the EFP was just such a fabrication. In Roudinesco's words, the cracks had begun to show between Lacan's legal family and his psychoanalytic one.[63]

In his letter of dissolution,[64] Lacan said, "Je persévère,"[65] a typical Lacanian pun on "I persevere" and "I severe-father" ("Je père-sévère"). But what did he persevere in doing? I read this statement as a reference to his ideal of setting the discourse of the analyst into a systematized movement, one firmly rooted in history. The EFP was incapable of meeting this ideal, but in the letter of dissolution, Lacan immediately declared the foundation of yet another school.[66] He doubtless intended to direct this

---

[59] "Letter of Dissolution", *Television: A Challenge to the Psychoanalytic Establishment,* trans. J. Mehlman (New York: Norton, 1990), 129-131.
[60] Unpublished.
[61] See Stuart Schneiderman, *Jacques Lacan: The Death of an Intellectual Hero* (Cambridge: Harvard University Press, 1983), 17; Roudinesco, 640.
[62] Schneiderman, 45.
[63] Roudinesco, *Jacques Lacan,* trans. Barbara Bray (New York: Columbia University Press, 1997), 402.
[64] "Letter of Dissolution", 130.
[65] *Autres écrits,* 318.
[66] "In other words, I persevere [no pun]".

school, not alive, but as Freud's "primal father", a dead "father severe".

Lacan appointed Miller his sole literary executor. The new school was initially called the Cause Freudienne, but reaction against Miller led to another succession of resignations, splits, and new schools, and in 1981, Miller responded to these developments by regrouping to establish yet another school, the École de la cause freudienne (ECF). In French as in English, "cause" has two meanings: the sort of cause that we judge worthy or otherwise, and for which we work or fight; and also "that which causes" a certain effect or result. The name of the new school thus recognized that Freud's life and death was the effective cause of the individual life of each person belonging to the school, as analyst. Lacan's famous "return to Freud", which he had advocated ever since his early days, here took a form more radical than ever before, and the ECF that bore this name continues today as the core organization of Lacanian psychoanalysis, with more members than any of its various rival groups.

The ECF still operates the *passe* system. Miller himself, however, had vague misgivings about the system from the start, fearing that it could be tantamount to imposing a second psychoanalysis on the candidate (the *passant*) if the *passeurs* themselves did not understand the real meaning of the system. Perhaps, indeed, the initial failure of the *passe* system to run smoothly bore out these misgivings. Although he represents the ECF in all practical matters, then, Miller has for these reasons never undergone the *passe* himself.

In September of 1980, Lacan noticed something amiss in his abdomen. He was examined, and his doctor said he found nothing out of the ordinary. Lacan, however, thought otherwise, and later pronounced judgment in typically blunt fashion: "He's an idiot. I know what's the matter with me." It was, in fact, cancer – and Lacan hated surgery.[67]

On July 15 1981, Marguerite Anzieu, alias "Aimée", the "protagonist" of Lacan's doctoral thesis, passed away at the grand old age of 89.[68] One month later, in August, Lacan was overcome by extreme abdominal pain, and surgery could be avoided no longer. The surgery appeared successful, but the sutures tore, leadings to peritonitis and blood poisoning.[69] Lacan plunged into agony once more, and after a deliberate overdose of morphine, finally drew his last breath on September 9.[70] His last words were reportedly, "I am stubborn . . . I am disappearing."[71]

"And call to an association once again those who, this January 1980, want to go with Lacan." "Letter of Dissolution", 130.
[67] Roudinesco, *Jacques Lacan*, 402-403.
[68] Roudinesco, 679.
[69] Roudinesco, *Jacques Lacan*, 407.
[70] Schneiderman, vii.
[71] Jeffrey Mehlman's translation. For this and all biographical details in this paragraph see Roudinesco, 679.

Six: Encore, Lacan!

According to Roudinesco, the young Lacan showed quite an interest in money.[72] Now money is an anal object, and Lacan died of bowel cancer; Freud, as a child, injured his mouth in trying to get something nice to eat, and died of cancer of the palate. This may all be pure chance – and then again, it may not be. Perhaps the place where desire is founded, when the human subject establishes itself as subject of that desire, is a particularly sensitive locale, and perhaps that is where we get cancer. Perhaps this empty, insatiable place can ultimately only be filled by the minions of death.

If we think that it was not mere chance – not contingent – then we bring necessity into the picture – the necessity of the *objet a*, running through the lives of Freud and Lacan like a constant thread from start to finish. The act of accepting this necessity, which is part and parcel of the path each person walks to death, is perhaps what is called "love" – or at least Lacan's definition of love invites us to think so.

The only necessity known to modern science, on the other hand, is the extreme necessity that everything is simply contingent. All laws are open to relativization. The arrangement that dictates that humans are made to die one day, therefore, also boils down to simple chance, and at least in principle, is an arrangement that can be altered. Science does not deny the possibility that humans might become immortal. Far less would it acknowledge that any relation other than chance could hold between infantile oral impulses, or a precocious interest in money, and cancer of the mouth or the bowel in later years.

Here psychoanalysis differs. Nothing is to stop someone on the road to becoming an analyst from taking the necessity that governed Freud or Lacan's way to death onto themselves, as the necessity that similarly governs their own death, through the mediation of the *objet a*. Indeed, it is probably the case that in her own particular fashion, each such person does precisely that.

In this book, I have taken up as my central thesis Lacan's late thesis, "the *objet a* is the golden mean", using it to reconsider the whole sweep of his thought from start to finish. In this sense, we could say that the *objet a* is an unbilled star of the book. Analysts regularly whisper among themselves that psychotic patients sometimes take the position of the *objet a*, just like the analyst. If this is true, then the encounter with the inner world of the psychotic can be constituted as an experience of the discourse of the analyst. This does not mean, however, that we can fondly expect to easily arrive at such experience in the course of treatment.

Word has it that the patient who said to me that she wanted "to start right from the very beginning" is now far away and leading a normal life. I brought her out

---

[72] Roudinesco, 103.

Chapter 8: THE DISCOURSE OF PSYCHOANALYSIS

from the wings once more when I set about writing this book, and in a sense, she too is its hidden protagonist, one of the foci around which the words in this book have been revolving. I would like to close the book by expressing my gratitude to her.

Bibliography

The books and articles listed here all existed before this book was ever read, or even written; here, however, they are also rediscovered after the book has been read. They are the origin of this book and its cause, but they are also its product, arising from the fact of its writing and reading. When a book is written and then read, therefore, we end up with a certain reversal of temporal order.

I wrote in my foreword that the past of an author is realized in the future where the reader reads. In light of this, we can see that I will inevitably rediscover my past in the items listed in this bibliography, and this is indeed the case. One of my first encounters with Lacan was through Sheridan's translation of his Seminar XI (lucky that Sheridan's translation had such allure!). It was only later that I learnt that the Afterword to this Seminar contains Lacan's own account of his encounter with the Japanese language. In other words, Lacan himself was pointing out to me what *my* encounter with language – my own native language, no less – had been like. The fact that Seminar XI is included in this bibliography hints at the fate that fell to my unconscious – to rediscover my first encounter with my own language, by way of Lacan's mediation.

In Sheridan's English translation, however, that afterword was omitted. This means that when I read this Seminar in the English, I in fact rediscovered my past *unknowingly*, in the form of something that quite literally was "all gone". Did Sheridan somehow know that eventually a certain Japanese man would read this Seminar and embark on Lacanian studies, and purposefully prepare for that Japanese reader a "missed encounter" such as that of which Lacan speaks? If so, we must admit that it was a superb analytic tactic.

This is, of course, nothing but my fantasy. However, insofar as a bibliography is predicated on "that which does not stop being written", we surely must grant that it is a device that anticipates such a fantasy, and allows for it, in its very make-up. Without further ado, then, this peculiar device is presented below.

* * * * * *

Abraham, Karl, *Selected Papers on Psycho-analysis* (London: Maresfield Reprints, H. Karnac, 1979).
Adachi, Tsuneo, $\sqrt{2}$ *no fushigi* [*The Wonders of* $\sqrt{2}$] (Tokyo: Kobunsha, 1994).
Anti-Climacus, *The Sickness Unto Death: A Christian Psychological Exposition for Edification and Awakening*, ed. Søren Kierkegaard, trans. Alastair Hannay (London: Penguin, 1989).
Anzieu, Didier, *L'auto-analyse de Freud et la découverte de la psychanalyse* (2 vols.) (Presses Universitaires de France, 1959).

Breton, André, *The Communicating Vessels*, trans. by Mary Ann Caws and Geoffrey T. Harris, with notes and introduction by Mary Ann Caws (Lincoln: University of Nebraska Press, 1990).
---------- *Nadja*, translated by Richard Howard (New York: Grove Press, 1960).
Conrad, Klaus, *Die Beginnende Schizophrenie* (Stuttgart: G. Thieme, 1958).
Davis, F. Hadland, *Myths and Legends of Japan* (London: G. G. Harrap and Company, 1913).
Dazai, Osamu, *Dazai Osamu zenshū* [*Complete Works of Dazai Osamu*] (Chikuma Shobō, 1976).
Evans, Dylan, *An Introductory Dictionary of Lacanian Psychoanalysis* (London: Routledge, 1997).
Fink, Bruce, *The Lacanian Subject: Between Language and Jouissance* (Princeton: Princeton University Press, 1995).
Freud, Anna, *The Ego and the Mechanisms of Defence*, trans. Cecil Baines (New York: International Universities Press, 1946).
Freud, Sigmund, *Briefe an Wilhelm Fliess 1887-1904*, ed. Jeffrey Moussaieff Masson, assisted by Michael Schröter and Gerhard Fichtner (Frankfurt: M. S. Fischer, 1986). Jeffrey Moussaieff Masson, trans. and ed., *The Complete Letters of Sigmund Freud to Wilhelm Fliess, 1887-1904* (Cambridge, Mass.: Belknap Press of Harvard University Press, 1985).
----------- *The Standard Edition of the Complete Psychological Works of Sigmund Freud*, ed. J. Strachey with Anna Freud, 24 vols (London: The Hogarth Press, 1953-1964).
Gay, Peter, *Freud: A Life for Our Time* (New York: Doubleday, 1989).
Gill, Christopher, trans. *The Symposium* (New York: Penguin, 1999).
Grosskurth, Phyllis, *Melanie Klein: Her Life and Her Work* (New York: Knopf, 1986).
Hegel, G. W. F., *The Phenomenology of Mind*, trans. J. B. Baillie (London: S. Sonnenschein, 1910).
Ichikawa, Hiroshi, "Yochō wo motomete", *Hihyō kūkan* (*Critical Space*) 1991, No 1.
International Psycho-Analytical Association, "Report on the Eighteenth International Psycho-Analytical Congress, President's Report", Dr. Heinz Hartmann, *International Journal of Psycho-Analysis* XXXV (1954), 271-279.
Johnson, Thomas W., "Far Eastern Fox Lore", *Asian Folklore Studies*, vol. 33 (1974), 35-68.
Jones, Ernest, *Sigmund Freud, Life and Work*, 3 vols (London: The Hogarth Press, 1980).
Jowett, Benjamin, trans., *The Dialogues of Plato* (Oxford: Clarendon Press, 1871).
Klatt, E. et al, *Langenscheidts Taschenwörterbuch: Englisch* (Berlin: Langenscheidt KG, 1983).
Klein, Melanie, *Envy and Gratitude* (New York: Basic Books, 1957).
---------- *La psychanalyse des enfants*, trans. J.B. Boulanger (Paris: Presses universitaires de France, 1958, 1998).
---------- *The Psycho-Analysis of Children*, trans. Alix Strachey (New York: The Free Press, 1975).
---------- *The Writings of Melanie Klein*, ed. Roger Money-Kyrle, Betty Joseph, Edna O'Shaughnessy and Hanna Segal, 4 vols. (London: The Hogarth Press and the Institute of Psychoanalysis, 1975).
Kojève, Alexandre, *Introduction à la lecture de Hegel*, réunies et publiées par Raymond Queneau (Paris: Gallimard, 1968).
Lacan, Jacques, "Actes du Congrès de Rome", *Psychanalyse* I (1956).
---------- *Autres écrits*, ed. Jacques-Alain Miller (Paris: Seuil, 2001).

Bibliography

---------- *De la psychose Paranoïaque dans ses rapports avec la personnalité, suivi de Premiers écrits sur la paranoïa* (Paris: Seuil, 1975).
---------- *Écrits* (Paris: Seuil, 1966).
---------- *Écrits: A Selection,* trans. Alan Sheridan (New York: Norton, 1977).
---------- "Logical time and the assertion of anticipated certainty: A new sophism", trans. Bruce Fink and M. Silver, in Ellie Ragland-Sullivan, ed., *Newsletter of the Freudian Field*, vol 2 (1988), 4-22.
---------- *The Seminar of Jacques Lacan, Edited by Jacques-Alain Miller: Book I, Freud's Papers on Technique 1953-1954,* translated with notes by John Forrester (Cambridge: Cambridge University Press, 1988).
---------- *The Seminar, Book II, The Ego in Freud's Theory and the Technique of Psychoanalysis, 1954-55,* trans. Sylvia Tomaselli, notes by John Forrester (Cambridge: Cambridge University Press, 1988).
---------- *The Seminar, Book III, The Psychoses, 1955-56,* trans. with notes by Russell Grigg (London: Routledge, 1993).
---------- *The Seminar of Jacques Lacan, Edited by Jacques-Alain Miller: Book VII, The Ethics of Psychoanalysis 1959-1960,* translated with notes by Dennis Porter (New York: Norton, 1992).
---------- *Le Séminaire de Jacques Lacan, livre VIII, "Le Transfert",* éd. Jacques-Alain Miller (Paris: Seuil, 1991).
---------- *Le Séminaire, livre XI: Les quatre concepts fondamentaux de la psychanalyse,* texte établi par Jacques-Alain Miller (Paris: Seuil, 1973). *The Four Fundamental Concepts of Psycho-Analysis,* trans. Alan Sheridan (London: Penguin, 1979).
---------- *Le Séminaire, livre XVII: L'envers de la psychanalyse,* texte établi par Jacques-Alain Miller (Paris: Seuil, 1991). Translation by Russell Grigg, *The Seminar, Book XVII: The Other Side of Psychoanalysis* (Norton, forthcoming).
---------- *The Seminar of Jacques Lacan: On Feminine Sexuality, the Limits of Love and Knowledge, 1972-1973 (Encore),* ed. Jacques-Alain Miller, trans. Bruce Fink (New York: Norton, 1999).
---------- *Television: A Challenge to the Psychoanalytic Establishment,* trans. Jeffrey Mehlman (New York, London: Norton, 1990).
Laplanche, Jean, and Jean-Bertrand Pontalis, *The Language of Psychoanalysis* (New York: Norton, 1974).
Legge, James, trans., *The Chinese Classics with a Translation, Critical and Exegetical Notes, Prolegomena, and Copious Indexes* (Hong Kong: Hong Kong University Press, 1960).
Lévi-Strauss, Claude, *The Savage Mind* (Chicago: University of Chicago Press, 1966).
Lévy-Valensi, J., Migault, P., et Lacan, J., "Écrits 'inspirés': Schizographie", *Annales Médico-Psychologiques*, XIIIe Série, 89e Année, T. II, No. 1(1931).
Lewis, Charlton and Charles Short, *A Latin Dictionary* (Oxford: Oxford University Press, 1979).
Masson, Jeffrey, *The Assault on Truth* (London: Penguin, 1985).
Matsuzawa, Tetsuro, "The death of an infant chimpanzee at Bossou, Guinea", *Pan Africa News*, 4 (1997).
Muller, John, and William Richardson, eds., *The Purloined Poe: Lacan, Derrida, and Psychoanalytic Reading* (Baltimore: Johns Hopkins University Press, 1988).
Nakamura, Hajime, *Shin bukkyō yōgo jiten* [*A New Dictionary of Buddhist Terminology*] (Tokyo: Seishin shobō, 1980).

Natsume, Soseki, *Light and Darkness,* trans. V. H. Viglielmo (London: Owen, 1971).
Nozaki, Kiyoshi, *Kitsune: Japan's Fox of Mystery, Romance and Humor* (Tokyo: Hokuseido Press, 1961).
Pascal, Blaise, *Pensées,* translated with an introduction by A. J. Krailsheimer (London: Penguin, 1966).
Rimbaud, Arthur, *Complete Works, Selected Letters,* trans. Wallace Fowlie (Chicago: University of Chicago Press, 1966).
Roudinesco, Elizabeth, *Jacques Lacan,* trans. Barbara Bray (New York: Columbia University Press, 1997).
--------- *Jacques Lacan and Co.: A History of Psychoanalysis in France, 1925-1985,* trans. Jeffrey Mehlman (London: Free Association Books, 1990).
Russell, Bertrand, *The Analysis of Mind* (London: George Allen & Unwin, 1971).
Sasaki, Ruth Fuller, *The Recorded Sayings of Ch'an Master Lin-chi Hui-chao of Chen Prefecture, Compiled by his Humble Heir Hui-jan of San-sheng* (Kyoto: Institute for Zen Studies, 1975).
Schneiderman, Stuart, *Jacques Lacan: The Death of an Intellectual Hero* (Cambridge: Harvard University Press, 1983).
Sharpe, Ella Freeman, *Dream Analysis,* introd. by Masud R. Khan (New York: Brunner/Mazel, 1978).
Shingu, Kazushige, ed., *Imi no kanata e: Rakan no chiryōgaku* [*Beyond Meaning: Lacan in the Clinical Setting*] (Tokyo: Kongō Press, 1996).
--------- *Muishiki no byōrigaku* [*The Psychopathology of the Unconscious*] (Tokyo: Kongō Press, 1989).
--------- *Yume to kōzo* [*Dream and Structure*] (Kobundō, 1988).
Shinran, *Tannisho: Notes Lamenting Differences,* translated and annotated in the Ryukoku University Translation Center (Kyoto: Tsuchiyama Printing Co., 1962, 1980).
Takemoto, Yasuyuki and Hiwahara Yoshiyuki, "The complexity of self-formation in psychoanalysis (Seishinbunseki ni okeru jiko keisei no fukuzatsusei)", Final dissertation, Ryukoku University, 1996 (unpublished).
Verlaine, Paul, *Oeuvres Poétiques Complètes,* ed. Y.-G. Le Dantec (Paris: Éditions de la Nouvelle revue française, 1938).
---------- *Poems by Paul Verlaine,* ed. Ashmore Wingate (London: The Walter Scott Publishing Co).
Wilden, Anthony, ed., *The Language of the Self: The Function of Language in Psychoanalysis* (Baltimore and London: Johns Hopkins University Press, 1968). Later republished as *Speech and Language in Psychoanalysis* (Baltimore and London: Johns Hopkins University Press, 1981).
Wittgenstein, Ludwig, *Tractatus Logico-Philosophicus: the German Text of Ludwig Wittgenstein's* Logisch-philosophische Abhandlung, trans. D. F. Pears and B. F. McGuiness (London: Routledge and Kegan Paul, 1961, 1988).

Index

A
Abraham 49
abortion 93, 110
absence 91, 92, 171
Adachi Tsuneo 127
AE 157, 185
agalma 49, 139, 140, 142, 144, 150, 157
Agathon 141
agency 168, 175
agent 163
Aimée 9, 102, 187
Alcibiades 141
Althusser,Louis 135
AME 158, 185
analysand 167, 183
analysis 73, 89, 101, 108, 110, 127, 140, 160, 168, 184
analysis interminable 51
analyst 27, 81, 82, 87, 106, 129, 133, 134, 137, 140, 152, 155, 160, 161, 167, 177, 183, 188
anxiety 18, 69, 112
Anzieu, Didier 12
Anzieu, Marguerite 187
Aristotle 178
arkhē 68, 69, 71, 73

B
bad object 142
Bataille, Georges 29
Bataille, Sylvia 29
beauty 120
beginning 68, 69, 84, 189
being 147, 149, 177
big Other 59, 61, 67, 107, 125, 127, 132
Bodhidharma 38
Bonaparte, Marie 5, 17, 30, 134
Bosch, Heironymous 75, 101
breast 49, 120
Breton 5, 132
Buddha 38, 79
Buddha Amida 79

Buddhism 74, 79, 82, 127
Buddhist 58, 173

C
calculation 53, 98, 118, 119, 128
castration 170, 174
castration anxiety 171
chaos 119
character 48
childhood 61, 152
Chinese thought 79
Christ 164
Claude, Henri 5, 8
Clérambault 9
cogito 59, 64, 65
Confucian 58
contingency 173, 178
contingent 171, 177
counting 107, 108, 129, 139

D
das Ding 26, 27, 91, 116, 120
dead 179
death 77, 81, 91, 98, 113, 188
deferred action 62, 109
demand 20
depressive position 20, 161
dereliction 99
Descartes 59, 64, 65, 67, 162, 164
desire 20, 58, 61, 76, 77, 79, 88, 89, 91, 139, 152, 159, 173, 182, 188
desire of the analyst 127
desire of the Other 2, 4, 14, 58, 59, 73, 75, 76, 77, 91, 92, 103, 127, 133, 152
desired 58
destitution of the subject 161
discourse 59, 161
discourse of science 162, 163, 165
discourse of the analyst 160, 167, 182, 183, 184
discourse of the hysteric 166, 167, 182

Index

discourse of the master 164, 165, 166, 168
discourse of the Other 67, 70, 71, 73, 75, 83, 108, 109, 122, 133, 144
discourse of the university 161
dissolution 186
Dolto, Françoise 135
dream 62, 69, 71, 72, 87, 93, 97, 101, 110, 111, 112, 144, 146, 147, 150, 160, 162, 177, 179
drive 20

E

Eastern philosophy 82
École de la cause freudienne (ECF) 187
École freudienne de Paris (EFP) 137, 180, 186
en 173
Es 71
excommunication 134
extimacy 119
extimité 70

F

family romance 71
fantasy 85, 165
father 179
feces 49
Fink, Bruce 41-3, 85, 116, 176
Fliess, Wilhelm 144, 148, 183
forclusion ("foreclosure") 174
fort-da 95, 119
fort-da game 86
four discourses 160
Four Fundamental Concepts of Psychoanalysis 88
fragmented body 75, 99, 101
fratricide 46
freedom 77, 104, 156
Freud, Sigmund 15, 38, 61, 71, 73, 86, 91, 129, 130, 140, 144, 147, 148, 151, 164, 179, 183, 184
Freud, Anna 22
Freud's son 150
full speech 45, 68

G

gaze 49

God 55, 68, 99, 173, 178
golden mean 52, 97, 98, 118, 119, 120, 121, 128, 188
golden section 52, 81, 149
good object 142
grace 99
Grosskurth 28
guilt 21, 172

H

Hegel 4, 57, 58, 77, 81
helpless being 99
helpless suffering 70, 71, 90, 99
helplessness 71
higan 58, 81, 150
human 49, 50, 55, 69, 104, 106, 165
human desire 77
humanity 80, 163, 178
hysteria 101, 145, 166
hysteric 77, 166

I

I 116, 119, 120, 121, 128, 139
Ichikawa Hiroshi 72
identification 83, 102, 112, 130, 132, 147, 148, 150, 158
identity 57, 58, 69, 83, 105, 108, 111, 113, 131, 153
images 113
imaginary 114, 124
impossible 61, 70, 120, 176, 178, 182
individual 131
infinity 118, 120, 126
inhuman 49, 50
instinct 20
interminable 65
International Psychoanalytical Association (IPA) 29, 32, 133
interpretation 41, 44
Irma 145-7, 151-2
irrational 56, 57, 59, 84, 121, 139
irrational number 57, 120
It speaks 108

J

Index

Japan 173
Japanese Buddhism 39
Japanese thought 79
Jesus 68
Jones, Ernest 145
jouissance 75, 159, 177

K

kirisute 47
Klein, Melanie 15, 22, 49, 91, 120, 134, 142, 161
knowledge 64, 68, 160, 162, 163, 164
kōan 44
Kojève 4, 81, 90
kū 74

L

La Rochefoucauld 181
Lacan, Jacques 9, 17, 24, 37, 49, 58, 65, 66, 68, 69, 70, 72, 73, 76, 77, 78, 79, 82, 83, 86, 88, 90, 97, 101, 104, 106, 111, 112, 114, 120, 121, 127, 129, 130-1, 134-5, 139, 140, 149, 152, 155, 159, 164, 167, 169, 170, 173, 176, 177, 178, 181-2, 183, 184, 186-7
Lagache, Daniel 30, 73, 134
language 61, 65, 67, 69, 70, 76, 91, 123, 129, 157, 160, 169, 178
Laplanche, Jean 135
Leclaire, Serge 134
Lévi-Strauss, Claude 111, 135
Lichtenberg 155
Lin-chi 78
love 55, 98, 110, 120, 131, 141, 173, 176, 177, 182, 188

M

madness 104
Magritte 124
Mannoni, Octave and Maud 135
master 166
master signifier 160, 165
matheme 85
Matsuzawa Tetsurō 80
metalanguage 129
Miller, Jacques-Alain 59, 136, 186, 187
mirror 99, 105, 121, 122, 124

mirror image 109, 110
mirror stage 24, 100, 106, 121-5
modal logic 178
Moebius strip 159
mother 142
murder 95
murder of the thing 90
Music Hell 75

N

Nacht, Sacha 30
nachträglich 63
Nachträglichkeit 62, 109
Nadja 5, 6, 132
Natsume Soseki 58
naturalness 79
nature 78, 79, 81, 162, 164
necessary 172, 176, 177
necessity 60, 69, 173, 177, 178, 188
neurosis 184
Nichiren 39
nirvāna 58, 79
not knowing 35, 40
nukegake 47
number 119, 130

O

objet a 49, 52, 73, 76, 78, 80, 83, 84, 88-90, 97-8, 109, 118, 120, 126, 127-8, 131, 132, 139-40, 144, 150, 152, 153, 160, 162, 163, 165, 167, 174, 178, 179, 188
obsessive compulsive 77
Oedipal 64, 173
Oedipus 34, 158, 161, 183
Oedipus complex 168, 170, 174, 177, 179
one 56-7, 130
One 128
ontology 172, 176
origin 63, 71, 73, 116, 120, 156
Other 59, 69, 70, 83, 97, 125, 152
other 83, 102, 163

P

paradox 66-7
Paranoia 11, 25, 47, 102, 114, 177

—197—

Index

paranoid-schizoid position   20
part objects   49
particular   56, 153
Pascal   104, 164, 181
pass   158, 168
passant   158
passe   180, 185, 187
passeur   158, 180
patricide   64
penis envy   171
personality   48
phallus   171, 174-6
Plato   141
pleasure principle   86
plus de jouir   115, 120, 159
point de caption   131
possibility   178
presence and absence   113
primal scene   63
prisoners   48, 50
product   163
projective identification   26
psychoanalysis   67, 93, 127
psychotic   74, 173, 188

R

ratio   53, 56, 117, 119, 120
rational   84, 120, 139
real   56, 61, 70, 76, 119, 149
Real   70, 119-21
reason   53, 57
rentai   47
repeat   86
repetition   87, 93, 110
Rimbaud   83
Rinzai   78
Rome Discourse   33, 37, 57, 68, 77, 78, 86
Roudinesco   10, 17, 183, 186
Russell   51, 112, 122

S

scansion   41, 108
Schema L   121
schizophrenia   74
science   139, 140, 162, 188

scientist   165
sekitate   42, 46, 50, 51, 52, 96
self   42, 104, 108, 131, 166
self-reference   109
self-referentiality   67, 83, 108, 112, 114, 122, 123, 155, 160, 164, 167, 169, 170, 174
self-referentiality, incompleteness of   67-9, 76
sexual relation   176
Sharpe, Ella   131
Shinran   38, 79
short session   30, 33, 44, 47
sickness unto death   81
signifier   69, 76, 83, 114, 118, 131, 155, 160, 167, 169, 170
Skriabine, Pierre   108
slip of the tongue   178
social   159, 161, 183
social bond   161, 170, 182
Société Française de Psychanalyse (SFP)   32, 134
Société Psychanalytique de Paris (SPP)   5
society   182
Socrates   141
solipsism   65
sonic boom   44
speaking being   69
structuralism   136
subject   65, 69, 76, 77, 89, 97, 107, 122, 126, 137, 157, 160, 162, 166, 170, 183
subject of science   162, 164
subject supposed to know   167
suffering being   99
surrealism   5
surrealist   9
symbol   61, 90
Symbolic   92, 112, 114, 115, 120-1
symbolic equation   17
symbolic matrix   107-8
symbolization   93, 96, 106, 112, 124-6

T

thing   115
three prisoners   42, 46, 53, 124, 125
time   34, 42, 52

Index

tōryanse 158
trait unaire 129
transference 4, 6, 7, 13, 61, 87, 106, 137, 141, 144, 167, 182
transference-love 177
trauma 62, 95
true person 156
true person of no status 78
truth 163, 174

U
unary trait 129-30, 131-3, 150
uncanny 120, 150, 158
unconscious 147, 159, 161

universal 55, 56, 98, 107, 112, 125, 130, 131, 139, 150
university 161
urination 46

V
voice 49
void 84, 85

W-Z
Wittgenstein 51, 65, 67
Yamaguchi Masaya 119
Zen 44, 74, 77, 78, 79, 127, 156